THE SEVEN LIGHTS

THE SEVEN LIGHTS

On the Major Jewish Festivals

Adin Steinsaltz
and
Josy Eisenberg

JASON ARONSON INC.
Northvale, New Jersey
Jerusalem

This book was set in 11 pt. Bookman Light by Alabama Book Composition of Deatsville, AL and printed and bound by Book-mart Press, Inc. of North Bergen, NJ.

Library of Congress Cataloging-in-Publication Data

Eisenberg, Josy.
  [Chandelier d'or. English]
  The seven lights : on the Major Jewish Festivals / Adin Steinsaltz
and Josy Eisenberg.
    p. cm.
  First French ed. co-authored by Josy Eisenberg and Adin Steinsaltz.
  Includes bibliographical references and index.
  ISBN 0-7657-6156-4
    1. Fasts and feasts—Judaism—Meditations. 2. Schneur Zalman of Lyady,
1745–1813. I. Steinsaltz, Adin. II. Title.

BM690 .E3813 2000
296.4'3—dc21

                                                                00–035539

Printed in the United States of America. Jason Aronson Inc. offers books and cassettes. For information and catalog write to Jason Aronson Inc., 230 Livingston Street, Northvale, NJ 07647-1726, or visit our website: http://www.aronson.com

This book is lovingly dedicated to

Our mother
Ruth Dubrofsky
Who continues to illuminate our paths

And to the eternal lights of our lives:
זכרונם לברכה

Our father
William Dubrofsky
An inspiration in life and beyond

Joshua Dubrofsky
Who gave and received so much love

Julia Weisz Teich Capon
A lady of immense courage

Ernest & Olga Weisz
So much lost, their legacies live on

Eva & David Goodman
Philip & Mary Dubrofsky
Our grandparents and luminaries who showed us the way

May their golden example always be a lamp unto our feet

On behalf of the
WILLIAM DUBROFSKY FOUNDATION

Harvey & Barbara Dubrofsky
Lorne & Sharon Dubrofsky
Montreal, Canada

Contents

Foreword   xi

The Days of Awe

First Gate—Rosh Hashanah, the New Year   3

The Head of the Year   5
   The Point of Origin, 9
   The Year Is Dead: Long Live the Year, 10
   A Programmed Moment, 13
   Who Made You King?, 14
   In the Name of the King, 19
   . . . And in the Name of the Father, 22
   Remember to Forget, 27
   Mostly Positive?, 29

The Royal Trumpets   32
   God Outside the Law, 34
   Rosh Hashanah: A New World Symphony, 37
   This Newborn World, 46

Second Gate—Yom Kippur, the Day of Atonement   51

The Weeping Waters   53
   Before YHVH There Is God, 56

vii

Contents

Where Are You?, 60
The Pure and the Holy, 66

The Haven of God   72
Thoughts Make the Man, 76
Spirit, Are You There?, 84
Up to God, 88
Reasons of the Heart, 95

The Three Pilgrim Festivals

Third Gate—Passover and the Exodus from Egypt   101

The Passage through Exile   104
Whoever Sows Israel, Reaps Humanity, 106
Dormant Israel, 109
Continuity in Change, 112
A Chromosome Called Israel, 113
Sow or Spread, 115
Exile, an Organized Disorder, 117
Memories from beyond Life, 121

The Great Crocodile   125
The Rejectionist Front, 127
The Clash of Worlds, 132
The Forces of Evil, 135

The Bread of Knowledge   140
To Eat Is to Know, 144
Tell Me What You Eat, 146
B-A-Ba: Abba, 151
The Leap into the Unknown, 154
The Leap, 159
The King Is Causality, 159
The King of All Kings of Kings Is beyond Causality, 160

The Bread with No Taste, 161
The Child and the Sage, 163
The Bread of Healing, 167

A Path in the Sea   170
In the Beginning Was the Sea, 174
Free as Water, 181
Our Mother the Sea, 187
Israel: A Pilot Fish, 191

Moses, the Human Fish   195
It's Him, I Recognize Him, 198
Moses: You Will Always Cherish the Sea, 203
Land of Men, 207
Like a Fish on Land, 210

Fourth Gate—Shavuot and the Giving of the Torah   213

Seeing Voices   215
The Secret of the Angels, 218
The End of Amnesia, 220
Hear What I See, 224
Know-How, 225
My Kingdom for a Mitzvah, 228
Hear O Israel, 230

Awe Yes, Fear No   233
Suddenly, So Close, 235
I, Anokhi, 238
A God Who Desires Me, 242

Fifth Gate—Sukkot   247

The State of Grace   249
God's Embrace, 253
Between Grace and Mercy, 255
The Dew and the Rain, 261

Seven Figures in Search of a *Sukkah*   267
  Substance and Subsistence, 272
  God's Friends, 275
  Reconstructed Man, 277
  The Princes of the Future, 281

The Times of Man

Sixth Gate—Purim   289

The Ace of Spades   291
  Totalitarianism and Idolatry, 294
  A Woman of Action, 298
  The Esther Syndrome, 302

The Pseudonym of God   306
  God in Hiding, 309
  Miracles Are Normal, 312
  The Healing of the Snake, 317
  Victory over Destiny, 322

Seventh Gate—Ḥanukkah   325

Man-of-Light   327
  Light, Lights, 331
  The Mark of the Commandments, 338

The Garments of Light   344
  Bittersweet, 347
  Clothe the Naked, 351

Index   361

Foreword

An ontology, a lifestyle, a system of values, Judaism is all of these things, but the backbone of its weltanschauung is a dual edification of time.[1] Time can be seen as the eschatological tension of world history paced by the great events of the biblical and postbiblical eras, which will culminate in the messianic age. Yet time can also be viewed in an astronomical or biological way. Its divisions—the day, the week, the month, the year—are punctuated by the rhythm of the Sabbath and a series of holidays.

There are seven such holidays, and we therefore felt that **The Seven Lights** was a fitting title for this book.

The seven major Jewish holidays can be categorized into three groups as a function of their tonality and origin. The first group includes the two major holidays that begin the Jewish year: Rosh Hashanah, the New Year, and, ten days later, Yom Kippur, the Day of Atonement. These solemn moments are known as the "Days of Awe."

There are three holidays in the second group. These holidays are called the "pilgrimage holidays" because the Bible commands all Jews to come to Jerusalem to celebrate them. These holidays are Passover, the Feast of Unleavened

---

1. Abraham J. Heschel, one of the great Jewish philosophers of our time, in his book *Man's Quest for God*, defines Jewish ritual as an "architecture of time."

Bread; Shavuot, the Feast of Weeks; and Sukkot, the Feast of Tabernacles. According to the Bible, the holidays of the first and second group were decreed by God and thus are holy. During these holidays, it is forbidden to work and virtually the same prohibitions as for the Sabbath apply.

The third group includes two holidays that were proclaimed by men and are considered to be less sacred than the preceding ones. The first is Purim, and the second, Hanukkah.

This book is the outcome of a dual encounter. Obviously, much has been written about the meaning of the Jewish holidays, but, in my opinion, no one has probed them with as much depth and originality as Rabbi Schneur Zalman of Lyady (1745–1813), one of the prime figures of Hasidism and the founder of the Habad[2] movement. This remarkable rabbi, who was a scholar, kabbalist, and spiritual leader, has countless readers and followers today, who call him either the *Admor Hazaken* ("our Old Master"), or the Alter Rebbe ("the Old Rabbi" in Yiddish). We will refer to him by the latter name. My encounter with the works of the Alter Rebbe[3] was a dazzling experience, and the hours spent studying his commentaries remain among the most rewarding ones of my life.

One of the mysteries, and certainly one of the charms, of the Torah is that one must always have a living master to explain the thought of a master who has passed away. I was privileged to meet Rabbi Adin Steinsaltz, who regularly gave

---

2. The acronym of the three *sefirot Hokhmah, Binah,* and *Da'at.* According to kabbalists, all reality is underpinned by the structure of the ten *sefirot,* the ten levels that extend from the infinite God to the finite world.

3. His main works include the *Tanya,* a collection of religious philosophy, and commentaries on the Torah (*Torah Ohr,* the *Likkutei Torah,* and a set of Torah talks ranging from 1802 to 1809 that are referred to by date).

radio talks and weekly lectures on the thought of the Alter Rebbe in Jerusalem. Philosopher, talmudist, and scientist, Rabbi Steinsaltz possesses an extensive background and an encyclopedic knowledge of Judaism. His insatiable curiosity and prodigious work capacity leave no area of the arts and sciences unexplored. He has that rare combination of strict orthodoxy and great open-mindedness. Thus, while reading the Alter Rebbe shed, for me, a new light on Judaism, I gained from Rabbi Adin Steinsaltz a new perspective on the teachings of the Rebbe that made him a true contemporary.

For several years Rabbi Steinsaltz appeared on a French television program, *The Source of Life*, to discuss the Jewish holidays. The intense interest expressed by the viewers, and their repeated requests for the texts used in our interviews, prompted me to write this book. It is a faithful rendition of the content of our interviews, and includes the necessary quotations that the rapid pace of the televised program prevented us from presenting.

Before delving into our subject matter, I would like to express my gratitude to Rabbi Adin Steinsaltz for the precious time he was willing to devote to this enterprise, to my assistant Pascale Kenigsberg-Cahen, whose skill and care were essential to the preparation of the original French manuscript; to Esther Singer, for her fine translation of the text into English; to Yaacov Tauber, who edited the translation, and translated all the citations from the Alter Rebbe's books; and to Ditsa Shabtai, who coordinated the production of this book in English.

Rabbi Josy Eisenberg

PART I

THE DAYS
OF
AWE

FIRST GATE

Rosh Hashanah
The New Year

THE HEAD OF THE YEAR

The Sages say: "The Holy One, Blessed be He, says: Recite the texts of Kingship before Me so that you may make Me King over you; recite the texts of remembrance before Me so that your memories may rise before Me for your benefit. And with what? With the shofar."[1]

For Rosh Hashanah is [the day of which it is said] "This day is the beginning of Your work, a remembrance of the first day." For on Rosh Hashanah man was created,[2] *and proclaimed: "God reigns, He is clothed in majesty,"*[3] *for it was then that His Kingship was revealed.*

Then, however, it was solely an "arousal from Above." Today, there must be "a remembrance of the first day" by means of an "arousal from below" through remembrance of the covenant and the bond which unites us with God, stirs the revelation of Kingship. This is achieved through the shofar, *which is on the level of higher teshuvah. It is a voice that cries out from the inner heart, so much so that no vessel of speech can retain it; for it is a pure voice.*

Likkutei Torah, Deuteronomy 44b

---

1. Babylonian Talmud, Tractate *Rosh Hashanah* 16a. The *shofar* (ram's horn) is blown in three sets of three blasts each: Kingship, Remembrance, and *Shofarot*. Each of these blasts is preceded by texts and blessings (in the Rosh Hashanah prayer) concerning its particular theme.

2. In Jewish tradition, Rosh Hashanah, the 1st of Tishrei, does not commemorate the birth of the world but the birth of Man. It falls on the sixth day of creation, which is the day on which Man was created.

3. Psalms 93:1.

> *Rosh Hashanah is the revealing of the Supreme Will; this is why this day is called the "head of the year." As every individual has a head, which is the head and brain of the body, so the year has a head, which is Rosh Hashanah, the head of the year.*
>
> Likkutei Torah, Deuteronomy 41c

> *This holiday is called Rosh Hashanah because it is like the head and the brain, which give the life force to all the parts of the body; similarly, on Rosh Hashanah the life force extends to all the days of the year.*
>
> Likkutei Torah, Deuteronomy 55c

Josy Eisenberg: The New Year is celebrated the world over, in all civilizations and cultures. It is generally a time for boisterous festivities. Judaism does not fully depart from the outbursts of joy that herald the birth of the New Year in Western society: in fact, it is recommended to feast on Rosh Hashanah. Although the holiday meal scarcely compares to a New Year's Eve banquet, all sorts of culinary traditions are observed.

Another, much more recent tradition, also characteristic of the universal manner of celebration, is the sending of New Year's cards with the traditional wish with which Jews greet each other on the New Year: "May you be inscribed and sealed for a good year."

This wish sets the stage for the special tone of the Jewish New Year. It is not so much a celebration of victory over death, of having lived, or survived, another year, as much as it is an apprehension—in all senses of the word—of the year to come.

Each of the holidays in the Jewish calendar has a name and an attribute. For example, in the liturgy, Passover

6

(Pesaḥ) is called "the Time of our Freedom"; Shavuot (the Feast of Weeks) is called "the Time of the Giving of the Torah"; and Rosh Hashanah is called *Yom Hadin*, "The Day of Judgment." In Jewish tradition, the Heavenly Court judges all humanity on Rosh Hashanah and inscribes us in the Book of Life:

Who shall live, who shall die,
who shall come to a timely end, and who to an untimely end;
who shall perish by fire and who by water . . .
Who shall be humbled, and who shall be raised,
who shall become poor and who shall become rich . . .[4]

Thus, from a religious perspective, the Jewish New Year is, above all, a bittersweet meeting with destiny. It is both the beginning of the year and the first day of a special cycle of ten days called the "Days of Awe," devoted to repentance, the righting of wrongs, and a return to God. These ten days culminate in Yom Kippur, the Day of Atonement. Traditionally, each person's fate is "inscribed" at Rosh Hashanah. This judgment remains "provisional" and hence open to appeal during this time, which is also known as the "Ten Days of Return (or Repentance)." On Yom Kippur one's fate is "sealed" permanently, which explains the New Year's greeting.

This extraordinary concept of an annual encounter with life and death is based on a highly specific view of Man's relationship to time.

Adin Steinsaltz: Contrary to conventional wisdom, Rosh Hashanah is not the start of the year, but rather a birthday, a date, a commemoration. In the liturgy it is called the

---

4. This passage is recited during the *Musaf* service on Rosh Hashanah and also, ten days later, on Yom Kippur.

"remembrance of the first day" or, in other words, of the birthday of the creation of the world.

The Sages say: "The Holy One, Blessed be He, says: Recite the texts of Kingship before Me so that you may make Me King over you; recite the texts of remembrance before Me so that your memories may rise before Me for your benefit. And with what? With the shofar."

For Rosh Hashanah is [the day of which it is said] "This day is the beginning of Your work, a remembrance of the first day." For on Rosh Hashanah man was created, and proclaimed: "God reigns, He is clothed in majesty," for it was then that His Kingship was revealed.[5]

However, we also use another expression in our prayers: *"This day is the beginning of Your work . . ."* This suggests that Rosh Hashanah is much more than a commemoration of the Creation. The text should be taken literally: Rosh Hashanah is the day on which the world is created anew.

J.E.: You are prompting us to go beyond the standard interpretation of the holiday. Rabbis have sought to determine when the world was created. The Talmud reports two opinions. The first is that the world was created during the month of Tishrei; the second is that it was the month of Nisan, the month of Pesah. We celebrate Rosh Hashanah in the beginning of Tishrei; in other words, the former opinion prevailed. Aside from the prayers you have mentioned, we also say the following:

---

5. *Likkutei Torah*, Deuteronomy 44b.

Today is the birthday of the world.
Today all the creatures of the world stand in judgment.[6]

One might assume that we are only dealing with a birth-day. You are saying that we should not interpret this verse as implying "the world was born," but rather, "the world is born."

This is a true birth. Nevertheless, we were just as alive yesterday.

The Point of Origin

A.S.: Rosh Hashanah reflects a concept of time that is very specific to Jewish thought. The day is neither an event, nor a commemoration, nor even a particular point in the time cycle. Rather, on Rosh Hashanah we witness a kind of absolute beginning of time, the onset of time as a series of strictly defined entities, rather than a continuous line extending on to infinity.

Each of these entities has a life of its own. In a certain way, time is like a living organism. This is why time can be born and then die.

For this reason, we often refer to an organic birth of time. For example, on Rosh Hashanah, annual time—the year—is born. We can truly say that the world is reborn. It is as though the creation of the world begins anew. In fact, all living things must be born.

On Rosh Hashanah the world returns to its point of origin. The pendulum of time also needs to be reset. The term "point of origin" is used because, in fact, on Rosh Hashanah we are not living at the beginning of time but rather before the

6. From the prayer for Rosh Hashanah and Yom Kippur.

beginning. Everyday time, our lifetime, contrasts, on Rosh Hashanah, with the time that preceded life, the time before Creation. Rosh Hashanah marks the crux of this dialectic.

The Year Is Dead: Long Live the Year

J.E.: A "time before time" merits further investigation. Before we examine this further, however, I would like to ask you to delve deeper into a slightly disconcerting topic you mentioned earlier: namely, the death of time. In the West we are accustomed to talking about the passing of time, wasting of time, loss of time. What is the death of time?

A.S.: Time is a pulsation. It resembles heartbeats: Each heartbeat is a singular phenomenon. Just because my heart is beating now does not mean that it is going to beat again one second from now. Every second, life surges forth once again. In the Kabbalah, this diastolic and systolic feature is called *Ratso-vaShov*, outpouring and contraction. It is characteristic of all forms of psychological and biological life and thus, as the Alter Rebbe points out, is also a feature of the life of time.

It is written: "Blow a *shofar* at the new moon, concealed to the day of our festival."[7]

The Supreme Will, which is revealed on Rosh Hashanah, emerges through the "concealment"—i.e., the withdrawal that occurs in the beginning of the Rosh Hashanah eve, which is the time of withdrawal of the general life

---

7. Psalms 81:4.

force of the bygone year; then, on Rosh Hashanah, through prayer and the shofar *blowings, another general life force is renewed.*[8]

It is as though the world has a heart whose continual beating enables the world to live. Because this beating is continuous, we are not aware of its real, dialectical structure, which is simply a chaining of discontinuities.

Thus, we can define the renewal of time as the emergence of a new heartbeat. In other words, life is reborn.

Let us note in passing that the word *pa'am*, which means "beat" in Hebrew, also designates a point in time.

J.E.: *Pa'am* means "once." In other words, the Hebrew language acknowledges the fact that time, like the heart, beats once, and then again, like a metronome. In fact, the heart is constantly dying and being born, and we are constantly between two beats of time. Inevitably, the day will come when no beat will follow the one before.

At Rosh Hashanah, one year clearly "follows" another. However, this succession also implies disappearance and death. We are at that crucial instant when a year has just disappeared—died—and a new year must be born to enable us to live.

A.S.: Time is both discontinuous and cyclical. For example, every day there are two cycles of twelve hours forming the hours of the day and the hours of the night. But no given hour is like another. Each has its own life, dimension, and tonality.

---

8. *Likkutei Torah*, Deuteronomy 54c–d.

According to kabbalists, this reflects the twelve different configurations of the four letters of the Tetragrammaton.[9] Each hour is governed by one of these configurations. In other words, each hour has its own code, a unique code, just the way each instant is unique.

Time was created to give life to the upper and lower worlds through the twelve configurations of the Tetragrammaton, which are renewed each day. Every hour a specific configuration gives form and life to the upper and lower worlds.

This is how the past and future are born. The first life departs and returns to its source, and another life descends from Above and becomes the time. This is why we use the term sha'ah *—hour—because the life force turns to the world[10] in a to-and-fro process.*

It is like the heart, the mainspring of man's life, which is a microcosm and which beats endlessly because it is within the process of to-and-fro.[11]

The second cycle is the cycle of days. Here again each day forms a complete cycle, a self-contained entity, and each morning is a new birth. This explains the importance of the prayer that celebrates this birth.

---

9. YHVH. There are twelve possible combinations of these four letters—YHVH, YHHV, YVHH, etc.

10. The word *sha'ah,* "hour," is derived from a verb that designates the act by which God acknowledges the actions of men by "turning" toward Him.

11. *Likkutei Torah,* Deuteronomy 61a.

In a similar fashion, the week has its cycle, and the month, whose birth is connected to the moon. Finally, we have the cycle of the year.

However, there is a fundamental difference between this cycle and the others. All the other temporal organizations are cyclical, but Rosh Hashanah is an absolute beginning. Recall that *shanah* ("year") comes from a root that means "doubling," "repetition."

J.E.: And "change."

A.S.: Indeed, what happens is a repetition of the act of creation and a total renewal of time.

A Programmed Moment

J.E.: It is obvious that no year is like any other. The years pass by and none are alike. The Alter Rebbe provides a good explanation of why this absolute beginning is called Rosh Hashanah, literally, the "head of the year."

Rosh Hashanah is the revealing of the Supreme Will; this is why this day is called the "head of the year." Just as every individual has a head, which is the head and brain of the body, so the year had a head, Rosh Hashanah: the head of the year.[12]

Every birth begins in the heads, the brains, of the off-spring's parents. The fertilization process initiates in the

---

12. *Likkutei Torah*, Deuteronomy 41c.

brains of the mother and the father. The child is the outcome of the genetic memory of his or her parents and of their desire.

On Rosh Hashanah, explains the Alter Rebbe, the new year is "conceived."

A.S.: Time is like a plant. The year only refines and develops the seed that is born on Rosh Hashanah and that will grow over the entire year. To borrow a metaphor from computer science, we could say that the "program" of the year is conceptualized and stored in memory on Rosh Hashanah and that the 364 other days of the year are simply spent running the program. Time is also like the body, in that it obeys the brain. This is clearly why Rosh Hashanah is called the head—the brain, program, principle—of the year. Rosh Hashanah is in some ways a "brain-day."

This holiday is called Rosh Hashanah because it is like the head and brain, which give the life force to all the parts of the body; similarly on Rosh Hashanah, the life force extends to all the days of the year.[13]

Who Made You King?

J.E.: Time is not given to us once and for all. Rather, it is doled out. Even its existence depends on the renewal of a lease, which is only seemingly tacit. The Sages grasped the fact that the creation of the world and the creation of time were identical. The decision to "renew creation" is made once a year, when God decides to recommence time.

---

13. *Likkutei Torah*, Deuteronomy 55c.

Let us clarify this further. First of all, this decision is not made haphazardly. Rosh Hashanah is the anniversary of the "first " creation. This event reflects both the natural and the universal. All humanity, regardless of belief or background, is dependent upon that point in time. Judaism is correct in stating that Rosh Hashanah is universal; God is concerned not only with the "time" of Jews on that day, but also with the time that each of the inhabitants of the planet has been allotted to live.

Nevertheless—and we will return to this in depth later on—Rosh Hashanah is primarily the holiday of Divine Kingship. The word *melekh*, "King," is mentioned extremely often in our prayers on Rosh Hashanah.

Nature has yielded to history. Accepting God's Kingship is not an innate, but rather an acquired, feature of time. Historical time is not identical with time in nature.

A.S.: In fact, there is a tight connection between nature and Kingship, and between the idea of the "beginning of the world" and the beginning of Divine reign. It is a closed circle in which the beginning and the end meet and merge. This is what the kabbalists call *Keter*, the Crown, and *Malkhut*, Sovereignty.

On each Rosh Hashanah, Divine Sovereignty is renewed, and it is written "They willingly accepted the yoke of His Kingship."[14]

Through arousal from below, by the nullification of one's own will so as to fully accept the yoke of Kingship, man

---

14. From the Daily prayer.

elicits the Will above to reign. This is what is called Keter Malkhut, *the crown of Kingship.*[15]

J.E.: In Kabbalah, the first of the ten *sefirot*, the ten Divine emanations, is Will (*Keter*). This will is creative and includes the will to begin. The tenth *sefirah* is Kingship (*Malkhut*), since the world was made to become the kingdom of God.

A.S.: The idea that the beginning (which naturally designates the beginning of time) and Kingship are fundamentally identical, is expressed by the kabbalistic axiom: *The end in action is the beginning in thought.*[16]

Whatever separates the first *sefirah* from the tenth are merely tools to accomplish Divine Will. They are the means, the techniques, to attain this goal. Thus, the world of intention, or Will, and the world of action, Kingdom, are one and the same. Thus, there is no duality between God the Creator (what you call "nature") and God the King. Nature is simply the instrument, the desired instrument, of Divine reign.

This is why Rosh Hashanah is both the birthday of the creation of the world and the special moment when God is proclaimed King. This proclamation is also a beginning, since Rosh Hashanah is God's coronation.

God is King, but He is a chosen King. In some ways, we choose Him again every year. Nothing is predetermined, "natural," nor is it guaranteed that God will accept the crown that man offers him. I will return to this point later.

---

15. The fact that God wants to rule: Immanence. See *Likkutei Torah*, Deuteronomy 56c.

16. From the liturgical poem *Lekhah Dodi*, recited every Shabbat eve.

During the Ten Days of Teshuvah we always say: O Holy King.[17]

Rosh Hashanah is the time of Kingship. This is because the world was created on the twenty-fifth day of the month of Elul, and man—on the first day of Tishrei.[18]

The revelation of Kingship begins the day man was created, since the concept of Kingship applies only to man and not to the animals, which were created before him. This is why Adam sang the Psalm: "God reigns, He is clothed in Majesty."[19] *Then God was robed in Majesty.*

On each Rosh Hashanah, all things revert to their point of origin, and Divine Kingship abounds from its source, as it did when the world was created.

This is what rose from the primordial thought (when God said to Himself, "I shall reign").

Kingship emanates from this will to rule; in other words, the ability to contract or conceal the Divine being for purposes of ruling over a separate being (or a being who imagines itself to be separate, since there is nothing but Him). What can God rule over? Nothing exists except for Him, as it is written: "I have not changed,"[20] *and "The Lord is King, the Lord was King, the Lord shall be King for ever more."*[21] *But since all existing things are nothing*

---

17. During the ten days between Rosh Hashanah and Yom Kippur, we replace the customary expression "Holy God" by "Holy King."

18. In other words, six days after the start of Creation. Man was created on the sixth day.

19. Psalms 93:1.

20. Malachi 3:6.

21. From the Morning Prayer.

*beside Him, every year His will to rule must be made to
abound.*[22]

J.E.: Thus, we find two homologous and complementary
concepts in Judaism. The classic concept is that of the
"chosen people." We are less familiar with the idea of the
"chosen King." What these two concepts have in common is
freedom. The choice of the Jewish people is neither natural,
necessary, nor predetermined: God chose us, and without
this choice we would not be Israel.

A.S.: The Talmud clearly shows that God first asked other
nations to be His people. Their refusal legitimizes the choice
of Israel.

J.E.: But on the other hand, God is only King if men freely
choose to recognize Him as such. The Alter Rebbe often refers
to the adage: "There is no king without subjects."[23]

In other words, God's essence and existence do not require us. He is everything and is capable of everything
without the existence of mankind. Everything, that is, except
being King. Without mankind, this concept is meaningless;
this is a sort of limit of Divine Omnipotence. Mankind "makes"
Him King.

All living things are affected by this concept of Kingship;
that is, man's conscious acceptance of Divine sovereignty.

---

22. Ruling, for God Who is omnipresent and master of all, is a type
of agreement, a "game" in which God consents to reduce His presence—to leave room, as it were, for the world to exist—and man must
ask God to renew this agreement. *Likkutei Torah*, Deuteronomy 51b.
23. See Rabbenu Beḥaye's commentary on Genesis 38:30 and
elsewhere.

Etymologically, Israel is the prototype. God chose Israel so that Israel would choose God. This is not a new idea. Even Moses stated it clearly:

> *You have affirmed this day that the Lord is your God . . . and the Lord has affirmed this day that you are . . . His treasured people.*[24]

It seems to me that Rosh Hashanah is precisely when this choice—or the renewal of this dual choice—takes place.

> *For Rosh Hashanah is [the day of which it is said]* "This day is the beginning of Your work, a remembrance of the first day." *For on Rosh Hashanah man was created, and proclaimed:* "God reigns, He is clothed in majesty," *for it was then that His Kingship was revealed.*
>
> *Then, however, it was solely an "arousal from Above." Today, there must be "a remembrance of the first day" by means of an "arousal from below" through remembrance of the covenant and the bond which unites us with God, stirs the revelation of Kingship.*[25]

In the Name of the King

A.S.: This is the discovery of transcendence. Why is the New Year period called the "Days of Awe," when it has nothing to

---

24. Deuteronomy 26:17–18.
25. *Likkutei Torah,* Deuteronomy 44b.

do with fear? The concept of "awe" refers to Divine transcendence, which is the true meaning of what is usually called "fear of God." "Fearing" God means being conscious of His transcendence. This explains why Jews go to the synagogue on Rosh Hashanah without quite knowing why. Divine transcendence, Kingship, is not always a conscious matter.

As the Sages say: "Even if they do not see, their star sees."[26] . . .

The flow originates from God Who encompasses the worlds,[27] and no human mind—created ex nihilo—can contain such a light without shattering; nevertheless, the Sages have said: "Even if they do not see, their star sees." The word star—mazal—comes from the verb "to flow." It means that which abounds, our soul, in the World Above.[28]

J.E.: The Sages of the Talmud, who, in my opinion, anticipated psychoanalysis, considered that part of man's mind, and his knowledge (or unconscious?), is located elsewhere, in what is termed his "star." The only apparent difference between this concept and the concept of the unconscious, as defined in psychoanalysis, is that the Sages situated the unconscious in a somewhat metaphysical location—the star—and not within the individual. This, however, may only be a question of phraseology.

---

26. Babylonian Talmud, Tractate *Megillah* 3a.
27. Divine transcendence, the *deus absconditus*, infinite being, beyond creation.
28. *Likkutei Torah,* Numbers 16a.

A.S.: When the Sages say that a man's star sees what escapes man's notice, they mean that if our souls were sensitive to everything that takes place in the universe or could perceive the immense range of phenomena around us, they would sense that the year is dying. Rosh Hashanah is both the last gasp of agony and the trauma of birth.

It seems to me that what motivates so many Jews to go to the synagogue on Rosh Hashanah is the uncanny, ill-defined feeling of experiencing the death-birth of time, and hence, Divine Presence. This is why they can proclaim Divine Kingship on Rosh Hashanah. It is a spontaneous, unplanned gesture, like so many kinds of human behavior.

J.E.: Granted, what fills synagogues on Rosh Hashanah is less a fear of death or punishment than the prompting of the collective unconscious. However, it seems to me that this act has strict logic behind it. On Rosh Hashanah, we proclaim the Kingship of God and we pray to be inscribed in the Book of Life. These two facets of the New Year are perfect counter-parts: because there can be no king without subjects, our "crowning" of God creates the need for our existence and survival.

A.S.: I would say that Rosh Hashanah is, first of all, a time of communication and this is precisely the real meaning of Kingdom. The kabbalists consider that the *sefirah* of *Malkhut* (Kingdom) is the place, the time, the channel or locus of a dual relationship where, in fact, the other *sefirot* are revealed.

This can account for the mutual dependence between the king and his people. This concept is not restricted to the philosophy of the *Ḥabad*[29] movement, where it plays a major

---

29. See Foreword.

21

role. It is found as early as in one of the most dramatic passages in the Bible: *"You are my witnesses, declares the Lord . . . and I am God."*[30]

The Talmud interprets this passage in the following way: "If you are my witnesses, I am your God." Only if you are my witnesses! Not only "there is no king without subjects,"[31] but also, if the subjects refuse to bear witness, they do not reduce the existence of God to nothing, but they narrow the vision of His sovereignty.

. . . And in the Name of the Father

J.E.: We should perhaps qualify our discussion of Divine sovereignty, since it might be misconstrued as suggesting that Rosh Hashanah is purely a holiday of Divine coronation. Of course, the liturgy is replete with words such as *King, Reign, Majesty, Crowning,* and so forth, as are the passages from the Bible that speak of God as King. The Rosh Hashanah prayers are constant variations on this wish for a universal acknowledgment of God's dominion, as expressed in the verse *"And may You reign, You alone, over all Your creation."*[32]

However, there is another tonality to the music of Rosh Hashanah. It is the feeling of filiation, an intimate connection between God and man. The main prayer of the holiday is an ancient one. Each of the lines starts by "Our Father, our King." God the King, yes, but also God the Father.

---

30. Isaiah 43:10.

31. See the previous section of this chapter titled "Who Made You King?"

32. From the Rosh Hashanah prayer.

It is written: "Blow the *shofar* on the new moon, concealed to the day of our festival; for it is a law *(hok)* for Israel, a judgment of the God of Jacob."[33]

The word hok[34] *means portion of food, or ration. This should be understood as meaning "I abound for Israel" so that Israel may become "My head."*[35]

Just the way the leg is ruled[36] *by the head and accomplishes its wishes without the slightest hesitation, . . . Israel is called the son of God; thus the son is called the "leg of the father,"*[37] *and he is under his rule.*

The verse says "portion" concerning Israel, and "judgment" concerning Jacob. This is because there are two categories: Israel is the son, the father's leg, submission, and self-annulment, whereas Jacob represents the servant. A servant may wish for someone else as his master, because his master is foreign to him. He nevertheless carries out his orders, and pays a heavy price by learning to curb himself . . .

Man is judged on Rosh Hashanah on his ability to "draw" God's Divinity into him.[38] *He is judged on his actions during the past year, which have made him worthy*

---

33. Psalms 81:4–5.

34. The literal meaning of the Hebrew word hok in this passage is "law." The Alter Rebbe provides a much deeper interpretation.

35. The word *Israel*, in Hebrew letters, is the anagram for the words *li rosh*, "my head."

36. Literally, "annuls itself." For more clarity, we have translated by the notion of "ruled."

37. *Yonat Elem* 282, and elsewhere.

38. To let Divinity enter into one's soul.

enough for God to be revealed in his soul. This is why it is said, "Judgment for the God of Jacob," because the conflict is there . . .

This is not the case for Israel—my head—the son: here, the portion is given outright.

Judgment, however, is merciful. This is why we have the ten Days of Awe and Yom Kippur: to allow us to cry for mercy and beg for forgiveness, so that the Supreme Will would reveal itself in our souls.

It is like a man who asks his friend to forgive him for the wrongs he has done. The real request is for the other person to lift up his heart and turn towards him. At the time of the wrongdoing, the other person turned away, as did his heart and will. Forgiveness consists of enabling (good) will to return.[39]

A.S.: There are two very different modes of relationship that unite man with God. Sovereignty implies subservience, while paternity involves intimacy.

The relationship to *Malkhut* is a hierarchical one. This is why the Rosh Hashanah rituals and liturgy deal primarily with a hierarchy, where God is the summit and men are the base. This forms a triple relationship associating the Creator, the world, and the Children of Israel. Based on the perception of a hierarchical structure, this relationship is not an intimate one. The fate of the world and the fate of Israel depend on the acknowledgment of a transcendent power and will. This is what the kabbalists called *Keter Elyon*, the source of Will—or, more accurately, the Divine crown.

---

39. *Likkutei Torah*, Deuteronomy 56a.

The second relationship, a close relationship with God the Father, is also part of Rosh Hashanah; but we experience it fully during Sukkot,[40] which celebrates our intimacy with God.

J.E.: It is no accident that the month of Tishrei converges on two key themes. Rosh Hashanah and Yom Kippur are focused on Kingship, and Sukkot focuses on fatherhood.

On Sukkot, we live in a small hut, whose roof is open to the sky. We place ourselves entirely in God's hands, trusting and living in an intimate relationship with Him. God is no longer perceived as a Judge but as a loving father.

On Rosh Hashanah, however, both these relationships intertwine. Divine fatherly love is necessary to temper the severity of judgment. Both these relationships appear clearly in one prayer we repeat often on Rosh Hashanah:

As children or as servants. As children, be merciful with us as the mercy of a father for children. As servants, our eyes look towards and depend on You, until You be gracious to us and release our verdict as light, O Awesome and Holy One.[41]

A.S.: Our real privilege is that we are both sons and servants. We are permitted to "stray" a little from God, an idea woven into the Rosh Hashanah prayers. When the observant Jew and the individual who is satisfied simply to pray on

---

40. Rosh Hashanah falls on the 1st and the 2nd of the month of Tishrei; Yom Kippur falls on the 10th of Tishrei; and Sukkot is from the 15th to the 22nd of Tishrei.
41. Rosh Hashanah prayer.

Rosh Hashanah stand in judgment before the King of Kings, they are both in the same situation and share the same degree of anxiety. Both are before God and say to Him: "Be my King." What did they do to deserve it?

Rabbi Aaron of Karlin was preparing for the morning service on Rosh Hashanah, which begins with the words, "O King." When he spoke these words, Rabbi Aaron fainted. When he regained consciousness, his followers asked him, "Why did you faint?" Rabbi Aaron replied, "Just as I was saying 'O King,' I remembered an anecdote. A rabbi came to Vespasian before the latter was made Emperor and greeted him with 'O Emperor!' To this Vespasian said, 'If you knew that I am the Emperor, why did you not come to see me sooner?'"[42]

The Emperor's question provides a good clue as to why these ten days are called the "Days of Awe." What could cause you to feel more riddled with anxiety than to hear your king ask: "Where have you been all this time? Where were you? Why didn't you come to see me sooner?"

This is how we feel as servants. As sons, however, we have the privileges of children. Regardless of what children do, even if they leave home for the whole year, they are still children. This is our only excuse. For in our position as servants, what could we say for ourselves on Rosh Hashanah?

J.E.: You can refuse to recognize God's sovereignty, but you cannot deny His paternity.

A.S.: In other words, you can revolt against sovereignty but not against paternity. I can rebel, but I remain a son.

---

42. See Tractate *Gittin* 56a.

This is, perhaps, what characterizes both the greatness and the tragedy of Jewish destiny: I cannot reject it all. I can rebel, have my revolution, commit violent acts against Divine authority, profanate, and so on. But I cannot cut the filial tie that unites me with God. This is beyond the power of my will. And this tie has existed throughout the generations.

Remember to Forget

J.E.: These two facets, fatherhood and Kingship, are brought together in Rosh Hashanah, the holiday of beginnings and the holiday of final outcomes. We said earlier that Rosh Hashanah is a new beginning and that the previous year is completely nullified. Yet Rosh Hashanah is also called *Yom haDin*, the day of judgment. Judgment implies memory, recollection of the past, and confrontation. The tone of the liturgy is that of remembrance.[43] We say, for example, "There is no forgetting before Your throne of glory," and "For You remember everything that has been forgotten."

So is Rosh Hashanah the day we forget the past, the day we make a clean slate, or is it the day of remembrance?

A.S.: The *ḥasidim* have a very beautiful interpretation of the second passage you mentioned, *"God remembers what men forget."* They say that if men only recall their merits and forget their sins, God only recalls the sins. But if men only remember their sins, God only takes their merits into account.

Nevertheless, remembrance and forgetting are not really antithetical. Both are recollections and are linked in subtle

---

43. For example, there are three series of *shofar* blasts during the morning service. The first series is called "Kingship" and the second series, "Remembrance."

ways. The first day of Rosh Hashanah can be seen as a day when we obliterate the previous year. It is a time of transition. The second day of Rosh Hashanah starts the New Year.

J.E.: Is this one of the reasons why the New Year lasts two days? Is the first day the day of forgetting and the second day the day of remembrance?

A.S.: They are two sides of the same active process. The modern term for this very old idea is sublimation. On Rosh Hashanah we sublimate the previous year. In other words, you can never forget without remembering. I need to remember what I want to forget. The sublimation process takes place in the following way: I need to relive and review the past year, so I can elevate it until it appears to have disappeared. This process of elevation, or sublimation, cannot occur unless we first recall faded memories. Thus, forgetting implies recollection.

This does not mean that Rosh Hashanah is a period of guilt. In fact, we hardly even talk about our sins. We are judged, but we do not confess.

J.E.: It is true that collective confessions are reserved for Yom Kippur when we recite the *'Al Ḥet* prayer, a confession (in alphabetical order) of all possible sins, and other penitential prayers. Though the mood of Rosh Hashanah tends not to be different from that of Yom Kippur, the two holidays differ at least on this point. There is only one prayer on Rosh Hashanah that mentions our sins. It begins with the words: "Our Father, Our King, we have sinned before You."

Mostly Positive?

A.S.: That is right. But do you know that in the hasidic liturgy of the *Ḥabad* movement this prayer is not recited on Rosh Hashanah? Since Rosh Hashanah is above all a holiday, a feast day when we are not allowed to be sad, we do not mention our sins.

J.E.: But it is the day of judgment!

A.S.: Correct; but in fact we are not being "judged for our sins." I would go so far as to say we are being "judged for our merits."

In fact, this judgment takes stock of who we are and what we have become. The purpose is not so much to make a list of all our daily shortcomings—this type of soul-searching should be done every day—but to make an overall assessment. On the Day of Judgment we attempt to balance the assets and liabilities of the world. The year comes to a close. God makes an inventory and wonders whether He should close up shop or whether it is worthwhile to start the creative process over again and "invent" a new year.

J.E.: I like the metaphor of the world as a store, a "business" where God wonders whether it is worth continuing or not. At times we have the feeling that this "business" is scarcely profitable and that God is continually covering the deficits so that it can stay open. In fact, the metaphor can be found in the Talmud in a slightly different form. The idea is extremely similar, and both expressions concern judgment.

Rabbi Akiva said: The shop is open, and the dealer gives credit, and the ledger lies open, and the hand writes, and whoever wishes to borrow may come and borrow, but

---

*the collectors regularly make their daily round, and exact
payment from man, whether he be content or not.*[44]

Does this world, this store where we live on credit, deserve another moratorium?

A.S.: This is the real issue, and this is why on Rosh Hashanah we plead with God to go on running the world's business and be our King. Our little self-examinations and personal soul-searching are not for Rosh Hashanah. We have the whole month of Elul, which comes before Rosh Hashanah, to devote to repentance and to return to God. Rosh Hashanah involves something else. Having finished the world's annual stock taking, we are ready, through forgetting and remembrance, to start a new page of history and welcome God. This is why most of the holiday rituals, including the *shofar* blasts, are designed to solemnly proclaim the arrival of the King and make way for Him.

This is the meaning of Psalms 24, which is recited often on Rosh Hashanah: *"O gates, lift up your heads! Up high you everlasting doors, so that the King of glory may come in!"*[45]

This is exactly what we do on Rosh Hashanah. We open the gates of the year, so that God may enter. To do so, everything needs to be in its place, the world must be worthy of receiving God. This is the meaning of our collective presence at the synagogue. By going there on Rosh Hashanah, Jews say, "Last year was more or less all right, we behaved more or less acceptably. But we want to continue, grant us

---

44. Mishnah, Tractate *Avot* 3:19–20 (Dr. Joseph H. Hertz translation).
45. Psalms 24:7.

one more year." In a way, the children of Israel go to the synagogue to reiterate their pledge of allegiance to their King and, beyond their shortcomings and expectations, to express the sole wish that God will, in turn, accept the crown from His people.

Kingship emanates from this will to rule; in other words, the ability to contract, or conceal the Divine Being for purposes of ruling over a separate being (or a being that imagines itself to be a separate being, since there is nothing besides Him). What can God rule over? Nothing exists besides Him. It is written: "I have not changed," *and* "The Lord was King, the Lord is King, the Lord shall be King forever more." *But because everything that exists is nothing besides Him, every year we must arouse His will to rule.*[46]

---

46. *Likkutei Torah*, Deuteronomy 51b.

THE ROYAL TRUMPETS

The shofar *is a pure voice stemming from the breath of the heart. It is not like speech, which is made up of letters that originate in thought . . . The inner heart is on a higher level than thought, and the voice of the* shofar *is like a heartfelt cry. It is written, "Their heart cried out to God."*[47] *This is the meaning of* teki'ah, *a continuous voice from the depths of the inner heart; it is followed by the* shevarim,[48] *a moan which expresses heartbreak; and finally the* teru'ah, *a wailing, tears destined to awaken Divine mercy.*

Likkutei Torah, Deuteronomy 58d

The shofar *unveils the Supreme Will. The* teki'ah *is a pure voice that reveals the inner heart; it is on the level of the Supreme Will, and is located above and beyond thought. It is written, "My Lord God shall sound the* shofar,"[49] *because the* teki'ah *represents the emanation of the Supreme Will of the Holy One, Blessed be He, which is higher than the letters which arise from thought, from which the Torah derives.*

Likkutei Torah, Deuteronomy 59a

Josy Eisenberg: Rosh Hashanah, the absolute beginning, is when we try to change the world by changing the year. The most spectacular change is God's new coronation, as though each year we needed to renew the lease on dominion that man's forgetfulness had almost rendered null and void. But

---

47. Lamentations 2:18.
48. From the root ŠVR, "to break."
49. Zechariah 9:14.

this also calls for a change in each of us. According to the Alter Rebbe, renewal implies plunging into the depths of our inner selves.

Adin Steinsaltz: He goes even further. His commentary is based on the well-known verse in the Psalms: *"Out of the depths, I call you, O Lord."*[50] Why do we say "depths" in the plural? The Alter Rebbe's explanation, one of the most poetic statements in his works, is that we need to reach the *higher depth*: the depth within the depth. Just as Rosh Hashanah is a renewal within a renewal, man can reach the true depths. This idea is based on the theory that when a man descends to the lowest point in his being, he can always go a little further down, until he reaches the source root of this being, the zero point before the beginning of his own history, in the depth of his being.

In the verse "From the depths I have called to You," *the word* miMa'amakim— *"from the depths," in the plural— is a reference to two "depths": (a) the quality of* Binah *in the heart, which is the innerness of the heart; (b) the quality of* Ḥokhmah *which shines into and illuminates the innerness of the heart, which is the quality known as "the mystery of the heart."*

An alternate interpretation is that the "two depths" are: Binah, *which is the "great love" [which motivates] the self-sacrifice in [the recitation of]* ehad; *and* Ḥokhmah illa'ah *(the higher wisdom), which is the higher awe.*[51]

---

50. Psalms 130:1.
51. Reverential fear. *Likkutei Torah*, Numbers 75b.

J.E.: Once again, the Alter Rebbe makes an original inter-pretation of one of the most classic texts in the Bible, *miMa'amakim*, which in Western society is known as *De profundis. De profundis* is understood as an abyss. When an individual is at the bottom of the abyss—something that can last a lifetime—we say that he is in a depression and that he grasps for God, his last shred of hope. This familiar interpre-tation is not entirely erroneous. When everything appears to be lost, is not God our only recourse?

However, the Alter Rebbe casts this passage in an entirely different perspective. I do not call out to God when I am at the lowest point in my life. Rather, I call on God by searching for Him from—or within—the depths of my being. This is ex-tremely logical, since the innermost part of man is necessarily the closest to God. On Rosh Hashanah we try to go back to the zero point of creation and, at the same time, to find the zero point of our souls.

God Outside the Law

A.S.: This twofold structure—*Hokhmah-Binah*—as found in the beginning of the beginnings, or the depth of the depths, represents the true structure of the individual and, by exten-sion, the structure of the universe. The Kabbalah helps explain this. The first of the Divine emanations—the ten *sefirot*—is *Keter*, the Crown, which represents Will. The uni-verse, and our world, come from this Will. This world is governed by laws that affect both matter and mind. But this well-organized and structured world also has a principle that the kabbalists call the Supreme Will, which existed before the establishment of the finite world. The Supreme Will was the first thing created, before any order of things, even before chaos. It is the absolute beginning.

> *On each Rosh Hashanah, Divine Kingship must be renewed. It is written: "They willingly accepted the yoke of His Kingship." By the arousal of the world below, by self-nullification in order to fully accept Kingship, man arouses the will Above to rule. This is what is called* Keter Malkhut, *the Crown of Kingship. During the rest of the year, this is done by submitting human will to the Torah and to the commandments which are (the expression of) God's will and thought. However, on Rosh Hashanah, this originates in the Infinite Will-of-Wills, the Will which is not even part of Supreme Thought.*[52]

In other words, there are two beginnings. First of all, there is the beginning described in the Bible. From something that exists—an idea, law, cell, matter, and so on—God creates the universe. But prior to this creation there was pure Will, the primordial Will, the source of all wills, which we call the absolute beginning.

This is what we are seeking at Rosh Hashanah. We are not seeking the source, but rather where this source springs from.

J.E.: The depth of the depths.

A.S.: The fountain of life itself, as is written in the Psalms:

> *With You is the fountain of life, by Your light do we see light.*[53]

---

52. *Likkutei Torah*, Deuteronomy 56c.
53. Psalms 36:10.

We should take this verse literally. The fountain of all life, the pure Will that precedes formative Will, is really found with God, close to Him, almost in Him. This is what we are seeking at Rosh Hashanah.

It is written: "With You is the fountain of life."[54] *Why "with you" and not "You are the fountain of life"? Because the world arises from Divine Immanence, from God Who "fills the worlds," and the life of all worlds arises from this Immanence. But nothing can exist in a cause-and-effect relationship with the transcendent God Who "encompasses the worlds," because the finite worlds cannot be born from the Infinite. This is why it is said "with You is the fountain of life," to show that the fountain of life is with You, and not You. It is entirely secondary (as compared to the Infinite).*[55]

J.E.: This is a fundamental distinction. In other words, God has two wills. One is a completely free will, the Supreme Will, because before creation everything was possible. The other will, causality, is the prisoner of laws that God desired and that henceforth constitute His will in action. In short, there is a will within the law and a will outside of the law. This is also true for men. In some areas, my will can be exercised freely and without restrictions, while in other areas, my will is governed by laws I cannot change. The only difference, but it is a crucial one, is that God can decide to move from one world to another, as is pointed out in the well-known saying in the Talmud: *"Whoever commanded oil to burn can com-*

---

54. Ibid.
55. Summary of *Likkutei Torah*, Leviticus 31a–c.

mand vinegar to burn."[56] This is what we call a miracle. Jewish thought—unlike Jews—does not like miracles and maintains that God generally adheres to the laws that He Himself decreed. But on Rosh Hashanah, we address ourselves to God's "free will."

Rosh Hashanah: A New World Symphony

A.S.: This is the real explanation for a beginning that is also a renewal. It calls for the abolition of the past. Eliminating the past, however, refutes the laws of life. I can try to change the future. But how can I change the past and cause something that existed to exist no more?

J.E.: This is exactly what we ask God to do in our New Year's prayers. *"Inscribe us in the Book of Life"* for one more year, without taking our past and our sins into account.

A.S.: This request only makes sense if I am out-of-time, in a place where the concepts of past, present, and future are devoid of meaning. There, and there alone, can I be reborn as a totally new person. This is precisely what happens on Rosh Hashanah. This re-creation, this total rebirth, is the coming of a new world. It is the true purpose of the main and most impressive rituals of Rosh Hashanah, the soundings of the *shofar.*[57] It is clear they will herald the Great *Shofar* one day—

J.E.: —which is something like the end of days: a new world is beginning.

---

56. Babylonian Talmud, Tractate *Taanit* 25a.
57. The ram's horn is sounded in remembrance of the ram sacrificed instead of Isaac; see Genesis 22.

A.S.: The World to Come announced by the prophets, a world of radical change for Israel and the world as a whole. The Great *Shofar* announces the first of these great upheavals: the return of Israel to its homeland.

> *And in that day, a great* shofar *shall be sounded; and the strayed who are in the land of Assyria, and the expelled who are in the land of Egypt, shall come.*[58]

But the prophet Isaiah goes even further. It is true that the fate of Israel will undergo the greatest upheaval in its history, with the ingathering of the exiles to the land of their forefathers. More than that, the whole face of the world will change: *For behold! I am creating a new heaven and a new earth.*[59] The world is thus destined to have a new beginning, and on each Rosh Hashanah we try to hasten its coming. Redemption means that today's sun will be different from yesterday's sun, that the skies will be new, and that new rules of the "game" will be set.

J.E.: In a completely natural process governed by nature's laws, this perspective is totally unfeasible. This approach can only be entertained within the framework of a theology that enables us to go back in time and place ourselves before the point zero of Will and before Creation, at a place where all the possibilities are open.

A.S.: In a number of branches of science, and particularly in mathematics, there is this idea that you cannot go beyond the

58. Isaiah 27:13.
59. Isaiah 65:17.

strict framework of certain laws unless you change the system. There is only a little leeway within the system itself, and the system cannot be changed from the inside. What you need to do instead is to get out of the system. This is what we try to do on Rosh Hashanah. We try to get out of the bounded system of our life and enter into a new heaven and a new earth.

J.E.: This is why the Alter Rebbe's explanation of the verse *"from the depths I call on You O Lord"* is so valuable. He is saying that this new world, our new virginity, is not located in a hypothetical future construction, as it is in most eschatologies, but rather can be found by traveling back to man's most distant past.

A.S.: In other words, to God. Just like the world, which is born on Rosh Hashanah, I need to delve into the deepest recesses of my inner self to find the point at which I draw my source from God. Rosh Hashanah, the birthday of the creation of the world, is first of all the birthday of the creation of man, and its primary concern is his new birth. You mentioned return. Although Rosh Hashanah is not specifically the day of *Teshuvah*, it is the beginning of the period of time devoted to this.[60] When we say "a return to God," we mean a series of acts of meditation, contrition, and soul-searching.

J.E.: We often call this period the "Ten Days of *Teshuvah*," commonly translated as "Ten Days of Repentance." The term is clearly erroneous. *Teshuvah* means "return." More than mere "repentence," this is a time of true return to God, a true turning backward.

---

60. The Ten Days of *Teshuvah* (literally: "return"), the first ten days of the month of Tishrei.

A.S.: There would be no existence if life were based on morality alone, because it is impossible to completely justify human existence according to ethical criteria. Our existence is linked to manifestations of the "supernatural" in our natural, deterministic world. This is the meaning of return. We return to a primordial source, beyond the bounds of nature and law and outside of causality. Ethics, like all other laws, has its own causality, and without return, the consequences of this causality would be devastating. One does not break an ethical law with any more impunity than any other law of life or society. This idea is developed in the Bible: *"One misfortune is the deathblow of the wicked."*[61] God does not punish man; rather, the act of evil itself is like swallowing poison, and death is merely the natural consequence of our wrongdoing.

If our moral conduct were governed only by causality, we would have died a thousand times for our behavior, our words, and our thoughts.[62] We go on living because we can escape the bounds of causality and enter into a world that is above, or beyond, causality. In a world where cause-and-effect relationships no longer hold, and where sin does not automatically result in death, we can be granted a new year of life.

J.E.: According to the Alter Rebbe, one can only go beyond causality by going beyond time. He contrasts two dimensions: time, which creates causality, and by extension, law and judgment; and beyond time, which is purely love.

---

61. Psalms 34:22.

62. In Judaism, ethics affect these three realms. We can do good or evil in actions, words, and thoughts, and there are commandments concerning each of these three areas.

It is written "For a little while I forsook you, but with vast love I will bring you back."[63]

In the times to come, when His Divinity will be revealed throughout the world, all flesh shall see that everything that exists is only an instant to God; this is why "For a little while I forsook you, but with vast love I will bring you back." *For when I take you back with vast love, you will understand that I only abandoned you for an instant . . . When man feels that the world is located in time, that time is itself only an* "instant" *for Him, because He is outside of time and before Him there is no division of time, his heart will flame and his soul will burn with desire to cleave to God.*

This is the meaning of the saying "Teshuvah *preceded the world." This does not mean that* teshuvah *existed before the world was created. Without the world there would be no sin and hence no repentance. What we need to grasp is that* teshuvah—*the consuming of the soul—is outside of time and the world.*[64]

The Alter Rebbe contrasts pure love, or pure will, the Supreme Will that preceded the existence of time, with rigor (in all senses of the word), which proceeded from the creation of time. He is, in fact, contrasting the Infinite with the finite. In kabbalistic terms, this is what differentiates the first *sefirah, Keter* or Will, from the second *sefirah, Ḥokhmah. Ḥokhmah* is already organized, whereas *Keter* is beyond any structure modeled on time. This search for a place-beyond-time prompted the Alter Rebbe to formulate one of his most

---

63. Isaiah 54:7.
64. *Likkutei Torah,* Deuteronomy 61a.

brilliant interpretations, his interpretation of the concept of wrongdoing.

On Rosh Hashanah we ask God to forgive *"all those who breached His will."* This phrase normally designates sinners, people who have exceeded the bounds and have gone beyond the law. In whose name, and how, can they be forgiven? Precisely, replies the Alter Rebbe, in the name of the world of pure Will, which is above and beyond all limits. "Regression," or return, is Divine love's response to wrongdoing. On Rosh Hashanah, we try to enter this world, which very different renowned philosophers and writers have called "beyond good and evil."[65]

A.S.: Think of an ever-flowing fountain where water is free. Each year is like a bottle of water that we have just emptied. We can refill our bottle with our share of life only at this unlimited fountain.

J.E.: I have gone beyond the law. I have exceeded the limits. I can only hope to go on living if, strangely enough, God also goes beyond the law and is outside of the law. We are not even talking about turning the clock back to zero, because there is no clock. However, although this opportunity, this grace of God, eliminates the effects of our wrongdoing, it does not eliminate us. We are not born again brand new. Once we are reprieved, we have the same potential, but we set off to improve it. This is one of the meanings of the *shofar* blasts. The liturgy makes a play on words and draws a connection between the word *shofar* and the root ŠPR, "to beautify." *"Beautify your deeds and let the covenant not be annulled."*[66] Thus, the past is not eliminated. Only the guilt is destroyed,

---

65. The concept of *teshuvah* will be discussed in detail in the Second Gate of this book.

66. From the Rosh Hashanah morning service.

and that destruction should serve as the springboard for our reconstruction.

A.S.: Rosh Hashanah is not Nirvana. Our primary aim is not to eliminate the past once and for all, but to have the opportunity to do things again and in another way. This is what we ask for in our prayers. All beginnings naturally imply change. The *shofar* prompts us to change. This is why the *shofar* blasts represent the feelings associated with Rosh Hashanah that we mentioned earlier, such as the death of time, the birth of the year, fear, the proclamation of sovereignty, the need for a fresh start. For example, let us take the third set of blasts, the *teru'ah*.[67] One of the most common explanations for *teru'ah* is that the sequence of highs and lows is evocative of the sound of a siren. It tells you that your life is in danger if you go on like this. The adage "improve yourself," which this set of blasts refers to, is a solemn warning. You need to change the future more than the past. You need to live differently.

J.E.: Change! Isn't that the key word of this whole holiday? Don't forget that the word *shanah* ("year," in Hebrew) is close to the verb *ŠNH* (to change), as are the other related words such as *yashan* = "old" (end of the old world), and *lishon* = "to sleep" (to stir from your slumber).

A.S.: And *sheni*, the second. This is because Rosh Hashanah occurs each year, and change also repeats itself.

J.E.: The Greeks believed that time was repetitive and cyclical. In contrast, in Jewish thought, repetition implies change.

---

67. The *shofar* blasts combine three types of sounds. The *teki'ah* is a long blast, the *shevarim* (broken sounds) alternate high and low notes, and the *teru'ah* is a set of nine staccato notes.

There is really no difference. God does not renew our lives for us to be carbon copies. If repetition does not imply change, it is only a terrible stutter.

A.S.: The *shofar* itself is a sign of a new beginning. What sign? We have already said that each of us goes down into our innermost reaches, to the depth of the depths. The *shofar* blasts express this descent. Not words, not even music, but pure sound. Traditionally, it is called *kol pashut*: a pure sound. This primordial, inarticulate sound returns me to a world before speech—

J.E.: —to the child who is the father of man?

A.S.: To the absolute beginning of things, to what preceded the first words and even the first music; in short, to the creation of the world.

The shofar *is a pure voice that comes from the breath of the heart. It is not like speech, which is made up of letters that originate in thought. The inner heart is on a higher level than thought, and the voice of the* shofar *is like a cry from the heart, as is written* "their heart cried out to God."[68] *This is the meaning of* teki'ah, *a continuous voice coming from the inner heart. It is followed by the* shevarim, *a moan that expresses heartbreak, and finally the* teru'ah, *a wailing, tears destined to awaken Divine mercy.*[69]

J.E.: The *shofar* expresses two types of purity, the purity of the human heart and the purity of the Divine Will. According

---

68. Lamentations 2:18.
69. *Likkutei Torah*, Deuteronomy 58d.

to the kabbalists, as channels of communication become more complex, they move further away from their primordial purity. Sound is purer than melody, melody less dense than thought, and thought is less complex than speech. We find all of these in the Torah, and the kabbalists have stressed the importance of musical notes, the *te'amim*, with which liturgical texts are cantilated. In its absolute simplicity, the sound of the *shofar*—a pure, "heavenly voice"—expresses what is the most primordial and fundamental in the individual: a pure cry of the soul. This cry comes from the depths that we try to reach during the Ten Days of *Teshuvah*.

Precisely because this pure sound is not part of any melodic structure, it also refers to the world before the creation. Creation is the Torah, and it is thought—*Ḥokhmah*—the second *sefirah*. The world before thought is the Supreme Will. It is unique, like a pure unstructured sound.

The shofar *reveals the Supreme Will. The* teki'ah *is a pure voice that reveals the inner heart. The inner heart is on the level of the Supreme Will, and is above thought. As is written:* "My Lord God shall sound the *shofar*,"[70] *because it stands for the abounding of Supreme Will of the Holy One, Blessed be He, that is higher than the letters that thought comes from, that the Torah comes from.*[71]

The *shofar* is thus an emotional, musical form of *teshuvah*. It expresses the return to man's "past anterior" in a way that is startling and full of pathos. But it also prepares for the future.

---

70. Zechariah 9:14.
71. *Likkutei Torah*, Deuteronomy 59a.

This Newborn World

A.S.: Yes, it does. Aside from the fact that it returns us to a past that precedes all pasts, the *shofar* always turns to the future. First of all, the *shofar* blasts herald the arrival of Divine dominion in the world. As was already said, on Rosh Hashanah we crown God. There is, however, a second feature. This is what the kabbalists call the "secret of the cutting." This is one of the basic tenets of the teachings of the Ari.[72] It deals with the relationships between the metaphysical and the physical in the process of creation. God created the world through what we call Kingship, *Malkhut*, a term that designates nature. Nature, the physical world, and its metaphysical origin, are not two different essences but rather come from the same "reality."

To separate the natural from the supernatural, this entity needs to be cut in two. The two halves cease to be contiguous and enter into a relationship of opposites. They can be side to side, or connected to each other, or dependent on each other. This surgical act is the *nessirah*, the cutting, the split.[73] The creation of man parallels the creation of the universe. Man also needed to be split. Man was separated from woman by "sawing" apart a single being to create two separate beings that are connected to each other and able to complement each other.[74]

All births imply delivery. This also happens at Rosh

---

72. Ari. Acronym of Ashkenazi Rabbi Isaac Luria (1534–1572), one of the great masters of the Kabbalah in Safed. His teachings, collected and transcribed by his disciple Ḥayyim Vital, have inspired the Kabbalah since the sixteenth century.

73. *Nessirah* comes from a verb that literally means "saw."

74. According to some talmudic interpretations, Eve was not taken from Adam's rib, but rather from one side of Adam. This gives rise to the theory of *nessirah.*

Hashanah, which is deservedly called the "day of the delivery of the world." The sound of the *shofar* is reminiscent of the voice of a woman in labor. This is the cry that announces the birth of a new world.

J.E.: It is a real delivery, and the metaphor is perfectly logical. The basic principle of Rosh Hashanah is, as we have said, a return to the embryonic state, to the Supreme Will. After this providential "regression" we need to be expelled, for life to start over, and the world to be reborn. A parturition must also take place, cutting off the fusional state we experience at Rosh Hashanah from daily life, which will begin anew in independence and freedom.

There is another relationship, however, between the *shofar* and this return to "time" before time. The return to the "Supreme Will" devoid of the features of reality, where man is at one with the Divine just as the embryo is part of the mother's body, is also a return to a single, indivisible Will, the Will of God. Here, in contrast to historical events, there cannot be any conflict between God's Will and man's. Is this not the prime meaning of the *shofar* blasts? They recall the sacrifice of Isaac and the complete submission of Abraham—Abraham's will—to the terrifying Divine command *"Take your son . . . and offer him there as a burnt offering."*[75]

A.S.: It is true that we sound the *shofar* on Rosh Hashanah because it is the day the *'akedah*[76] took place. Deeper still is the idea that the *shofar* is blown because on that day, a new birth took place, the birth of Isaac. In a certain way, the

---

75. Genesis 22:2.

76. *'Akedah*—literally, "binding." This is the traditional term for what is incorrectly called "Abraham's sacrifice." Isaac was not sacrificed but rather bound on the altar. The binding is a symbol of Abraham's ability to restrain his feelings of fatherhood.

47

'akedah is less a definition of the mutation of Abraham (the one who bound) than that of Isaac (the one who was bound). Strangely enough, many commentaries refer to the ashes of Isaac as though the sacrifice really took place, suggesting that Isaac died and was resurrected.

J.E.: This is what we mean when we say "rise from the ashes."

A.S.: A new Isaac is born after his will had been reduced to ashes. Some commentaries even say that this resurrection happened during the *'akedah*. This implies that the key moment in the *'akedah*, for both Isaac and Abraham, is in the total annulment of human will to Divine Will.

J.E.: Let me point out that this biblical passage hints repeatedly that Isaac was as involved in the *'akedah* as his father. They walked together to the sacrifice, and Isaac let himself be bound. This is why this passage is called the *'akedah*, to stress the "binding" of the will.

A.S.: What happens here goes far beyond the annihilation of human will. We are witnesses to the total destruction of established values. The ethical laws that forbid murder and human sacrifice are disregarded—not to mention the ties of the father–son relationship. In other words, the *'akedah* is an attempt to go beyond all laws and all love, in order to reach a level where the only law is Supreme, primordial Will. This is what produces the new Isaac, on the ruins of the old order that he was asked to destroy without his complete annihilation. The only annihilation man is requested to carry out is his desire to prolong the old order. When this desire self-destructs, the abounding Will Above awakens. This Will can re-invent the world.

J.E.: This helps explain why the Midrash says that Isaac died. Living is wanting to live. If I renounce all forms of will, I am virtually dead. I would lose my identity, because I would no longer have any autonomy. My will merges into the Supreme Will.

A.S.: This is the true return to the Primordial Source. What happens, or should happen, for each of us on Rosh Hashanah is very much like what happened collectively to Israel during the revelation on Mount Sinai. There, as well, death is mentioned: *"At each of the Ten Commandments, the soul of each of them departed."*[77]

J.E.: The soul departs, frees itself of the body in a climax that goes far beyond the climax of love, to the ecstasy of the Supreme Revelation.

A.S.: It starts in the *'akedah.* In the narrative, revelation is mentioned twice. *"And Abraham named the site* haShem-yireh, *which is the source for the present saying, 'On the mount of the Lord there is vision.'"*[78] This enigmatic passage implies that the seed of the second revelation, the one at Mount Sinai, is contained in the revelation to Isaac. In both instances, the man "dies" because he has seen God.

The Midrash goes even further. It states that the *shofar* is derived from the ram that was sacrificed on the altar instead of Isaac. A ram has two horns and thus two *shofars.* The first is the one that proclaims the revelation on Mount Sinai, which was made to the sound of the *shofar: "The blare of the*

---

77. Babylonian Talmud, Tractate *Shabbat* 88b.
78. Genesis 22:14.

horn grew louder and louder. As Moses spoke, God answered him in thunder."[79]

The second horn is the *shofar* of the final redemption, the ingathering of the exiles, the *shofar* that will proclaim a new heaven and a new earth; the taste of this new world we experience each Rosh Hashanah.

J.E.: You are prompting us to look at the Jewish New Year in a new way. Traditionally, the holidays are divided into two clearly defined categories: the historical holidays, dealing with revelation, and the "Days of Awe," the days of judgment. You are saying that Rosh Hashanah is fundamentally a time of revelation. The old year is dead, and with it dies what screened our will from the Divine Will. Our will did more than hinder the Divine Will: It restricted it. Thus, in the interstice separating the death of time from its rebirth, humility and return call forth the primordial time of the revelation, when God was undisputed King of the universe. Then, everything may begin anew.

---

79. Exodus 19:19.

SECOND GATE

Yom Kippur
The Day of Atonement

THE WEEPING WATERS

The origin and beginning of revelation is alma d'itgalia *("the revealed world"), which comes to vitalize and bring into being the revealed worlds.*

Now, the revealed worlds, which derive their vitality from the level of alma d'itgalia, *are called the "lower waters"; they are also referred to as the "weeping waters," as it is brought down in the* Zohar *that the lower waters weep, "We desire to be before the King," because of the knowledge and apprehension [that they would then attain]. For there are waters which are higher than them, which are on the level of "hidden worlds which have not been revealed." They, however, are called the "lower waters," since "God divided between the waters . . . and the waters . . ."[1] so that the hidden worlds derive their vitality from hidden forces and effusions. Therefore the [lower waters] weep over their descent to lower and lower places, their entire desire and craving being to be before the King.*

This, then, is the attribute of compassion, as expressed by each of the Twelve Tribes, that is within every person: to arouse great compassion upon the divine spark which descended from its place of glory from a lofty place to a lowly place, "from a high roof [to a deep pit]."
Likkutei Torah, Numbers 3b

The world has a misconception in regard to the essence of teshuvah, *thinking that* teshuvah *is something for persons of lowly worth and for sinners. The truth is otherwise, for* teshuvah *is primarily associated with the*

---

1. Genesis 1:7.

*lower and upper heh [of the Tetragrammaton],[2] which "a
brutish man does not know."[3]*

*In truth, [the essence of teshuvah] applies to "dwellers in
the tent"[4] of learning and Torah scholars. For the Written
Torah is the upper heh, and the Oral Torah is the lower
heh, and when one interrupts [one's occupation with]
these and occupies oneself with the vanities of the world,
one must "return" and restore these heh's to their
source, this is [teshuvah] in the general sense.*

*In the specific sense, meditation upon the greatness of
God, contemplation in prayer and the concentration of
thought is the upper heh; and when these are expressed
by the mouth in the endeavor of Torah learning and
prayer, this is the lower heh.*

*Now, the Sages have said that seven things preceded the
world, and one of them is teshuvah,[5] the concept being
that teshuvah is primarily in the heart, which is the upper
heh—that is, the soul's dissolution [in quest of] God.*
       Likkutei Torah, Drushim leRosh Hashanah,
       Deuteronomy 60d–61a

Josy Eisenberg: The ten days between the rebirth of time
on Rosh Hashanah and the atonement on Yom Kippur, which
open the year for us, are called the "Ten Days of *Teshuvah*"—

---

2. The second and the fourth letters of the Tetragrammaton YHVH.
The former denotes the Lower World, which needs to return to its
source, and the latter denotes the Upper World, where we need to
return. One of the functions of life is to unite these two heh's.

3. Psalms 92:7.

4. An appellation for Torah scholars, based on Genesis 26:27.

5. See Midrash, *Genesis Rabbah* 1.

ten days of "return." We will refer to the teachings of the Alter Rebbe to develop the principles of *teshuvah*, which is one of the most important concepts in Jewish religious thought. We mentioned earlier why *teshuvah* is much more than a classic "return to God" of the wayward person who rediscovers the path to faith.

Adin Steinsaltz: *Teshuvah* is hard to define because of its complexity. To understand its essence, we first need to contrast it with the concept of law. A "law" is something we cannot transgress without causing or experiencing the consequences. This is obvious regarding, for example, the laws of nature: I cannot put my hand in a flame without getting burned or walk barefoot in the snow without getting chilled. So it is for the laws of the spirit. Worlds other than the physical world are also governed by laws. I cannot sin without it having an impact both on my soul and on the world as a whole. The entire universe, both physical and metaphysical, is profoundly affected by causality. All of our actions have effects. These effects are generally irreversible. I can jump off a roof and then exclaim, "That's not what I wanted to do, I'm sorry I did it, let bygones be bygones . . ." Obviously, I may be sorry I jumped off, but that does not make any difference. What is done is done.

What is true for matter is true for the spirit and ethics as well, because they, too, are governed by causality. If I commit a sin, if I transgress a Divine prohibition, if I neglect a Divine duty, what is done is done, and what has not been done has not been done. My actions, or lack of them, change reality.

Teshuvah runs counter to these starkly obvious examples and irrefutable logic. *Teshuvah* consists of saying to God, "I didn't want that to happen," or " I am sorry I did that," and then, to obtain Divine forgiveness, to behave as though these events never occurred. How can something that took place, that exists, be no more? This is the crux of the problem. The first step in *teshuvah* does not consist of standing before God and hearing Him say, "I have forgiven." Before this happens, I need to tell Him about my life, my past, my world, and ask Him for something much more radical than forgiveness: I want my sin to be blotted out. It's much more than changing the future.

J.E.: Much more than "a better tomorrow."

A.S.: It is changing the past, so that yesterday is no longer yesterday. In a world governed by causality, this cannot take place. It can only happen when we come before God.

Before YHVH There Is God

J.E.: We are always before God.

A.S.: Yes, indeed, but for the Alter Rebbe, the phrase has a very specific meaning. It refers to a certain stage in Divine life, before all causality.

The Supreme Will has two aspects: one aspect is vested in Ḥokhmah (the Divine attribute of Wisdom), which is the first point of the hishtalshelut (the "chain of evolution" by which God created the entirety of existence). This level of Will is drawn out via the Torah and the mitzvot, this being the Supernal Will clothed in Ḥokhmah, for the Torah emerges from Ḥokhmah. [The Divine attribute of Ḥokhmah] is represented by the yod of the Tetragrammaton, and the Supreme Will that is clothed within it by the kutzo

shel yod [the yod's upper serif].[6] *The second aspect is
that aspect of Divine Will that is above and beyond the
order of* hishtalshelut *and is not at all enclothed in the
supernal wisdom. . . . This aspect is called "the Will of
all Wills" . . . and is revealed in* ba'alei teshuvah *(peni-
tents or "returnees") through their [stimulation of the]
depth of the heart. . . . Regarding this it is written,
"Before HaVaYaH (as the Tetragrammaton [Y-H-V-H) is
represented in Hasidut (due to the prohibition of writing
or pronouncing it as it is), you* shall be *purified" (Leviticus
16:30), that is, on the level that precedes and is above the
level of HaVaYaH . . .*[7]

J.E.: This is one of the Alter Rebbe's most subtle and original
interpretations. The key verse of the Yom Kippur liturgy is
captured in one sentence that forms the leitmotif of all our
prayers: *"For this day atonement shall be made for you, to
cleanse you of all your sins; you shall be pure before God."*[8]
The Alter Rebbe suggests that we interpret "before" as a time
rather than a place; before God, or more precisely, before
YHVH, since the Tetragrammaton appears in the text. What
does this imply? The interpretation hinges on the fact that
kabbalists consider the Divine Name and the Divine Essence
to be radically different.

The Essence of God—His real nature—is totally beyond
our comprehension. No name can name Him or, in other
words, define Him. In the word *de-fine* there is the "finite,"
which is incompatible with the Infinite. Nevertheless, the

---

6. The yod is the first letter of the Tetragrammaton YHVH; there is
a dot above it, called the *kutzo shel yod,* which refers to Divine hidden
Will.

7. *Likkutei Torah, Drushim l'Rosh Hashanah* 54b–d.

8. Leviticus 16:30.

Bible gives God a variety of names, starting with the Tetragrammaton. YHVH is considered to be the most sacred of all the Divine names, *haShem haMeforash*, the "substantive Name," which we are forbidden to even try to pronounce. According to the kabbalists, this is because the Name of God, like all the other names, is only an instrument invented by God to create the living world. This name is, in fact, a code. It is the substrate of all reality and hence of all causality. The real point of origin was the time[9] when the Name did not yet exist, and there were no laws. It is the "time" when God was alone, when He made all reality, the time outside and beyond all space and creation. Let us return to a passage from the Alter Rebbe that we have already quoted.

When man takes this to heart—that the entire universe is under time, while the entirety of time is but as a single moment before God, Who is above time and before Whom time's divisions do not apply at all—his heart will burn as a flaming fire and his soul will dissolve [in yearning] to cleave to Him.

Thus, "Teshuvah preceded the world." This is not to say that it existed before the world was created; for if there is no world there is no sin, no iniquity, and no teshuvah. Rather, this means that teshuvah with a dissolution of the soul reaches higher than time and space.[10]

J.E.: *Teshuvah* is a return to this primordial stage when reality has no reality and where the concept of sin is mean-

---

9. If it can be formulated this way. In fact, time was itself created by the Name and is a "time" that preceded the existence of time.

10. *Likkutei Torah, Drushim l'Rosh Hashanah 61a.*

ingless. It is beyond the bounds of ethics and law; an Eden before any sin. The God before the Creation, *before YHVH*, is also the God before Judgment. Return can be likened to total reversibility. We go back to square one, and the impossible annulment of the past becomes possible, because it is natural.

A.S.: It is as though we could alter our lives like filmmakers and say: "Cut! That sequence was terrible; let's film it again." This is *teshuvah*: saying, "That last sequence was no good, the actors were in the wrong places, the light was not right, let's start over again." In a film, what is unreal in our lives can be turned into something real. The paradox of *teshuvah* is similar. In other words, I can change my past and make it over. I am authorized to act retroactively. I can act as though what happened did not happen; likewise, I can also conduct my life as though I actually did what I neglected to do.

J.E.: This is what we call atonement, a return to the point in time before I acted.

A.S.: I return to the primordial source, to the embryonic state where all avenues are still open. Here, our life, time, and deeds are nebulous. Here I can start anew. This idea is materialized in a specific ritual that takes place on Yom Kippur. On the day before the holiday, it is customary to immerse oneself in the ritual bath.

J.E.: This tradition is based on an interpretation attributed to Rabbi Akiva. Playing on the double meaning of the word *mikveh*, which designates both "ritual bath" and "hope," Rabbi Akiva interprets the verse in Jeremiah: *"O Hope of*

Israel, O Lord. Those who forsake You shall be put to shame[11] as referring to God, the ritual bath of Israel, in which the Jew immerses himself to be purified. *"Fortunate are you, Israel: Whom do cleanse yourself before and Who cleanses you!"*[12]

A.S.: I return to the primordial source. I immerse myself completely and I disappear beneath the water. It is as though I drowned, and a new person emerged from the waves. I am like a newborn baby who was born twenty or fifty years ago.

J.E.: *Teshuvah* is the key to atonement. Divine atonement ceases to be forgiveness and becomes the natural outcome of the human effort involved in returning to the point of origin. It can be likened to watching a movie of a race while it is rewinding. *Teshuvah* is reparation, because it is a new beginning.

Where Are You?

A.S.: The opportunity to "remake" our souls is a boon in itself. However, *teshuvah* is more than a process involving our inner lives. As we have said, transgression not only affects us subjectively but impacts on the world as well. Thus, doing *teshuvah* not only consists of changing ourselves but is also an attempt to rewrite cosmic history. I rewrite my own personal history, but by doing so I also rewrite the history of the world around me. *Teshuvah* is return, reparation, and re-examination at the same time. First of all, it obviously involves the relationship each individual establishes between him- or herself and his or her sins and omissions.

---

11. Jeremiah 17:13.
12. Babylonian Talmud, Tractate *Yoma* 85b.

But fundamentally, *teshuvah* goes far beyond the problem of sin and each individual's perception of his or her acts. The real issue one must come to grips with is not one's list of sins but defining one's place in one's personal history. The real question is not "Is this man good or bad?" but rather, "Who is he?" "Where is he?" The crux of the matter is to decide whether he is "only" a man. If this is the case, there is a real lapse, a sin in the etymological sense of the word.

J.E.: In other words, something is missing. The word ḥet, which we translate as "sin," comes from a verb that the Bible uses to refer to the archers of King David and that means "miss the target." Sin thus differs radically from a breach or a violation: It is a failure to fulfill something to oneself. The sinner is a man who has missed out on his life, a failure.

A.S.: On Yom Kippur, in addition to taking stock of the year and repenting for various acts, we address the much vaster issue of "Where are you?" and "What kind of person have you become?" This is a question we ask ourselves and that God asks us, too. At times, God challenges us: "Why are you merely men? Why is the world merely the world?" In our moments of lucidity, we address this same criticism to ourselves. We reach the point where we are no longer satisfied with our human condition. In Jewish tradition, man's cries join forces with the cry of the world as a whole. When God made the world, He separated the waters, the first raw material of the universe.

In Genesis it is written: "*God made the expanse and separated the water which was below the expanse from the water which was above the expanse.*"[13] From this time on,

---

13. Genesis 1:7.

there were two types of waters: the waters close to their Creator, or Upper Waters, and the Lower Waters, which are far from Him. The *Zohar* teaches us that after this separation, the Lower Waters began to weep and said: "*We, too, want to be in the presence of the King.*"[14] The waters want to return to their source. This is the essence of *teshuvah.* Beyond being a reexamination of our sins, *teshuvah* is a bewailing of the separation and the cry, "Why am I not in the heavens?"

The origin and beginning of revelation is alma d'itgalia *("the revealed world"), which comes to vitalize and bring into being the revealed worlds. Now, the revealed worlds, which derive their vitality from the level of* alma d'itgalia, *are called the "lower waters"; they are also referred to as the "weeping waters," as it is brought down in the* Zohar *that the lower waters weep: "We desire to be before the King.*"[15]

J.E.: So *teshuvah* is not so much a return to one's sins as a return to God. The interesting thing in the notion of "the weeping waters" is that water is often used in the Bible as a metaphor for man; for example, the well, the fountain, the river.

A.S.: Man is a river. The waters of our lives flow ever onward. The notion of return reflects the idea that the river wants to reverse its direction and head back to its source, rather than merge into the sea. A river must follow its course, but it would like to flow backward, since as it flows it collects dirt.

---

14. *Tikkunei Zohar, Tikkun* 5.
15. *Likkutei Torah,* Numbers 3b.

J.E.: A good description. We are all rivers that would like to become sources again. The dream of the fountain of youth, becoming children again. This is one of the Alter Rebbe's most cherished ideas. He frequently mentions the desire for purity in the Jewish soul, which he sees as a form of yearning for the absolute or as thirst for God. This desire tends to be overridden by our daily lives, but it is nevertheless a fundamental trait in all Jews. Within, though sometimes unconsciously, all Jews bewail the absence of God. This idea has always surprised me; and I wonder, with all due respect, whether the Alter Rebbe is not being a little too naïve or optimistic.

A.S.: On the contrary. I think crying is the hallmark of the Jewish condition. Crying is neither tearful nor whining but is like the weeping of the Lower Waters. I have always been struck by the story of Moses who was rescued from the waters. The Bible describes Pharaoh's daughter, as she opened the basket: *"When she opened it she saw that it was a child, a boy crying. She took pity on it and said: This must be a Hebrew child.'"*[16] How did she know that he was Jewish?

J.E.: As if no Egyptian babies cried. Statistically, in fact, that child was more likely to have been abandoned by an unmarried Egyptian.

A.S.: Of course. But because he was crying, he was Jewish. And Jews do not cry as individuals.

J.E.: You mean they do not cry over their own personal fates?

16. Exodus 2:6.

A.S.: They cry because a basic characteristic of being Jewish is to represent the "human" part of the human race and to be the individual who is sensitive to the world's sufferings, its existential pain, and who feels this pain that punctuates reality. This is neither a personal tragedy nor an existential drama. Each individual is called upon to surpass himself, and this applies to everyone, regardless of his or her achievements in this life. This is why the Alter Rebbe defines two categories of *teshuvah*. The first is the *ba'al teshuvah*: the repenting sinner. But he adds that the righteous man, the individual who has never sinned, must also do *teshuvah*.

To understand the essence of teshuvah:

There is a common error that only lowly people and transgressors need to do teshuvah. *The truth, however, is otherwise, since* teshuvah *relates primarily to the upper and lower "hehs" [of the Tetragrammaton], and this applies particularly to the "tent dwellers"[17] and students of Torah; for the Written Torah is the upper "heh" and the Oral Torah is the lower "heh," and when one disrupts these "hehs" to occupy himself with worldly vanities, he must return (i.e., do* teshuvah) *and restore them to their place. More specifically, meditation upon the greatness of God and concentration and kav-vanah,[18] these being functions of the faculty of thought, are of the upper "heh," and when this is expressed verbally in Torah study and prayer, it is of the lower "heh."*

---

17. An appellation for Torah scholars, based on Genesis 26:27.

18. Lit.: "direction," i.e., the turning and focusing of the mind and heart on the significance of prayer, from the simple meaning of the words to its most esoteric meditations in prayer.

> *Now our Sages have said that seven things preceded the world and one of them is* teshuvah.[19] *The meaning of this is that the main part of* teshuvah *is in the heart, on the level of the upper "heh"—namely, the soul's dissolution [in yearning] toward God.*[20]

Because *teshuvah* is one of the seven things that existed before Creation, it follows that its essence is not connected to sin.

J.E.: Do you mean that *teshuvah* is on the level of ontology rather than morality?

A.S.: Precisely. The fact that we are alive means that we are living far from the source. The ability to return needs to be inscribed in human nature. When doing *teshuvah*, I retrace the whole history of the world and I go back before YHVH, to the "time" before Creation. All *teshuvah* means returning home, yet not to the home of one's ancestors or parents but rather to the home of the soul. This is the meaning of one of the most beautiful verses in the Song of Songs: "*Draw me after you, let us run; The king has brought me to his chambers.*"[21]

J.E.: In Jewish mystical tradition, the lover's words are really the words of the soul that wishes to enter the Divine palace.

A.S.: Why does it deserve to? Our Sages have tried to answer this question by establishing a cause-and-effect relationship

---

19. Midrash, *Genesis Rabbah* 1.
20. *Likkutei Torah, Drushim l'Rosh Hashanah* 60d.
21. Song of Songs 1:4.

between the beginning and the end of the verse. They deduce that because I have already been in the King's chamber—or, in other words, in an intimate relationship with God—I can once again ask to be led there, to be made to return.

The Pure and the Holy

J.E.: There is both the eternal return and reminiscence. We always return to where we came from.

This clarifies the leitmotif of Yom Kippur: "*For on that day He will forgive you, to cleanse you that you may be clean from all your sins before God.*"[22] However, in addition to another reference to "before God," the term *purification* needs more explanation. There are two concepts in Judaism that play an important role in Yom Kippur: purification and holiness. One of the reasons Jews are asked to fast on Yom Kippur is to distance themselves from the material world, to be more like angels who are said to be *kadosh*, "holy." Yom Kippur is a holy day, but it is also a time for purification. What is the difference between these two terms?

A.S.: The Alter Rebbe suggests the following distinction. Being holy is being different than others and on another level. This is why we say the angels are holy, or that Israel is holy, and that there are various degrees of holiness. The term that best captures the meaning of holiness is *transcendence*. In contrast, purity is a state that is devoid of all else; it is nothingness.

J.E.: In other words, holiness is relative and purity is absolute. If I am holy, I differentiate myself from the profane. My

22. Leviticus 16:30.

life is governed by other matters; I am different. On the other hand, a pure product is intrinsically pure. We could say that holiness is based on difference, whereas purity is based on indifferentiation. What is pure is not combined. Everything is equal and homogeneous. Incidentally, the Sages have drawn a parallel between the word *tahor* ("pure") and the word *tsohar*, which means "clarity" and "light." The latter term gives rise to the word *tsohoraim*, literally "double light," which means "noon." Thus, there is a close connection between purity and the dazzling light of noon.

A.S.: Purity is perfect clarity, immaculate whiteness, with no other colors, shapes, or forms. It is totality, plenitude, indifferentiation. This is why white is the color of Yom Kippur. The observant wear white *tallits*,[23] and traditionally under the *tallits* people wear white robes.[24] This is because white—purity—is the symbol of the world before the separation. It orients us back to that stage before Creation where we hope to receive atonement—that is, purification.

J.E.: The Alter Rebbe provides an interesting comparison between purity and holiness, suggesting that they are two stages in the progression of the soul. This passage, which contains issues that were crucial to the Alter Rebbe, deals with the problem of the "descent" of the soul to Earth and the motivations for incarnation.

Now we will understand the elevation achieved by souls after their descent to clothe themselves in a body. For the source of the soul is from the inner aspect of the vessels, which is the inner dimension of the ten sefirot of the

---

23. Prayer shawl.
24. A white shroud.

world of Atzilut *(Emanation),*[25] *which are as a body to their soul, the light of* En Sof *(Infinity) that dwells and clothes itself within them. As it exists in* Atzilut, *the soul is called the "pure one." Then "You created it, You formed it," and so on.*[26] *It descends to* Beriah *(the world of Creation),* Yetzirah *(the world of Formation) and* 'Asiyyah *(the world of Action). This is a descent for the sake of ascent for, as we say regarding the fulfillment of the mitzvot in the physical world, "Who has sanctified us with His commandments"—sanctity (*kadosh*) being loftier than "purity" (*tahor*), as is known [as is evidenced by the fact that] "purity" is said regarding the Levites, while "sanctity" pertains to the* Cohanim *(priests).*[27]

"Purity" as in the verse "pure as the sky"[28] *or as in the* Targum's[29] *translation of* tzohorayim *(noon) as* tihara,[30] *implies "brightness." [In its pure state] in* Atzilut,[31] *the soul is as the brightness of light. And yet, this description*

---

25. The first of the four worlds that arises from the En Sof (the Infinite), the world of Emanation.

26. "My God, the soul You placed within me it is pure. You created it, You formed it, and You breathed it into me . . ."—from the morning prayers. The Alter Rebbe is saying that this passage describes the various states of the soul as it descends from Atzilut ("it is pure") through the three other worlds, which are finite, and which are Beriah ("You created it") and Yetzirah ("You formed it") to our world of 'Asiyyah ("You breathed it into me").

27. The Cohen (priest) is the superior of the Levite, the priestly assistant.

28. Exodus 24:10.

29. Onkelos's Aramaic translation of the Torah, which has the authority of talmudic commentary.

30. Deuteronomy 28:29 (the same root as tohar, "purity").

31. In other words, the ten sefirot or Atzilut, the purity of the human soul. The soul reaches the light of En Sof itself by fulfilling the mitzvot.

applies only to something that is an existence, and to which there is a certain substance; it is only that this is a very bright and pure substance; namely, the vessels of Atzilut. On the other hand, "sanctity" implies transcendence (lit., apartness), meaning that it is removed and abstract of all definition and substance, so that one cannot even describe it as "bright." This is the light of En Sof *itself, which no thought can grasp and which possesses no attributes[32] at all. The ascent [to this level] is through* teshuvah *and good deeds. This is the concept of* tashuv heh[33] — *the return of the upper heh — as opposed to yod.[34]*

J.E.: I felt it was important to quote the whole passage because it clarifies everything we have just said, while also highlighting certain points. For example, it discusses the play on words in *teshuvah,* which is one of the Alter Rebbe's favorite themes. Each letter of the Tetragrammaton refers to a specific world. The yod — the first letter — designates *Atzilut,* the world of Emanation, absolute transcendence. The heh, the second letter, begins the world of Creation, the definite and the finite. Life begins by a traumatic delivery of the Divine Name: The yod delivers the heh, and the soul is separated from its womb. Through *teshuvah* (the heh) our lives return to the yod. This is reunification that kabbalists call *Yihud,* the supreme unification.

---

32. The light of *En Sof* is absolute indifferentiation, and the ten *sefirot,* its instruments, are not of the same nature; they are conceivable in thought.

33. The Alter Rebbe is reading the word *teshuvah* as an acronym of *tashuv heh* (as it can indeed be read in Hebrew letters).

34. *Likkutei Torah, Re'eh* 27a.

A.S.: Life is replete with separations. Time, which sets the boundaries of the past, present, and future, is one example. The supreme unification is the state in which all these boundaries are dissolved and where there is no differentiation between what was, what is, and what will be. Through *teshuvah*, we attain the Divine Being, which the kabbalists call the *'atik yomin*. This is generally translated as "the Ancient of Days." But the real meaning of the word *'atik* is "cut," "cut off," "torn from," or "separated." We should translate *'atik* as "the one who is separated from the days."

J.E.: Older than time.

A.S.: Completely beyond time, and thus, existence. However, beyond time, change does not exist. In this primordial stage, nothing ever existed. God is presented as:

> *You are [the same] before the world was created, You are [the same] since the world has been created, You are the same in this world; You are the same in the World to Come.*[35]

J.E.: On Yom Kippur we are prior to any event, we are outside of time and hence outside of existence. For this reason, we are before any sin. Atonement is possible because at this stage, just as when a movie sequence is filmed over, nothing has in fact occurred. The kabbalists also call the "Ancient of Days" the "long face," meaning the God of patience. Being patient means being able to bear something, and in Hebrew the verb *naso* means both "bear" and "forgive."

---

35. From the Morning Service.

A.S.: That is right. God can bear everything, as is written: "*It is I who carry, I was the Maker and I will be the Bearer and I will carry and rescue you.*"[36]

In other words, God bears the world in His outstretched arms, which is the meaning generally attributed to the verse: "*A support are the arms everlasting.*"[37]

Teshuvah enables us to return to the absolute transcendence of God, which in Kabbalah is called the *Sovev kol 'almin,* God Who encompasses the worlds, the supreme circle, where above and below do not exist. It is where, according to the famous dictum, the great and the small are identical, where nothing that occurs in time or space has any meaning compared to absolute Divine transcendence. Nothing ever existed, so I can freely decide and choose what will be.

When man takes this to heart that the entire universe is under time, while the entirety of time is but as a single moment before God, Who is above time and before Whom time's divisions do not apply at all—his heart will burn as a flaming fire and his soul will dissolve [in yearning] to cleave to Him.

*Thus, "*Teshuvah *preceded the world." This is not to say that it existed before the world was created; for if there is no world there is no sin, no iniquity, and no* teshuvah. *Rather, this means that* teshuvah *with a dissolution of the soul reaches higher than time and space.*[38]

---

36. Isaiah 46:4.
37. Deuteronomy 33:27.
38. *Likkutei Torah, Drushim l'Rosh Hashanah* 61a.

THE HAVEN OF GOD

The third [level of] teshuvah *applies even to one who refrains from evil absolutely, and does good absolutely; and this* teshuvah *is greater [than the first two]. This is [the* teshuvah*] referred to in the verse "Return to Me and I shall return to you."*[39] *The meaning of this is that which we have explained in another place in explanation of [the expression of the Sages] "all his days in* teshuvah*,"*[40] *which does not refer to* teshuvah *over transgressions, God forbid; for if this were the case, how can it be in "all his days"?*[41] *Rather, this* teshuvah *is over one's distance [from God]. For even though he does good and fulfills mitzvot, he can nevertheless still be an "existence" and a "something"; even [his] love [for God] is still on the level of "a being who loves." And the primary point of* teshuvah *is, as it is written, "and the spirit shall return to the God,"*[42] *namely, that he should desire to return to his source and root . . . in the essence of the light of* En Sof, *which is above and beyond the [Divine light] that fills the worlds and the [Divine light] that encompasses the worlds, for it is of no relation to the worlds at all.*[43]

Thus it says regarding the splitting of the Red Sea, "Till Your nation passes HaVaYah,"[44] *meaning that they reach higher than [the level of Godliness represented by] the name HaVaYah. For at the splitting of the Red Sea the*

---

39. Malachi 3:7.
40. Babylonian Talmud, Tractate *Shabbat* 153a.
41. No one can sin twenty-four hours a day.
42. Ecclesiastes 12:7.
43. God's immanence (which fills) and His transcendence (which surrounds) remain connected to the existence of the world. The idea is to reach the Infinite itself, which is above these two categories.
44. Exodus 15:16.

revelation was above and beyond the [Divine light] that encompasses the worlds; this is how the "sea" was transformed into "dry land," the hidden world[45] being literally revealed.

Likkutei Torah, Balak 74a

Josy Eisenberg: We have already seen that the purpose of Yom Kippur is to enable us to move from a more mundane relationship with God to an extraordinary one, one of transcendence. I would say that 364 days a year we face God the Creator, the Divine Immanence. This God is also our Judge, because the creation of the universe implies the existence of values and morals. Thus, everything we are capable of doing during our lives is important, significant, and to be taken into account. Whoever says "taking into account" also says "being accountable."

And then, once a year on Yom Kippur, it is as though we say to God, "Forget all that, pretend nothing happened, and let us go back to the starting point of the universe."

This is the meaning of the verse we recite solemnly when we open the Ark, and which is even recited three times:

Lord, Lord, a God compassionate and gracious, slow to anger, abounding in kindness and faithfulness, extending kindness to the thousandth generation, forgiving iniquity, transgression and sin, and cleansing us.[46]

45. The sea is the symbol of the concealed world, and the earth represents the revealed world. More on this is in the chapters that deal with Pesaḥ.

46. Exodus 31:6. This passage, which is known traditionally as the "Thirteen Attributes of Mercy," was spoken by Moses when he begged God to forgive Israel for the sin of the Golden Calf.

The Sages point out that the Tetragrammaton is repeated twice in this passage. Why? They say that You are God—love—before sin, and You are love after sin. This interpretation confirms what we were saying. We address God's transcendence, a God Who is "above" all and Who does not change even when events and acts in this world change, since they have no meaning or reality in comparison to the transcendence of God.

The Jewish definition of mercy is thus less an act of indulgence, or a decree of amnesty, than a shift from the usual state of Divine life—immanence—to that state of transcendence that we cannot hope to reach in our daily lives. One day a year, God agrees to play this sort of surrealistic "game," which in itself is an act of grace and in fact constitutes Divine mercy. But to obtain this Divine mercy, man has a role to play, and this is what I would like us to discuss here.

This role is, of course, *teshuvah*. We have seen how it operates ontologically. But what does it mean for us concretely? The Alter Rebbe provides us with one clarification. He says that the triple dimension of *teshuvah* should affect man in his thoughts, his words, and his deeds.[47]

Adin Steinsaltz: As we said earlier, there are several levels of *teshuvah*. The most elementary but nevertheless indispensable is contrition. It involves "repairing" my acts. This encompasses the individual as a whole and not just the physical. We repair the soul in the same way that we repair the body. It is like caring for the ill: We need to treat the wounds, stop the bleeding, set in a cast or sew stitches, as need be. This level of *teshuvah* tackles the various symptoms

---

47. In Jewish tradition, ethical values and the commandments of the Torah are rooted in this triplet. We are expected to do good and to eschew evil in our thoughts, words, and deeds.

of disorder in an individual, in order to get him back into shape.

However, there is a second and more radical form of *teshuvah*, which in fact probably no one can fully achieve. This is the *teshuvah* of my personality, my inner self. In this case, we are no longer examining the quality of my acts but rather the nature of my thoughts. Where exactly are they located?

In other words, in the abstract and outwardly, I seem to be perfect. I have always done what I said I would do, I have refrained from doing what is forbidden. Everything appears to be in order. Fine! But where was the real me in all this? What world were my thoughts and intentions wandering in? The issue is not whether I had what is termed "evil impulses," but whether my impulses were truly human. Sometimes you can be faultless and still not really be human. We are part of the animal kingdom. We are simply animals that are more intelligent than the others. But is this being human?

J.E.: This is perhaps how we should interpret one of the most disconcerting passages in the book of Ecclesiastes:

Who knows if a man's life breath does rise upward and if a beast's breath sinks down into the earth?[48]

King Solomon's question, which appears skeptical about differences in destiny between man and animals, has always seemed a little heretical. But your words suggest that the text can be interpreted in the following way: Men's thoughts do not always fly high, and in particular, higher than those of animals.

---

48. Ecclesiastes 3:21.

I thought about this passage once on a train ride. There were two businessmen in my compartment who, for the entire trip, talked about good restaurants and tasty dishes. I thought to myself that I had not heard a conversation between two people but between two stomachs. If cows could talk, I am sure they would discuss the respective merits of their pastures in the same way.

A.S.: There are people who are closer to zoology than to anthropology.

J.E.: A very banal model of "barbarism with a human face."

A.S.: When God made man, the Bible tells us that He breathed a spirit into him, a breath of life.[49] The *Targum* translates this verse as a "spirit that speaks."

J.E.: A thinking reed, but one that truly thinks.

A.S.: Only a man like this is worthy of being called a man, worthy of the Divine plan to be made "in God's image." And this is why the fundamental purpose of *teshuvah* is to bring our thoughts back to what they should be.

Thoughts Make the Man

J.E.: If true *teshuvah* consists of purifying my thoughts and placing them on a level of preoccupation that is worthy of man's ideal nature, a question arises. On Yom Kippur we hold a vast collective confession, repeated ten times during the five services of this High Holy Day. This liturgy includes a certain number of passages related to sins of the spirit: trickery,

---

49. Genesis 2:7.

lying, hypocrisy, concealment, and misuse of language. However, the emphasis seems to be more on a failure to obey laws concerning the body and on violations of prohibitions. I do not need to tell you that in many Yom Kippur sermons, rabbis talk more about respecting the Sabbath or the holidays or the dietary laws, than about the quality of our thoughts or our intentions.

A.S.: That is true, but it is easy to explain. First of all, it is sometimes hard to ask someone to amend his spirit when he still needs to repair his actions. Second, it is clearly easier to talk about actions; in other words, to address something we can label or virtually point to, such as "Do you keep the Sabbath?" This is easy to check. But if I say to someone, "Are you truly a man?" "Are you positive you belong to the human race?" I am certain to create confusion. The offense when I criticize someone is greater than when I criticize a particular act; in addition, the accuser cannot prove anything, and neither can the accused.

This is why appeals for *teshuvah* start from the most elementary level, in order to elicit the soul-searching that alone can make the question "Who are you?" meaningful to me.

J.E.: When the Alter Rebbe refers to the need for "repair of thoughts," is he referring to the problem of the purity of intent? We know that Jewish tradition has always stressed carrying out the commandments for the love of God and not for the love of the self; that is, without seeking reward or personal gain.

A.S.: It is much more than that. We need to know what we really value, the way we think about these things, and how we judge them. For example, a man can be a good father, a good husband, a good citizen. But in his heart of hearts, maybe none of this has any value for him.

J.E.: In other words, he does it all mechanically, by rote. It is a truism that sinning sometimes calls for imagination and courage, which are not within everyone's grasp.

A.S.: The really crucial items of importance for this man may be on another level. I am not referring necessarily to sins or perversions, but to things that are incompatible with our notion of humankind. This is why what we must "repair" is not only what we are thinking about, but also how we think.

J.E.: It is striking that in Hebrew, the word *ḥashuv*, "important," comes from the verb *ḥashov*, "to think."

A.S.: That is right. What matters is what is important for thought. The question can be framed in the following way: What does an individual really consider valuable?

J.E.: What are his values?

A.S.: What is decisive for him? What has an impact? We have already mentioned the verse from Psalms *"From the depths, I call You, O Lord."*[50] This verse, and the plural form of "depths," had a profound effect on the Alter Rebbe. He even goes so far as to speak not only of a depth within the depths, but of ten depths through which we pass successively, between Rosh Hashanah and Yom Kippur.

There are ten "depths" corresponding to the ten at-tributes of the soul—the seven traits and the three intellectual faculties.[51] *The "depth" of each attribute is its*

---

50. Psalms 130:1. See the section "The Royal Trumpets."
51. Three of the ten *sefirot* deal with matters of the spirit, and

root, which is called the "depth of darkness"—to say, the darkness which has not yet come to be revealed in the soul . . . These derive from the supreme attributes, coming from above, which are higher than the faculties manifested in the soul. It is only through [man's service of God on the level of] "with all your might"[52] that these "depths" are revealed.

It is from this state that "I call you HaVaYaH," renewing the HaVaYaH in the soul and causing the HaVaYaH of the "depths," that have yet to manifest themselves in the soul, to be in the soul. Through this [one achieves that] "God transformed the curse into blessing,"[53] for from this place is drawn forgiveness for sins. . . .

We therefore recite the psalm "From the depths I call You HaVaYaH" on the Ten Days of Teshuvah, for each day draws down another "depth," until Yom Kippur—[of which it is written] "Before HaVaYaH you shall be purified"[54]—when the level of "Before HaVaYaH," from which is drawn down the effect that "you shall be purified," is manifested in the soul.[55]

A.S.: Sometimes a person can exhibit all the outward manifestations of well-being. But when you scratch the surface, the picture changes entirely. Repairing the soul involves going to its very depths. We need to reach this inner depth in

---

seven, called *midot*—"measures"—represent the world of ethics and values.

52. Deuteronomy 6:5. The Alter Rebbe uses this term to refer to the ability to surpass oneself.

53. Deuteronomy 23:6.

54. Leviticus 16:20.

55. *Likkutei Torah, Ki Tetze* 39b.

order to achieve what the Alter Rebbe calls the "ultimate and supreme repair": the repair of the soul.

For each of us, this involves thinking globally about our place in the world, to pierce our existence, to reach the depth of the depths: the inner depths. This form of knowledge calls for understanding rather than contrition. This is because the soul itself can never sin. It has nothing to repair. Sin can affect the other levels of our lives. Our self, our *nefesh*, can sin; our spirit, *ruah*, can be impure; but the soul is always pure.

J.E.: What an astounding claim! Isn't the perversion of the soul found in all of literature? The Alter Rebbe, however, makes the immaculateness of the soul one of the hallmarks of his thought. Let us try to sort things out. In traditional Jewish psychology, man is clearly composed of a body and a soul; but what is conventionally known as the "soul" corresponds, in fact, to the three dimensions you mentioned earlier; namely, man has a *nefesh*, a *ruah*, and a *neshamah*.

Nefesh designates the individual's set of vital functions; in other words: physiology, instincts, libido, and so on, or what I would call his will and ability to live. This is the level of human biology and the individual as a living being. The word *nefesh* happens to be used in the Bible in contexts when people are counted. It is said that there are so many "souls," *nefesh*, in a given locality.

Second, man has a *ruah*. The word, which means both "wind" and "breath," refers to an individual's spirit. Another translation would be the individual's intellectual and moral abilities, his values, his ideology, beliefs, and so on. *Ruah*, like *nefesh*, is associated with the body. In fact, it connotes bodily functions that are restricted by the same limitations and bounds as the body. Man's immortality comes from the presence of a spark of the *En Sof*, the Divine Infiniteness, which is called *neshamah*. It is the highest of the three human components, and the word *soul* should be reserved for it alone. Every morning, when, according to Jewish tradition, the Divine soul re-enters the human body that it left during the night, we recite a prayer that begins:

> *My God, the soul which you have given within me is pure. You have created it; You have formed it; You have breathed it into me.*[56]

The classic interpretation is that my soul *was* pure before Creation. Not at all, says the Alter Rebbe. Because the words *created* and *formed* designate the second and the third of the four worlds, he deduces that the word *pure* designates the first of these worlds, the world of Emanation. This is the world of Divine light that nothing can blot out, and this is why we should read: *My God, the soul which You have given in me is pure.*

The soul is a tiny gem hewed from a diamond, a spark of Divine light that nothing can cut. It is set in the *nefesh* and the *ruah*. If they are sullied by life, the soul gets spattered like a diamond that has fallen into the mud. It loses its brilliance but not its purity. It would be dulled but not scratched or broken. In other words, and the Alter Rebbe often refers to this theory, this "part of God" within man may appear to be missing if the individual has erred. People live through *nefesh* and *ruah*. In contrast, *neshamah* is a virtual presence in each of us. We can push it aside or exclude it from our field of vision altogether. In some of his writings, the Alter Rebbe states that sometimes the soul hovers about the individual, waiting for him to open the door to his inner self.

56. Babylonian Talmud, Tractate *Berakhot* 60b.

> . . . the upper soul, which is not vested within the body.
> For not the entire soul is vested [in the body], only a
> reflection and extension of it, while the essence of the
> soul hovers above [the body]. This [transcendent essence
> of the soul] is called mazal.[57]

A.S.: The concept of *teshuvah* incorporates the idea that we also need to make our soul "come back."

J.E.: "Returned to himself" is an expression we use when someone recovers from a fainting spell. Sometimes our soul faints.

A.S.: It is as though the individual were separated from his soul. The soul is exiled. It exists in one sphere, and the person in another. Nothing connects them any more. *Teshuvah*, return, consists of bringing the soul back to the person, as though the person were dead, and we needed to resuscitate his soul.

Here, *teshuvah* does not involve an act of contrition (the first type of *teshuvah*) or "repairing" the soul (the second form), but rather a desire to seek it out. The soul is like a tiny spark buried in the "depths," hidden in the ashes, the coals, or the dross, that I need to dig out to bring back to life. The third level of *teshuvah* does not consist of returning to a childhood state but, rather, regaining my true adulthood.

> The third [level of] teshuvah *applies even to one who*
> *refrains from evil absolutely, and does good absolutely;*
> *and this* teshuvah *is greater [than the first two]. This is*

57. *Likkutei Torah*, Numbers 16a.

[the teshuvah*] referred to in the verse, "Return to Me and I shall return to you."*[58] *The meaning of this is "all his days in* teshuvah,*"*[59] *which does not refer to* teshuvah *over transgressions, God forbid, for if this were the case, how can it be "all his days"? Rather, this* teshuvah *is all over one's distance [from God]. For even though he does good and fulfills mitzvot, he can nevertheless still be an "existence" and a "something"; even [his] love [for God] is still on the level of "a being who loves." And the primary point of* teshuvah *is, as it is written, "and the spirit shall return to the God."*[60] *Namely, that he should desire to return to his source and root . . . in the essence of the light of* En Sof, *which is above and beyond the [Divine light] that fills the worlds and the [Divine light] that encompasses the worlds, for it is of no relation to the worlds at all. Thus it says regarding the splitting of the Red Sea, "Till Your nation passes HaVaYah,"*[61] *meaning that they reach higher than [the level of Godliness represented by] the name HaVaYah. For at the splitting of the Red Sea the revelation was above and beyond the [Divine light] that encompasses the worlds; this is how the "sea" was transformed into "dry land," the hidden world being literally revealed.*[62]

In the teachings of Hasidism,[63] the word *adam* (man) is said to derive from two sources. The first, more biblical,

---

58. Malachi 3:7.
59. Babylonian Talmud, Tractate *Shabbat* 153a.
60. Ecclesiastes 12:7.
61. Exodus 15:16.
62. *Likkutei Torah, Balak* 74a.
63. And also in the works of several other writers prior to the advent of Hasidism, such as Rabbi Isaiah Horowitz, the Shelah (1565–1630), in his commentary *Shnei Luhot haBrit* ("The Two Tablets of the Covenant").

interpretation, links Adam to *adama* (Earth). Man was drawn from the Earth. He is a terrestrial being, an earthling, and a mortal. The second, more etymological interpretation is that Adam comes from the phrase *edame la'elyon*: I resemble the One Above. Man is in the image of God. In other words, man aspires to the image that God has of man. To do *teshuvah* is to return not to the person that I was, but to the person that I should be, and to recover the quintessential purity of my being.

Spirit, Are You There?

J.E.: What the Alter Rebbe has to say about the soul should clarify some ambiguities concerning spiritual life. He makes a radical distinction between the life of the spirit and the life of the soul. There is a tendency to combine the two and to assume that beautiful spirits, or great spirits, are great souls. The words themselves are confusing. The words *spirit* and *spiritual* have the same root, and the word *spiritual* is in itself ambiguous: someone can be spirited, but the spiritual life of a saintly man is usually not spirited.

In other words, Western thought may have too strong a tendency to confuse culture and spirituality. However, the former is no guarantee of the latter. An individual can be spiritual in the sense of being refined, but this does not mean that he or she has a spiritual life, unless the soul (which has fainted) comes back to itself. Perhaps one of the most striking examples in our generation of the dichotomy between the culture and spirituality is that of Nazi Germany. Germany is one of the most refined countries in the world in the arts and letters, yet it was the country that operated the gas chambers.

A.S.: Western culture places so much value on culture that it calls it "spiritual life." In Judaism, what happens in my *ruaḥ* is not necessarily superior to what happens in my *nefesh*. Why should an individual's brain be more sacred than his body? Spirit and matter are two forms of life, two different modes of the same reality.

I would say that Judaism anticipated somewhat the theory of relativity. Before Einstein, matter and energy were thought to be two entirely different entities. We know today that they are basically the same and are simply two facets of the same reality. Similarly, there is a conventional distinction between mind and matter. Judaism has always refused to accept this division. Mind and matter are only two phases of the same reality. One cannot be associated with good and the other with evil.

J.E.: For the simple reason that matter, our body, our minds, and our souls are all desired and created by God and bear the mark of the Divine.

A.S.: In Judaism, the real opposition is not between mind and body, or body and soul, but between the sacred and the profane. And it is clear that many facets of "spiritual" life are unrelated to the sacred. Only the sacred and the profane are two different worlds. In contrast, the differences between the various facets of existence, both material and spiritual, are only quantitative. This is why we can be totally absorbed in the "spiritual" life of the mind—for example, devoting our life to philosophy or music—and nevertheless live completely in a nonsacred world. Hasidism emphasizes the close connections between thought and matter. Thought is the outcome of the functioning of a physical organ, the brain. This is why thought is one thing, and the soul, another.

J.E.: This is also one of the Alter Rebbe's favorite topics. All thought has a material substrate. Thought is not completely abstract or immaterial. Only the soul is "pure spirit."

A.S.: Thought is dependent on various physical, chemical, and biological functions of the brain. Thought thus belongs to the world of the profane. The soul, on the other hand, is part of the sacred world, and this is why the soul can remain sacred even when it acts or manifests itself in the world of matter. But the soul can also be totally cut off from the sacred if the individual is caught up in a "spiritual" world.

J.E.: Let me try to reformulate. I can cut wood and be immersed in the sacred, and I can listen to Bach and be in the profane. This said, I would like to come back to the problem of the "repair of the soul." It is easy, in theory at least, to repair one's acts. If I cause damage to someone, I can compensate the damage: I apologize, I pay, I repair. If I had evil intentions, I can try to change them. But how can I "repair" my soul?

A.S.: Very simply, by letting the soul return; since, as we said, it can take its leave. The other "repairs" are only the halfway houses where the soul can reside. One day a rabbi asked his followers, "Where is God?" They answered, "What a question! God is everywhere." The rabbi shook his head and in a very simple and disconcerting way said, "Oh, no. God is where you let Him come in." The same is true for the soul. We need to make room for Him to enter. But things do not stop there. We cannot be satisfied with an existence where the soul comes and goes, giving us moments of ecstasy and then departing—

J.E.: —or when we abandon the soul.

A.S.: This relates to what the Alter Rebbe said about the two depths. Our deepest desire is to find our soul in the depths of our inner selves. The individual can then extract all the impurities from his inner self and finally reach the most intimate, almost fusional, place where his Ego is connected to God. This is the basic motivation of *teshuvah*. The prophets express this as follows: *"Why are You like a stranger in the land?"*[64] Sometimes, God feels like a stranger in our world.

J.E.: You remind me of a teaching by the Maggid of Dubno, one of the great masters of the nineteenth century, regarding the following verse: *"You are but strangers resident with Me."*[65] According to the Maggid, God speaks to the Jews and says, "If you consider yourselves to be citizens, settled in this world, I become a stranger. But if you consider yourselves to be strangers, temporary residents, in the world, then I will reside here completely."

A.S.: The real function of *teshuvah* is to put an end to God's exile. To achieve this, I need to search inside myself and find the core of my existence, by searching ceaselessly day and night:

Upon my couch at night, I sought the one I love.[66]

I can only encounter God in the depths of my being, once I have ridden myself of all the veils, dross, and lies, the lies I tell myself. In the Psalms God is called *"the strength of my*

---

64. Jeremiah 14:8.
65. Leviticus 25:23.
66. Song of Songs 3:1.

87

heart and my portion for ever."[67] We should understand this as meaning that my real strength, the core of my being, is God, forever.

Up to God

J.E.: This search for my soul, in a continual dialectic of presence and absence, and the seeking of authenticity, is one of the Alter Rebbe's interpretations of the splitting of the Red Sea.[68] The following text links this event to the revelation of a higher reality that is crucial to achieving atonement on Yom Kippur.

Thus it says regarding the splitting of the Red Sea, "Till Your nation passes HaVaYah"[69]—*meaning that they reach higher than [the level of Godliness represented by] the name HaVaYah. For at the splitting of the Red Sea the revelation was above and beyond the [Divine light] that encompasses the worlds; this is how the "sea" was transformed into "dry land," the hidden world being literally revealed.*[70]

The earth represents the revealed world, and the sea is the concealed world. The visible ego and the concealed soul exist in all individuals.

---

67. Psalms 73:26.
68. See the sections "A Path in the Sea" and "Moses the Human Fish."
69. Exodus 15:16.
70. *Likkutei Torah, Balak* 74a.

A.S.: That is right. The Red Sea split to reveal the "depths of the depths." In this historical circumstance, there was a miracle: God split the sea for the Children of Israel. This miracle can happen again. God will not reveal Himself directly to us, but rather a light will penetrate us, our eyes will be opened, and the black holes of reality will dissipate. Most of the time, however, we must make the effort ourselves.

J.E.: We would all like to be granted such grace, but you know that the Sages of the Talmud, as paradoxical as it may seem, did not like miracles. The Alter Rebbe takes the same approach when he emphasizes searching rather than grace.

To understand how this is reflected in [man's] service of God:

We see that there are two levels of [Divine] service. One is an arousal from below,[71] through toil of the soul and toil of the flesh with an in-depth meditation of the mind and a broken heart, through which [the person] brings about an illumination, a closeness to God, in his soul. In other words, arousal from below [achieves] an arousal from Above. The second level is that, at times, there can be an excitement of the soul without any preparation or toil at all. As we see, there are many people who are aroused suddenly and their hearts and souls become fervent during prayer, for a certain stretch of time, without them knowing whence this arousal came to them. After a short while, the strength of this arousal wanes.[72]

---

71. When the initiative for illumination comes from man.
72. *Likkutei Torah, Vayikra* 2b.

A.S.: This is because illumination, or grace, as its name suggests, is only on loan. We are allotted a grace period of an hour, or a month, but we never possess grace. To integrate something we need to build it ourselves, to weave the threads of its existence ourselves. Naturally, we can sometimes be helped, but this does not solve anything permanently. There is a verse that we recite often:

Take us back, O Lord, to Yourself, and let us come back.[73]

Whatever happens, we have to come back by ourselves. It is like a child learning to walk. You have to give him a hand, so he can learn to overcome his fear, but you cannot give him your hand all the time.

J.E.: There are three levels of *teshuvah* repair: I need to repair my actions, my *nefesh*; I need to repair my thoughts, my *ruah*; and I need to repair my soul, my *neshamah*.

Our Sages have said, "Better one hour of teshuvah *and good deeds in this world than in all the life of the World to Come."*[74] *What is meant here is not physical* teshuvah *over transgression, that is, only the abandonment of sin; for if so, why "one hour"? Rather, the meaning of "*teshuvah *and good deeds" is that in order that one's deeds should be good and luminous, with the light of God* En Sof, *Blessed be He, it must be on the level of* teshuvah *which is the endeavor to return the soul to*

---

73. Lamentations 5:21.
74. Ethics of the Fathers 4:17.

its source and root, and to literally cleave to the light of En Sof, Blessed be He. For "teshuvah preceded the world"[75] — the world being drawn from the [Divine] name HaVaYah, which is only an effulgence.[76]

The Alter Rebbe has an original approach to action. He says that what is really important is not to repair one's sins — to make amends for what one has done — but rather to repair what one has not done.

A.S.: At times, I need to go even further and ask myself how to repair my beliefs. It is not any easier to repair what one assumes to be "good deeds." In fact, there are two facets of *teshuvah.* On the one hand, I need to repair my sins. As is said in the Prophets: *"I wipe away your sins like a cloud, Your transgressions like mist."*[77]

The figure of speech is elementary. There were clouds, and the wind blew them away. The sky is blue once again; we do not even remember that there were clouds. This is atonement: The thing is abolished. But on the other hand — and this is the Alter Rebbe's concern — there is everything that I did not do. This raises a serious question: How can I repair my omissions, my lapses, my shortcomings? What can I do in order to do something I have not done?

J.E.: This, in my opinion, is the only really meaningful existential question. The things I did not do weigh more heavily than the things I did do.

---

75. Midrash, *Genesis Rabbah* 1.
76. *Likkutei Torah, Drushim l'Shmini 'Atzeret* 85a.
77. Isaiah 44:22.

A.S.: This is true, and it is easy to understand why: Life should attain some added value. Take, for example, a completely righteous person. He has never transgressed a prohibition. He is innocent. When he dies, his soul returns unchanged to the starting point. Did his life have a meaning? All that investment, all that struggle, all that effort, to remain the same and to return intact!

J.E.: This is one of the questions that the Alter Rebbe dealt with extensively. He continually dealt with the classic response that Jewish tradition gives to this question, namely, that *yeridah tsorech 'aliyyah,* literally, "you need to go down to go up." This saying means that the incarnation of the soul in the body is designed to enable the soul to rise higher than when God created it. Existence on earth has a surplus value. This statement is somewhat surprising. What can the soul aspire to that is "higher" than Divine birth? The kabbalists reply that while the soul comes from the second *sefirah,* Ḥokhmah, Divine thought, during its stay on earth the soul carries out the Divine commandments, or Will (*Keter*)—the first *sefirah.*

We must first understand [the answer to] the question why did the soul descend to this world in order to receive reward afterwards in Gan Eden *(the Garden of Eden), when before its descent it certainly was in* Gan Eden *and certainly enjoyed the effulgence of the* Shekhinah *(Divine Presence). So what advantage is there in its descent? Now there are many answers to this. But the ultimate answer is [expressed] in the saying of our Sages, "Better one hour of* teshuvah *and good deeds in this world, than all of the life in the World to Come,"*[78] *and the saying of*

---

78. Ethics of the Fathers 4:17.

> our Sages, "In the place that ba'alei teshuvah *stand, the*
> *perfectly righteous cannot stand.*"[79] *Now, before their*
> *descent into the body, the souls were certainly "perfectly*
> *righteous." But therein lies the advantage of their de-*
> *scent into the body—that they become* ba'alei teshuvah,
> *and thus above and beyond the righteous.*[80]

A.S.: The purpose of life is not to avoid sinning. A rabbi asked his students, "What is the purpose of man on Earth?" His students answered, "To repair his soul." "But before its birth, the soul is very happy where it is," rejoined the rabbi, adding, "That is not it. The goal of life is to raise the heavens."

This is the classic theme of the soul that descends in order to rise up higher. The meaning is that we need to change life itself. And to do so, it is not enough to avoid evil: We must also act. We need to have enriched our existence. This is the image of the sower. God only "sows" in worlds where there can be a harvest, a surplus value.[81]

J.E.: I need to take stock of what I neglected to do.

A.S.: And here, the problem of *teshuvah* is a serious one. This is because doing something that was never done is contrary to all the laws of nature. How can I introduce into time, and into my past, actions that I never accomplished? The Alter Rebbe's response corroborates everything we have said so far about Yom Kippur. This type of reintegration is only possible if we are united with the Infinite, if we ascend to "God before sin," if we are "before God." In these cir-

---

79. Babylonian Talmud, Tractate *Berakhot* 34b.
80. *Likkutei Torah, Balak* 73a.
81. This theme is discussed more fully in the section titled "The Passage through Exile."

cumstances, where there are no limitations on time and space, everything becomes possible—including performing the omissions of the past.

[It is written,] "For as the earth brings forth its growth, and a garden grows its seeds."[82] *This refers to the growth from the deed of the mitzvot and the meditations (*kavvanot*) of the mitzvot . . .*

But when a person sins, God forbid, and abnegates a positive commandment, he is called a "lacker" (ḥote'), meaning that [he has caused] a lack and a void in the above sowing. How much more so is this the case when he transgresses a negative commandment . . .

But also for this there is a remedy, through the revelation of the thirteen attributes of mercy through teshuvah, *especially in the Ten Days of* Teshuvah, *which are the prime time for the acceptance of returnees. [The revelation of the thirteen attributes of mercy] fills all the defects and all the lacks that were made, by drawing down the light of the supreme sanctity.*[83]

A.S.: All in all, the life of the soul is similar to life in the physical world, and we sometimes need to get out of the system. The Talmud gives an astonishing definition of *teshuvah*. *Teshuvah* "transforms sins into good deeds."[84] This is a qualitative alteration, which is similar to the classic problem in physics, that in no system can the left be turned into the right. Whatever changes are made, there are always con-

---

82. Isaiah 61:11.
83. *Likkutei Torah, Nitzavim* 51a.
84. Babylonian Talmud, Tractate *Yoma* 86b.

stants, and I can only reverse them by changing the system or by entering the fourth or the fifth dimension; there, the left can be the right and vice versa. The same is true when we need to accomplish the real revolution of turning evil into good, darkness into light, nothingness into being: We need to leave the finite system in which we are locked.

Reasons of the Heart

J.E.: The prophet Hosea expresses this in a strongly worded verse: *"Return, O Israel, to the Lord your God."*[85] The Sages have commented often on this verse. It does not say "Return toward God," but rather "to God," as though through return we could really reach Infinity itself.

A.S.: According to the Alter Rebbe, this is what is demanded of Man in the basic prayer we recite three times a day, the *Shema'*. We recite, *"You will love the Lord your God with all your heart, with all your soul and with all your might."*[86] *"With all your heart"* is the repair of our actions; *"with all your soul"* is the repair of desires, thoughts, and intentions; it is the repair of the soul to be able to give one's life for God.[87]

As regards *"With all your might—*

J.E.: Let me point out that this is the customary translation, but it is a poor rendition of the initial meaning of the term *meod* used by the Torah. *Meod*—which in Hebrew, by the

---

85. Hosea 14:2.
86. Deuteronomy 6:4.
87. This is one interpretation of the verse "With all your soul." Rabbi Akiva suggests that we read it as "Even if He takes your soul." Babylonian Talmud, Tractate *Sanhedrin* 61b.

way, is an anagram for the word *Adam*—is an adverb that means "exceedingly" and "very much." We should translate "You will love your God with your veryness." The Alter Rebbe sees this as the supreme form of love, which surpasses all categories of heart and mind.

A.S.: The Alter Rebbe says: You should do what you can, and afterward, do a little more; in other words, learn to go beyond your limits. This is real *teshuvah*, being able to go beyond what you are (ordinarily) able to do.

"You shall love . . . with all your soul."[88] *Just as Above there are ten* sefirot *through which sustenance is drawn down from* En Sof *into the worlds, so, too, are there in a person ten attributes of the soul, the mind, and the traits.*[89] *And this is the work of man—to bind all attributes of his soul with the "mind" and "traits" of God, which are the ten* sefirot. *This is achieved by binding his mind and intellect with the* HaBaD *(Hokhmah, Binah, and Da'at, the three faculties of the mind) of God, which is the Torah, and by cleaving to His traits. This is love of God "with all your soul," with the ten attributes of the soul.*

But there is also a level that is higher than the ten sefirot *and is not counted among them at all, for it, too, is infinite. This is the Supreme Will. Likewise, this attribute is found in the soul [of man]—the will that is beyond the intellect. This is the concept of [loving God] "with all your might."*[90]

---

88. Deuteronomy 6:5.
89. The three *sefirot* of the intellect, and the seven *midot* (measures) that represent the seven categories of emotions, values, and virtues.
90. Deuteronomy, ibid. *Likkutei Torah, Song of Songs* 49b.

If I am able to open this door in myself, then I can commend myself to the Divine infinity. Everything can change and full repair can take place. In our prayers we say "You treat small and great alike."[91] The mighty and the small are only equal in one instance: before the Infinite.

J.E.: Job, when speaking of the world above, says: *"Small and great alike are there."*[92]

A.S.: There is no great and no small, and no guilty or innocent party. Through *teshuvah*, we reach that point where Job also said: *If you sin, what do you do to Him? If you are righteous, what do you give to him?*[93]

Everything is nothingness, and hence everything is possible.

---

91. From the Prayer for the High Holidays.
92. Job 3:19.
93. Job 35:6–7.

PART II

THE THREE
PILGRIM FESTIVALS

THIRD GATE

Passover and the Exodus from Egypt

Josy Eisenberg: Three times a year, all Jewish males were commanded to go up to Jerusalem to celebrate three festivals: Pesaḥ, the Passover; Shavuot, the Feast of Weeks; and Sukkot, the Feast of Tabernacles. These holidays are traditionally known as the "pilgrimage festivals." We will comment upon them in this order, which corresponds to their chronology in the Bible.

In many respects, Pesaḥ (Passover) can be viewed as the central holiday in the Jewish calendar and is perhaps more important than the "Days of Awe." In contrast to the other holidays, which we observe at set times and which kindle our memories and experiences once a year, Pesaḥ is a constant feature in the life of the Jew.

The Bible says: *"So that you may remember the day of your departure from the land of Egypt all days of your life."*[1] This indeed has been so. There is no major prayer that does not mention the event that constitutes the birth of the Jewish people. This birth is paradoxical, because Israel was not born in its own land but rather in exile. It was accompanied by a surprising dietary ritual, eating unleavened bread, and was followed by an astounding miracle: The Red Sea parted to let Israel through. Thus, there are three key phases of Passover: before the Exodus (exile), during (unleavened bread), and after (crossing of the Red Sea). We will devote the next chapters to each of these three topics.

---

1. Deuteronomy 16:3.

THE PASSAGE THROUGH EXILE

Regarding Israel in galut *(exile) it is written: "And I will sow her to me in the earth."*[2] *And our Sages have said: "He who sows a* se'ah *harvests many* korin.*"*[3]

To understand the concept of "sowing" and the growth and increase generated by the galut: *It is written: "Israel is holy to God, the first fruits of His grain."*[4] *His grain—for the people of Israel are called God's grain. In the same way that a person sows grain because of the manifold increase that will grow [from it], so, too, when God desires that the revelation of His Divinity the world should increase and multiply . . . He "sows" the people of Israel, who are His grain.*

Torah Ohr, Beshallaḥ 61a

Josy Eisenberg: Jewish history is articulated around the polarity between the Holy Land and exile, or, as some define it, between Jerusalem and Babylon. Jewish history is a long series of exiles and enslavements, interspersed with brief returns to the land and to national and religious independence.

Jewish history has been shaped by its three main exiles: to Egypt, to Babylon, and to Rome. The exile to Rome refers to

---

2. Hosea 2:25. Note that the literal meaning of this verse is the absolute antithesis of the interpretation given to it by the Alter Rebbe. It describes the return of Israel who will be "sown," replanted, in its land.

3. Babylonian Talmud, Tractate *Pesaḥim* 87b. A *se'ah* is a measurement of solids and liquids; approx. 13.3 liters. A *kor* (singular of *korin*) is about three times as much.

4. Jeremiah 2:3.

the exile caused by the destruction of the Second Temple in 70 c.e. and the dispersion that followed it. To this day, all Jews in the diaspora—with the rare exception of the few Jewish communities that survived in Moslem countries—still live in "the Roman exile."

Why exile? Why does our history start with an exile? Commentaries make it clear that these exiles, including the first one, Egypt, were not mere historical or geographical accidents. Exile is a part of our lives, literally and figuratively.

Adin Steinsaltz: The enslavement of the Israelites by the Egyptians and their exodus from the land of Egypt have a dual meaning, depending on whether we look at it from a macrocosmic or a microcosmic standpoint. If we view exile as a microcosmic feature—

J.E.: —in other words, from the standpoint of the individual, who is seen as a world in miniature; he experiences the phenomena we experience in the real world on his own scale—

A.S.: —on this level, the concept of exile no longer bears a relationship to history. It is no longer in the realm of time, but rather within the individual himself. Instead of being an event, exile becomes an experience every individual must go through during the course of his or her life.

Exile is an experience we live through, and the cycle of the Jewish year is its model, its framework, and its locus. This cycle creates a parallel between external, or "objective," time and time as we experience it. It calls upon the individual to relive history within himself. This specific inner experience of time bears much in common with development on a biological level. According to biologists, every individual relives the course of development of *homo sapiens* from its beginnings.

Similarly, each of us individually relives the historical evolution of the Jewish people. Thus, on a microcosmic level, exile is an individual experience and a certain way of living one's life.

J.E.: Let us define this experience, starting with the macrocosmic view.

A.S.: Exile is a basic feature in the history of the world and a crucial feature in its evolution. The macrocosmic is no less of an accident or a chance occurrence than the microcosmic. On the contrary, it is one of the building blocks in the evolution of the human, and in particular the Jewish, being. It is a phase in time that the history of the world must necessarily pass through.

J.E.: The macrocosmic level is on the planetary scale, suggesting that exile is a universal phenomenon. Nevertheless, it is a specific dimension of the Jewish experience. One way of defining the Jewish experience is to say that it is specific yet necessary to the universal experience of exile. This universal experience would be inconceivable without the role played by Jews. The Alter Rebbe defines this role very precisely.

Whoever Sows Israel, Reaps Humanity

Regarding Israel in galut *(exile) it is written:* "And I will sow her to me in the earth." *And our Sages have said:* "He who sows a se'ah *harvests many* korin." *To understand the concept of "sowing" and the growth and increase generated by the* galut, *it is written:* "Israel is holy to God, the first fruits of His grain." *His grain—for the people of Israel are called God's grain. In the same*

106

> way that a person sows grain because of the manifold
> increase that will grow [from it], so, too, when God
> desires that the revelation of His Divinity the world should
> increase and multiply . . . He "sows" the people of
> Israel, who are His grain.[5]

J.E.: The Alter Rebbe is attempting to respond to one of the key questions in Jewish existence: Why does the history of Israel begin by the long and painful exile in Egypt? Why has the Jewish people lived the greater part of its history in exile, which seems so absurd? Even today, four-fifths of the Jewish people still live in exile. The question is made more acute by the suffering of the Jewish people in exile. The Jewish exile has been, and still is, greeted with violence, racism, and xenophobia. Nevertheless, the Alter Rebbe's response is that Israel is the staff of wheat that God planted in the world to increase its value.

A.S.: This is a very optimistic view of exile. It makes more sense, however, when you realize that the concept of exile is hardly ever dealt with singly in Jewish thought. Rather, *galut* (exile) tends to be coupled with *geulah* (redemption). The roots of these two terms are very similar, which explains why countless texts have established a dialectical relationship between *galut* and *geulah*. It is worth reiterating that exile is not an accident but rather a cyclical phenomenon. In other words, it is one of the basic building blocks of life. However, this does not imply that exile is normal. It appears to be necessary and inevitable, but all the definitions concur that exile is abnormal. It is beyond the norms of existence and its duration does not make it any more normal.

---

5. Torah Ohr, *Beshallah* 61a.

J.E.: A sick man can spend the greater part of his life in bed or in a sanatorium. This state ends up by being the "normal" one, but that does not make it any the less pathological.

A.S.: In fact, there are two modes of existence. We call the first the normal mode and the other, exile. There is a variety of different ways of differentiating these two situations. To start with, let us define "normal" as a completed, finished situation and "exile" as a situation where things are still in the making.

J.E.: This prompts two questions. First of all, it is a bit paradoxical to say that something is both abnormal and necessary. Second, if this abnormality is really necessary, must it occur in a situation of such excessive violence as the one the Israelites were subjected to in Egypt?

A.S.: Exile, by definition, is a phenomenon constantly fed by emotions, the unpredictable, radical change. It makes sense that exile should reflect absurdity and paradox. Furthermore, the Alter Rebbe defines exile as absurd. The Maharal of Prague,[6] however, stresses the paradoxical nature of this situation. Exile is a whole series of paradoxes. In the final analysis, what accounts for the Alter Rebbe's optimism is the permanent dialectical reversal of exile and its fundamentally rich and constructive nature. Exile is always linked to its complement, redemption.

---

6. Rabbi Judah Lowe ben Bezalel, the famous commentator. He lived in the sixteenth century and his name is associated with the tale of the *Golem*.

Dormant Israel

J.E.: Redemption has an eschatological significance. Israel will be redeemed from exile in the messianic era. However, there is a very specific meaning of redemption related to birth—namely, delivery. The Alter Rebbe associates *galut* and *geulah* with the process of pregnancy and birth, confirming your definition that exile is gestation.

> The galut *is analogous to pregnancy and the redemption of the messianic era, which will be speedily in our day, is comparable to a birth, as it is written:* "For Zion has gone into labor, has also given birth to her children."[7] *And regarding the times when these people of Israel are to be found in dire straits, God forbid, it is written:* "For the children have come to the birthing stool, and there is no strength to give birth."[8]

J.E.: A lifetime is a continual series of gestations and deliveries. If we interpret exile in this way, in terms of physical or emotional life, or life in any form, it ceases to be a specifically Jewish problem and becomes a metaphysical necessity, in that all life is first of all an exile.

A.S.: I would say that there is some exile in all lives. A beautiful definition of exile, encompassing a whole range of concepts, says that exile is sleep and dreaming, while redemption is the awakening. Life cannot be entirely composed of periods of wakefulness. Day and night are the two basic features of reality. We must pass through the night of exile.

---

7. Isaiah 66:8.
8. Isaiah 37:3; *Torah Ohr, Vayera* 55a.

This state can be more or less comfortable. Jews can feel more or less content in exile. Sometimes this is simply a matter of personal luck.

J.E.: The exile of Jews in the United States is much more comfortable than the exile of their brethren in the former Soviet Union.

A.S.: That is not the real problem. The critical feature is that all individuals must go through slumber to reach a state of wakefulness, just as we must go through different changes to reach stability. "I am asleep but my heart is wakeful."[9] The *Zohar*, commenting on this text, says, "I sleep in exile." Exile is like sleep. When you are asleep, your eyes are shut. It is written, "No signs appear for us."[10]

J.E.: The Alter Rebbe refers to this idea often. The life of the children of Israel is split into two phases, or two states of consciousness. One phase is when Israel "sees." Its history is studded with diverse revelations, the high points of lucidity. One example is the exodus from Egypt, where it is written that Israel "saw the wondrous power which the Lord had wielded"; another is the giving of the Ten Commandments, where it is written that Israel "saw that I spoke to you from the very heavens."[11]

Israel "sees" when there are face-to-face encounters with God. At the end of time, this vision, this knowledge of God, will be total and permanent: *"For every eye shall behold the Lord's return to Zion."*[12] The other phase is exile. Here Israel no longer "sees" God. God is concealed, and Israel is no longer

---

9. Song of Songs 5:2.
10. Psalms 74:9.
11. Exodus 14:31 and 20:19.
12. Isaiah 52:8.

clairvoyant. It feels, it perceives—because sleep is not unconsciousness—but it no longer knows. This is the exile of consciousness: "No signs appear for us."

The Alter Rebbe concurs with the *Zohar* but goes beyond the comparison of sleep with exile. He also describes exile as a dream, drawing our attention to a point that the commentators have, perhaps, neglected. Exile is directly related to dreams. Because of his dreams, Joseph is sold by his brothers and is brought into Egypt, thus preparing the way for the exile in Egypt. Joseph rises to a position of power because of his ability to interpret the dreams of Pharaoh's ministers and then Pharaoh's own dreams. The immediate outcome of Joseph's position of power is that he has the Israelites brought to Egypt, thus laying the cornerstone of exile. Exile, in this case, is much more than life caught in slumber: The imaginary goes beyond reality.

"A Song of Ascension: [when God returns the returnees to Zion], we will have been as dreamers."[13]

A dream joins two opposites into a single subject, and combines two opposite concepts as if they were one. This is due to the fact that, during sleep, the intellectual faculty of discrimination departs, and there only the faculty of imagination remains; and the faculty of imagination can combine two opposites, e.g., a ship flying through the air.

Such is the concept of galut. *The spark of Godliness in the soul of man is in a state of "sleep" and "departure of the intellect," and can therefore combine two opposites . . . [a person] can imagine that he loves God, and at the same time, love his physical self.*

---

13. Psalms 126:1.

111

In truth, however, this "dream" has a supernal source, and is founded upon the loftiest peaks of holiness . . . where everything is equal, and all realities are integrated and unified without any diversity or division.[14]

Continuity in Change

J.E.: This text clearly takes a very different, and even sur-realistic, view of Divine sowing, which according to the Alter Rebbe appears to be the prime motivation for the exile of Israel. This calls for some clarification.

A.S.: Although the formulation is new, the idea is a very old one. The world is a place for sowing, seeds, planting. The "descent" of the souls refers to this. This idea is found in another form in the Bible, when Ezekiel describes Israel as an abandoned child that God takes in to raise and then to marry.

Similarly, the pains of the messianic era are called labor pains; and it is written: "Pangs of childbirth assail him."[15]

Another example: The Prophet Ezekiel compares the redemption from Egypt to the history of a child on the day of his birth: "As for your birth, when you were born your navel cord was not cut, and . . . you were not rubbed with salt."[16]

The basic idea is that God uses the people of Israel to attract other peoples to Him. It is worth pointing out that from this perspective, the name "Israel"—beyond referring to the Children of Israel—designates a function, and this func-

---

14. *Torah Ohr, Vayeshev* 28c–d. This text is lengthy and complex. The second part only summarizes the main ideas rather than providing a direct quote.

15. Hosea 13:13.

16. Ezekiel 16:4; *Torah Ohr, Vayera* 55a.

tion is the capacity for change. This is the surplus value you mentioned earlier. The aim is not to increase the number of Jews, but rather to change the nature of the world by introducing Judaism into it. The idea is not to turn Gentiles into Jews but to make reality Jewish by changing reality.

This is the Divine investment. Through the existence of the Jewish people, God expresses the need for another reality to emerge. By doing so, He thrusts Israel into the chaos of the world to hasten the coming of this other reality, which is the purpose of creation.

A Chromosome Called Israel

J.E.: What you call reality, basic reality, is the world in its raw state. To structure and civilize the world, there must be change. This will result in the second reality, which fulfills the Divine purpose and can only be achieved through the final process described in the sentence: "*What is accomplished at the end is what God willed at the beginning.*"[17]

Israel is thus defined as the instrument and the vector of change from the Stone Age to the messianic era. How does exile enable Israel to accomplish this change? It is not easy to specify all the modes of intervention, but one thing at least is clear: Israel must be sown in the land.

In Hebrew, the term *zera'* means "seed." By extension it has come to mean filiation and posterity. For example, the expression *zera' Israel* is often used to refer to the Jewish people in history. The Alter Rebbe's use of the word *sow* refers, however, to the literal meaning of the word *zera'* as seed.

---

17. From the song *Lekha Dodi*, which is part of the Sabbath eve prayers.

A.S.: For the Alter Rebbe, the word *zera'* refers not only to the internal continuity of the Jewish people but mainly to the fructification of the Jewish people and to its capability to influence its environment. This concept of *zera'* can be explained in biological terms. There are two facets of any *zera'*. First, it is a carrier. In biological terms it is the envelope for the genetic code. In and of itself, it is only one component that preserves the code or the program of the entire system. However—and this is its second feature—if it stays inactive, it becomes inert. Its function is to release the code and transmit the message. In other words, the *zera'* preserves internal identity and transmits it.

J.E.: Israel is thus the genetic memory of what the world should be; it is, perhaps, the last chromosome it needs to be normal. Nevertheless, the world exists; and if it did not have its own genetic code, albeit incomplete, there would be no life at all. Israel needs to contribute the final chromosome, so carefully preserved throughout its entire history. This implies that there are deep affinities, or compatibilities, between the code of the world and the Jewish code. For if not, there would be total rejection (partial rejections, unfortunately, have not been lacking) and the sowing would fail to take. This suggests that there is a certain kinship between the world in its raw state and the Divine idea that Israel is entrusted to spawn.

This is what the kabbalists wanted to express in the theory of the "sparks of holiness." Let us summarize this theory very briefly. At the time of Creation, the Divine vessels shattered because the universe could not bear the flood of Divine light. Fragments of light, the sparks of holiness, fell into matter and formed a kind of sacred and infinite nucleus within the finite world. The world became a fenced-in arena in which knowledge of God and forgetfulness of God wage war.

Knowledge is day, forgetfulness is night. Knowledge is light, and forgetfulness is shadow. But darkness is never total, because the night is full of flashes of light. Even when God seems to be absent, He always finds a spark in man or in matter to rekindle knowledge.

Exile is the darkness where God seems to be absent but in fact is only "sleeping." When men forget God, the kabbalists do not adopt the Nietzschean position that God is dead, but rather that He is "on hold." The mission of Israel is to reestablish communication and release the sparks. It is said that each time Israel goes into exile, the Divine presence is exiled, too. This presence is the Divine spark that shines in the soul of Israel. This spark aspires to return to God. The strength of this desire enables it to gather up the other sparks that fell into matter when the vessels shattered.

Sow or Spread

A.S.: One of the cornerstones of Jewish mysticism, which is also found in many other forms of mysticism, is that creation in general and the presence, or descent, of the soul into the body in particular, all form a long process of exile. Thus, the exile of the Jewish people is more than a special case or even a symbol. In exile the Jewish people act as human seeds, which come from the body and which carry the highly concentrated message of the body as a whole. Each chromosome is a perfect replica of the whole organism. The true function of the Jewish people is to encode and constitute the genetic system of the world.

J.E.: In the Bible, Israel is often called "the seed" or "the holy seed." There are other versions of this idea, in which Israel is called a plant or a messianic bud:

115

"But a shoot shall grow out of the stump of Jesse, a twig shall sprout from his stock."[18]

The word *seed* can refer to both sowing (planting) and disseminating (spreading). The actions can either complement each other or conflict. Sowing can refer to planting in a specific place, and disseminating can mean dispersal. Sowing can represent implantation in the Holy Land and return.[19] Dissemination would, then, designate the diaspora, a term that itself means "dispersion."

Jewish history tends to be viewed more in terms of dispersion than in terms of sowing. The Alter Rebbe rectifies this somewhat by reminding us that exile is more often sowing than dispersion. He frequently mentions the fact that the first leader of the Jews in exile was called Zerubabel; quite a title, when you realize that his name breaks down into *zara'*—he sowed, and *babel*—Babylon, the dispersion.

The meaning of the name Zerubabel ("Sown in Babylonia") is that the community of the souls of Israel are seeds from the "seeding light" of the tzaddik (righteous one) who vitalizes the worlds. For [the souls of Israel] are "a portion of God"[20] and "My firstborn son,"[21] and as it is written, "And I shall sow the house of Israel and the House of Judah with the seed of men and the seed of

---

18. Isaiah 11:1.

19. This image is often used by the Prophets of Return: Isaiah, Ezekiel, Jeremiah, Hosea, and others.

20. Deuteronomy 32:9.

21. Exodus 4:22.

cattle";[22] and since Zerubabel was the prince of Israel and the head of its communal soul, he was called "Sown in Babylonia," in reference to [the souls of Israel] being sown in the Babylonian Exile. For, as is known, in each exile they are "sown"—subjugated in that particular exile—in order to achieve the refinement in the transformation of evil into good.[23]

I have always thought that the diaspora, a Greek term, reflects the feeling of non-Jews when they examine the history—and perhaps more so, the geography—of Israel. Jews, on the other hand, only refer to the *galut*; and they place more emphasis on the phenomenon of exile than on dispersion itself. In the final analysis, dispersion is an accident or an epiphenomenon. For example, in Egypt, during the first exile, the Israelites were not dispersed; they were all grouped together, or concentrated in the sinister sense of the concentration camps that their enslavement so much resembled. What counts above all is exile itself.

Exile, an Organized Disorder

A.S.: The Alter Rebbe's greatest concern was this facet of exile. His purpose in writing about exile was not to make a litany of suffering; rather, he emphasizes its positive side. In his opinion, exile is a revolutionary process that involves radical transformation of the essence of things. In other words, what is crucial as regards the exile of Israel is not what happens to Israel, but what changes when Israel is in exile.

---

22. Jeremiah 31:26.
23. *Maamarei Admor HaZaken*, 1802, p. 215.

117

This perspective forms the backdrop for the question of the sparks within the two worlds, or two states, which form one of the basic polarities in Kabbalah: the world of *tohu*, the world of disorder; and the world of *tikkun*, the world of reparation.[24]

What the kabbalists call *'olam ha-tohu*, the world of *tohu*, is a world without order, lacking system and organization, a world where there is still no dividing line between the possible and the impossible; in short, a world where anything can happen.

It is remarkable that the difference between the world of *tohu* and the world of *tikkun* corresponds, in the Alter Rebbe's view, to the relationships between the Jewish world and the world of non-Jews. The latter world is perceived as a world in a state of chaos: everything is possible because nothing has really been delineated.

J.E.: In other words, this is a world without Torah and hence, in a certain way, without law, or at least deprived of *the* law?

A.S.: It is indeed a world without Torah; in other words, without that guideline or thread that maintains men on the winding paths of life. The world of *tohu* is that place where chaos engenders perplexity, since it is directionless. When we look at the world today, it does not seem to be heading anywhere. Where is the world going?

J.E.: You are also a physicist. Can we compare *tohu*, and its rectification, *tikkun*, to what happens in the structure of the atom?

---

24. When God created the world, it is written that *"the earth being unformed and void, with darkness over the deep . . ."* (Genesis 1:2). This led to the idea that the world was created from a state of chaos and that it is up to Israel to "repair" it.

A.S.: Absolutely. Even though the Alter Rebbe obviously does not employ the same terminology, he hints at this. In physics, there are electrons that can move in any direction. If these electrons are placed in a magnetic field, the presence of the piece of metal is enough to make them all move in the same direction. This is what we call polarization. The magnet will now orient the electrons toward a specific point and make them part of an organized system. In other words, what changes is not the nature of the electrons but rather their state. They go from a state in which they were oriented randomly to a state in which there are cardinal points, an up and a down, and where they themselves are oriented. Catalysis took place.

J.E.: Matter is, perhaps, one of the first places where there is constant interplay between *tohu* and *tikkun*. Life at all levels is made up of this dialectic between disorder and order. In biology, people often refer to the "structure of living things." The Maharal of Prague based his entire philosophy on the conflict between the unorganized world and the world of Torah, which he specifically called the world of *seder*, that is, order.

Israel is thus the catalyzer of these lost "electrons" that the Kabbalah calls "sparks." As you have said, these electrons not only are disorganized but also go in all directions. They are everywhere. This dispersion may be one of the keys to the problem of exile.

A.S.: Dispersion, the diaspora of the Jewish people, is frequently associated with exile. In fact, and as you pointed out, in Egypt there was an exile without dispersion. The essence of exile is dissemination and disorder.

J.E.: In other words, there are two kinds of dissemination. The first is the dissemination of the sparks of Divinity, dispersed in the disorder of the world; and the second, the dissemination of Israel. On the one hand, reparation, on the other hand, disorder. It is crucial to realize, however, that this disorder is Divine in origin. The world of *tohu*—matter and life in their primitive, crude state—was created by God even before the world of *tikkun*. Chaos precedes light.

. . . the earth being unformed and void [tohu-bohu], *with darkness over the surface of the deep and a wind from God sweeping over the water. God said,* "Let there be light."[25]

A.S.: By creating it, God gave the world infinite possibilities and, in particular, that complex and problematic thing we call free will. The world is free to go in any direction it wishes. Being able to choose one's direction is one of the specific prerogatives of the human race. This is what differentiates people from angels, who are always described in Jewish literature as being perfectly organized, in rows of four, standing rigidly at attention. Ezekiel describes them as having only one leg. They cannot go forward: "*The legs of each were [fused into] a single rigid leg.*"[26]

Man, by contrast, walks. In Zechariah's vision, this contrast is heightened: "*If you walk in my paths and keep my charge, you in turn will rule my house and guard my courts, and I will permit you to walk about among these attendants.*"[27] Walking, choosing one's direction, is one of the consequences of the freedom that God granted us.

---

25. Genesis 1:2–3.
26. Ezekiel 1:7.
27. Zechariah 3:7.

It is important to realize that our world is not a vacuum, as the Mayas, for example, believed. The world of *tohu* is simply a world where nothing is delineated. All the elements are there, but they are not arranged in a coherent order. To use a human metaphor, I would say that these elements are disoriented; they do not know which direction to choose.

J.E.: What very striking images! Frenzied particles of matter, moving in all directions, something scientists often see under the microscope, and that make up, in their disorder, as many sacred potentials. In the final analysis, evil is disorder; but this does not imply that the world came from a diabolical power, a kind of Divine anti-matter. These elements, the world of *tohu*, were created by God.

Memories from beyond Life

A.S.: The theory of *tohu* and *tikkun* is the most rigorous form of monotheism, the diametrical opposite of dualism. The most fundamental premise of Jewish faith is that everything comes from God. No form of existence is possible without the Divine Presence.

We could easily paraphrase the Divine *cogito*. The Alter Rebbe would not say, "I think, therefore I am," but rather "I think, thus God is." This is because all reality is the manifestation of the Divine Presence. The forces that emanate from God are in exile in the world, in the sense that matter has no awareness of its Divine nature. It does not know where it comes from, and it does not know what it wants or where it is going.

J.E.: To be in exile is to be unaware or amnesic.

121

A.S.: The world is like someone who has lost his bearings and does not even know that he comes from somewhere else. The Divine in the world is what emanates from another reality, from another dream, but which the world is unaware of and hence cannot find. On the cosmic level exile is identical. The Divine sparks are present in the world. They are responsible for life at all levels and all the details of existence. They act in the world but are unaware of their origin, and this is why they act in an unstructured fashion. This leads to disorder in the world.

J.E.: The main difference between nature—and more precisely, everything that belongs to the natural order, including certain men—is that nature, like man, comes from God but does not know it. Man, however, can and must know this.

A.S.: Exile is the situation of being deprived of memory and will. This produces anarchistic behavior, including self-destruction. The world of reparation, of redemption, *geulah*, which will end the *galut*, closely resembles the process of psychoanalysis but operates in the opposite direction. In psychoanalysis, the patient needs to talk about himself to discover his own truth. Here, to deliver him, to cure him, someone needs to reveal his origin and his identity to him. The world suffers from the complex of thinking that it is the world.

J.E.: And nothing more than the world.

A.S.: To cure the world, Israel must go into exile. Its mission is to free the world of its complex.

J.E.: This idea is something like Plato's myth of the cave. The prisoners only see a shadow but believe that this shadow is reality.

A.S.: In certain respects there is a similarity, but the Alter Rebbe's ideas go much further. Unlike the myth of the cave, in the Jewish perspective, light is not elsewhere: It is within reality.

J.E.: In the heart of the shadows.

A.S.: Simply, it operates poorly because its particles are poorly oriented. In the Alter Rebbe's view, the world is not a place of shadows and darkness like a void. Rather, it is poorly lit. The floodlights—the sparks—shed light in an unstructured and diffuse way, and we need to bring them together and focus them correctly to produce a single beam of light.

J.E.: This is a movie and television problem. If the projectors used to light the studio or a film location are poorly oriented, they produce a horrible combination of shadows and lights. This combination really characterizes life. It is written concerning Creation: "*God saw that the light was good and God separated the light from the darkness.*"[28]

A.S.: This separation is, however, far from being radical and complete. Light and darkness, Good and Evil, are in constant interplay, and one of the functions of exile is in fact to separate them. In all his writings, the Alter Rebbe defines darkness as a lack of knowledge and stupidity. Darkness is not a separate essence; there is no Manicheism or combat between darkness and light. What happens is simply that the part that knows is combined with the part that does not know. Actually, this is not a mixture of positive and negative, but rather of conscious and unconscious. Because of their unconsciousness, the unconscious parts can even harm

---

28. Genesis 1:4.

themselves. We have mentioned self-destruction. This is precisely what happens in biology. Certain cells "forget" their function, and although they cannot be termed completely bad, they start to act in the wrong direction. Instead of contributing to the normal functioning of the system, they destroy it.

J.E.: You cannot find a better definition for exile than a cancer—which can, luckily, be cured. This is the function of Israel. Missionary, psychiatrist, physician: all these metaphors apply. Israel must liberate the conscious particles and activate them to make the others conscious. This accounts for exile.

Why, however, did exile start in Egypt, and why is this country both the archetype and the prototype of all exiles? I suggest we devote the second chapter on Passover to this question.

THE GREAT CROCODILE

In the tenth year, on the twelfth day of the tenth month, the word of the Lord came to me: "O son of man, turn your face against Pharaoh king of Egypt and prophesy against him and against all Egypt. Speak these words: Thus said the Lord God: I am against you, O Pharaoh king of Egypt, Mighty crocodile, sprawling in your rivers, who said, 'My Nile is my own, I created myself' " . . .

Therefore, said the Lord God: "Lo I will bring a sword against you and will cut off man and beast from you so that the land of Egypt shall fall into desolation and ruin. And they shall know that I am the Lord—because he boasted, 'the Nile is mine, and I created myself.' "

Ezekiel 29:1–9

Josy Eisenberg: All individuals run the almost constant risk of inner exile. The strongest part of my ego slips away or lets down its guard, and the dark, incoherent forces lurking within me take over, like in dreams where the "other" rationality dominates. Exile is a battlefield where man's capabilities do combat, a black hole from which man must emerge to discover light. It is also the place where the forces of holiness are the prisoners of the forces of evil, and it is Israel's mission to free them.

The saga of exile begins in Egypt. Jewish texts depict Egypt as the place where the forces of darkness prevail. This explains why the presence of Israel in Egypt is a necessity, and why Israel will inevitably suffer. But why Egypt?

Adin Steinsaltz: In Jewish thought, Egypt, ancient Egypt, is the archetype for a whole set of attitudes.

125

First of all, the name *Egypt—mitzrayim—*is grammatically dual.[29] It is the plural of *meitsar,* which means "narrowness," or "anguish." Egypt symbolizes narrow-mindedness. Ancient Egypt and its paganism are the model for the individual who fabricates an entire system to refute real knowledge. The system upholds its false reality in the face of Divine reality. Egypt is the prototype of a world that proclaims itself to be autonomous and announces that it owes nothing to others because it is self-sufficient.

J.E.: It could be termed a "self-made land."

A.S.: This is exactly the mentality that the Bible attributes to the person who incarnates Egypt, the Pharaoh. Egypt is known as the gift of the Nile. The river is its genitor, and hence its God. The Pharaoh claims no less than to have fathered the Nile.

> In the tenth year, on the twelfth day of the tenth month, the word of the Lord came to me: "O son of man, turn your face against Pharaoh king of Egypt and prophesy against him and against all Egypt. Speak these words: Thus said the Lord God: I am against you, O Pharaoh king of Egypt, Mighty crocodile, sprawling in your rivers, who said, 'My Nile is my own, I created myself'" . . .[30]

---

29. Indeed, geographically, there are two Egypts: Upper and Lower Egypt. In Hebrew grammar there is the singular form, the dual form, and the plural form. The word *mitzrayim* is the dual form meaning, literally, "two Egypts."
30. Ezekiel 29:1–3.

The Rejectionist Front

J.E.: Exile represents the existence of paganism, the antithesis of monotheism. Egypt, the first great civilization of the East, developed the most sophisticated form of ancient paganism. The Egyptians had a pantheon of divinities, including the Pharaoh, who himself was divine. If exile implies Divine absence, God was never more in exile than in Egypt. For this reason alone, it makes sense that Egypt was the theater for the spectacular demonstration of God's existence through the ten plagues.

A.S.: The deeper the darkness, the more dazzling the victory of light. Humbling the Pharaoh meant ending the fantasy of autonomy or self-creation that so many civilizations develop. But let us not fool ourselves: Pharaoh is not an ordinary opponent of God.

J.E.: It would not be a fair match.

A.S.: In Jewish mysticism, Evil is a very powerful reality and the forces within it are necessarily powerful as well. In the Bible, Egypt is called the "nakedness of the land,"[31] a place of extreme decadence. The contrast is extremely striking, since the greatest powers of holiness lie buried precisely where the darkness is the most impenetrable.

J.E.: The conflict between Egypt and Israel is characterized by the metaphor of a battle between two crocodiles, or aquatic beasts. The battle is between the Pharaoh, the crocodile of impurity, and Moses, called the crocodile of holiness. This

---

31. Genesis 42:9: "You have come to see the nakedness of the land."

clearly points to the fact that the opposing forces are complementary.[32] To understand this theme, I suggest we examine a remarkable text by the Alter Rebbe. First of all, in Jewish mysticism, souls are represented by fish.[33] The Egyptian crocodile symbolizes souls in their primeval, bestial, and untamed state, with no obedience to God. In contrast, Moses incarnates self-abnegation. He remains the "most humble man, more so than any man on the face of the earth,"[34] and he is represented by a special kind of crocodile—the Leviathan, a messianic fish.

Thus will be understood what is written in Zohar, Torah Portion Bo *34a, in the verse "Come to Pharaoh":*[35] *"To the crocodile . . . and Moses was afraid of him . . ." For "One opposite the other, God created."*[36] *Just as there is the concept of "leviathan" and "fishes of the sea" in the realm of holiness, so, too, do they exist in the realm of impurity . . . But these are "one opposite the other"—complete opposites. For the "leviathan" and the "fishes of the sea" in the realm of holiness are in a state of utter self-abnegation within their source in the Blessed Infinite,*[37] *while regarding the leviathan of the* kelipah[38] *it is written "[Pharaoh] . . . the mighty crocodile [that crouches within his rivers], who says, 'My river is my own, and I created myself' " . . . Now regarding*

---

32. According to the major premise of the Kabbalah, God created holiness and the "other side" as counterparts, and "one opposite the other" (see Ecclesiastes 14:7).

33. This topic is dealt with in depth in the chapter "Man-of-Light."

34. Numbers 12:3.

35. Exodus 10:1.

36. Ecclesiastes 7:14.

37. *En Sof, Baruch Hu,* Infinite God.

38. Literally, "husk," the symbol of evil.

Moses it is written, *"For I drew him from the waters,"* for Moses is from the tribe of Levi, from the leviathan of holiness.[39]

J.E.: This, however, should not be misconstrued as a form of Western Manicheism, opposing God and the Devil. On the contrary: the world only exists through Divine energies, which all derive from the same source. At times, however, these forms of energy malfunction. In our last interview, we alluded to cancer cells. This is exactly what happened in Egypt. Egypt is strong because it derives its nourishment from healthy Divine energy. But at a certain time, like healthy cells that begin to malfunction, these energies are used to reject God.

A.S.: All the forces in the world have their source in God. All forms of power, whether physical, intellectual, or political, necessarily derive from Divine power. The real issue is the direction these forces will take. They can obey their laws and remain loyal to their original principle. In this case, they are forces of health and order. However, these forces can also create their own order, in which case they become self-destructive. Egypt is the prime example of a power that proclaimed itself totally independent, bowing to its own will alone, living for and by itself. This new order, which legitimizes disorder and anarchy, is the radical opposite of the

---

39. The Alter Rebbe associates leviathan with Levi, which means "attachment." The leviathan is joined to God instead of to Pharaoh; and Moses, being a Levite, is the best example of someone who is connected and who connects to God. *Likkutei Torah, Vayikra* 8c.

forces of holiness that show obedience to God. This is why Pharaoh is called the *'oref.*[40]

J.E.: You are alluding to a famous play on words in Jewish exegesis, in which the letters of the word *par'oh*—the Pharaoh—are the anagram of the word *'oref*, the back of the neck. When the children of Israel revolt, they are called "stiff-necked people." Pharaoh also adopted this attitude of disobedience. To accept the yoke, the neck must be bent. Pharaoh refuses. He says to Moses: "*Who is the Lord that I should heed him and let Israel go? I do not know the Lord, nor will I let Israel go.*"[41]

It takes ten plagues to demolish his pride. The Alter Rebbe refers frequently to the Pharaoh-*'oref* anagram. He associates it with two other readings of the root *par'oh*. The verb means "discover," "reveal" (in the very specific context of revealing the genital organ after circumcision), and is also the anagram of *'aphar*, the "dust of the earth."

The neck is part of a larger kabbalistic concept of Divine Will. The clearest manifestation of will occurs in face-to-face encounters, because the listener is the direct recipient of what the speaker has to say. However, there can also be a "face-to-back" encounter, in which the recipient of the message does not care. In kabbalistic terms, this attitude is compared to someone throwing the message over his shoulder or behind his back.

The neck symbolizes the fact that someone only derives secondary benefit from the Divine Will that enables him to be. The Pharaoh-*'oref* symbol represents human existence in which the power that derives from Divine Will turns its back on it. Communication is reestablished when this attitude is

---

40. Exodus 32:9.
41. Exodus 5:2.

modified and the genitalia are uncovered. Communication must be rooted in a land, a history, and a geography, yielding the four-pronged association *Pharaoh-neck-uncovering-land.* This symbolism also inspired the classic comparison between the face-people and the back-of-the-neck-people.

The righteous are called "eyes"[42] *. . . Eyes are in the face, which is the seat of the primary faculties—sight, hearing [etc.]; also a person's thoughts lie with the things he sees. This is not the case with the back [of the head], where there is but a minute amount of vitality, which derives from a mere reflection and effulgence from the vitality of the face . . .*

The letters of the word Pharaoh *also spell the word* ha'oref *("the back of the neck"). This means that he does not possess a "face" at all, and all his vitality derives only "from behind," as one who casts something over his shoulder.*

This is the meaning of "we were slaves to Pharaoh . . . and God took us out"[43] *[granting us] the element of "face." This is why the perpetual desire of every Jew is to cleave to the one God, and under no circumstances does he wish to be separate from Him. Also, at the time he is doing business, he only "forgets," which is also from the element of the "back"; for in the midst of his business, as soon as he reminds himself of the one God, his heart is very much aroused [with the desire] for the one God.*[44]

---

42. See Psalms 33:18, and Deuteronomy 32:10.

43. Deuteronomy 6:21. Israel is freed from the yoke (neck) of forgetfulness.

44. *Likkutei Torah, Shir Hashirim* 36a.

> *As is known, the name* Pharaoh *is related to the word* peri'ah, *meaning "exposure" and "revelation"—a reference to the attribute of* Malkhut *(sovereignty) which reveals all illuminations, and which is the faculty of speech.*[45]

The Clash of the Worlds

A.S.: Pharaoh is the diametrical opposite of the Jewish being, yet his energy is drawn from high up in the "back" of the creative Will. This is what makes him the absolute opponent of Israel. It was more important to destroy the idea of a self-sufficient world, which the Pharaoh represented, than to demolish Pharaoh's pride. A self-sufficient world is a world without change. When the miracles take place in Egypt, the world discovers that change is possible.

J.E.: Change implies that the natural order can be modified. All the commentaries state that Pharaoh could know God as God of nature, but not as beyond nature. In a way, Pharaoh represents the atheist whose concept of God is similar to a concept in physics. There are laws, and no one is beyond the law. This position is the negation of Divine omnipotence and Providence. How could a man like this, with this kind of ideology, exercise such power over Israel? The Alter Rebbe hints at a reply to this question in the previous passage, when he says that Evil lodges in the highest levels of existence.

A.S.: Nature as a whole derives its substance from primeval energies, the primitive forces of Creation. Egypt obviously

---

45. *Maamarei Admor haZaken,* 1812, p. 112.

derives its energies from these sources. These "forces of the jungle" preceded all order, or organization, in the world. According to the Kabbalah, the world of raw elements preceded the creation of the world as we know it. It is a lawless world, where anything can happen.

J.E.: You are referring to the world of *tohu*, which we mentioned concerning Yom Kippur as well as exile. *Tohu* is the primeval state of matter but is also the raw material of the spirit and society. Pharaoh is a perfect incarnation of the world of *tohu*, characterized by anarchy[46] and, at times, by murderous madness.

A.S.: The Alter Rebbe compares exile to a dream. In a dream, anything can happen, because the customary laws of logic no longer hold. Exile is a separate world that functions according to its own laws, the laws of outlaws, in a world of disorder. When a world such as this encounters the Jewish world, which represents knowledge and awareness of God's Presence in the world, confrontation and clashes are inevitable. Israel, who believes in the existence of a specific order, faces Pharaoh, who cannot even imagine that a world like this exists.

J.E.: Must all conflicts of ideas or intellectual debates end in persecution? This is the real issue. The clash with Pharaoh caused real genocide. Was it really necessary for the founding of monotheism?

A.S.: What is tragic in the history of the Israelites in Egypt is precisely the inevitability of tragic events. Had Egypt cloaked

---

46. See the previous chapter regarding the relationship between *tohu* and the atom.

itself in elegant and appealing trappings, the Israelites would never have recognized its true nature. Bondage in Egypt was a form of pedagogy.

J.E.: What a lesson!

A.S.: A lesson that had to be learned. In order for the Jewish people to fully understand the forces and ideologies that formed the essence of Egypt, they had to suffer. If they had not reached that level, which the Bible describes as bitterness, they might have forgotten that they needed to be saved. Even in a world in disorder, there is room for Israel. In actual fact, ancient polytheism was fairly tolerant and was not at all opposed to making room for a different religion.

J.E.: The Romans would have been delighted if they could have included the God of the Jews in their pantheon. The problem was that this God was unclassifiable.

A.S.: In Egypt, Israel was on the brink of forgetting its mission. If Egypt had been more tolerant, and less hostile and xenophobic, the Israelites probably would have. However, when Israel suffers, it becomes aware of the extremes of persecution and begins to realize that persecution is neither accidental nor a random occurrence of history. Israel grasps that it is the victim of deliberate antagonism and sees that Israel and Egypt are two different essences. Unfortunately, the greater the persecution, the stronger this awareness. Suffering was thus the key to the necessary polarization that enabled Israel to discover its own identity and disentangle itself from its identification with Egypt.

The Forces of Evil

J.E.: There is a classic argument, expounded in particular by Jean Paul Sartre, that anti-Semitism is the main factor in Jewish survival or, in any case, in Jewish awareness. In my opinion, this type of reasoning is extremely dangerous, because it implies that without persecution, the Jews would have been assimilated years ago, and it turns anti-Semitism into a form of *felix culpa*. I have always countered this idea, by showing that the number of Jews who remained faithful to their religion as a result of persecution was much lower than that of Jews who vanished because of it. Nevertheless, Egypt can be seen as a special case, because Israel needed to witness a visible, spectacular form of evil in order to distance itself from it. This view concurs with the Bible, where the Israelites are frequently taught to love strangers because they were once strangers themselves in Egypt. In other words, there is no better way to prevent racism than to have suffered from it. It is clear that the memory of the concentration camps motivates many Jews today to fight for human rights.

However, the Holocaust forces us to ask why, from ancient Egypt to Nazi Germany, the combat between henchman and victim was so imbalanced. Alter Rebbe suggests a metaphysical reply. The forces of evil emanate from a primeval world of absolute disorder, *tohu*, and precede the coherent organization of reality. They form a set of unchannelled forces and primary instincts, a sort of archeo-humanity that, like the jungle, is uncontrollable because it is primeval and basic. In other words, evil possesses greater energy than the energy contained in Good. Is this why Israel has so often emerged as the weakling in the course of history?

A.S.: Imagine that Israel had power. In this case, the world around it would not have had the ability to choose. It is written in the Torah that Israel is small in number.

135

It is not because you are the most numerous of peoples that the Lord set His heart on you and chose you— indeed you are the smallest of peoples.[47]

One of the motivations for this numerical inferiority, and this weakness, is that it enables the rest of the world to exist. To employ the classical vocabulary of the prophets and Jewish mysticism: Without this disparity between Israel and the nations, light would have quickly eliminated darkness, and the world of order would have destroyed the world of disorder.

J.E.: Israel would have been tempted to impose its law by force and its faith through arms. There have been precedents. However, this is not the way the "Jewish model" is meant to be exported.

A.S.: Despite this imbalance, we hope that one day the whole world will adhere to the plan for humanity in the Torah. This will necessarily take time, the time the world takes to exercise its free will. This explains why Israel suffered in the land of Egypt. The chosen people needed to deal with a great civilization and with a powerful, rich, and cultivated people. No other nation would have been able to dominate Israel. Exile implies the clash of two cultures, or else the battle is skewed from the outset.

J.E.: Jewish literature tends to adhere to the Manichean vision of Israel and Egypt you just described.
    However, things are less clear cut than they seem, since

---

47. Deuteronomy 7:7.

there were defections on both sides. It would be more accurate to describe the relationship between Egypt and Israel as one of attraction and repulsion. Despite the hardships of bondage, a certain number of Israelites adapted perfectly to their condition of slavery. The Midrash compares the exodus from Egypt to being ripped out, and even in some places to a real delivery: "*Like a calf torn from the belly of its mother.*"[48]

The Maharal of Prague considered this image to be of major importance. The calf belongs to the same family as the cow. Over the centuries, a real relationship of kinship had developed between the Israelites and Egyptians. In the desert, one of the many complaints voiced by the children of Israel was that they were sorry to have left Egypt.

"We remember the fish that we used to eat free in Egypt."[49]

A.S.: Jews have always been attracted by the world of *tohu*. This world is not fundamentally bad. We have seen that it contains many holy elements.

J.E.: The sparks.

A.S.: This is why there has always been reciprocal, or at times a unilateral, attraction between the world of *tohu* and the world of *tikkun*. The light in the heart of Israel discovers the kindred lights held prisoner in chaos, eliciting sympathy and compassion between the two worlds. The more sparks of holiness, the stronger the attraction.

---

48. *Midrash Rabbah*, Exodus 3:17.
49. Numbers 11:5.

J.E.: We could easily extrapolate and cite any number of poles of attraction, such as the French Revolution or Marxism, which have held great, and sometimes deleterious, attraction for Jews. In Egypt, the attraction was apparently very strong. Moses had to negotiate with the people step by step to kindle the idea of freedom in them, make them aware of their uniqueness, and give them the strength to throw off the chains of bondage. The Talmud says that in Egypt, Israel had reached the forty-ninth level (out of fifty) of impurity— that is, assimilation. At this stage, only violent persecution could make them revolt. The Sages confirm this idea by commenting that Pharaoh had "*brought the heart of Israel to their heavenly father*"[50] and that each time Israel wavered, God imposed "*a king as hard as Haman*" on Israel.[51] Does this imply that we need to suffer to know or acknowledge God?

A.S.: Fortunately not. Suffering is only one alternative we can exercise. If we acknowledge our identity spontaneously, we do not need to be tortured to admit it. In contrast, if we try to be like the people around us, we will end up being rejected, and we will finally grasp that we are us, they are them, and that we have to start the process of saving the world over again. If we forget our mission, the world unwittingly finds various ways of recalling us to our duty. In other words, the world is like a giant self-regulating mechanism that calls to order the parts of its organism that malfunction. When a piece of the mechanism shirks its duty, the mechanism has an almost physiological need to constrain it in order to fulfill its function. But, once again, this is a reflex function, and the body sets it in motion without knowing why. In the mecha-

---

50. *Exodus Rabbah* 21.
51. Babylonian Talmud, Tractate *Sanhedrin* 97b.

nism of the world, the function of Israel is the knowledge of God. This is what the world reminds Israel to do, just the way the body protects the brain so that it can continue to play its role in the processes of life.

J.E.: When there are toxins in the body, the cells secrete antibodies. Exile is a kind of antibody that serves to remind Israel that it is, and should be, Israel and enables it to gather the lost sparks. Antibody, as we see, starts with the prefix "anti."

A.S.: Many versions of this idea can be found, in particular in the writings of the Maharal of Prague and Rabbi Yehudah Halevi.[52] The latter uses the image of the heart in his well-known statement that Israel is the heart of the world. The heart is the most important and the most fragile of all the organs. It is tuned to all the suffering of the body, but is also the best preserved. One of the functions of the body is to ensure correct heart function and safety; the very existence of the world depends upon it.

---

52. Jewish philosopher and poet who lived in Spain (1075–1141), author of the *Kuzari*.

THE BREAD OF KNOWLEDGE

"The sound of my beloved, here it comes, leaping over the mountains, skipping over the hills. My beloved is like a deer."[53]

This verse refers to the exodus from Egypt, at which time the redemption came about in a manner of "leaping,"[54] [the galut having been reduced] from 400 to 210 years, as explained in Midrash Shir Hashirim *(Song of Songs) in this verse.*

To understand all this [we must first explain what] we say in the Haggadah, *"Why do we eat this matzah? Because the dough of our ancestors did not have time to ferment before God, King of all Kings of Kings, revealed Himself to them and redeemed them"* . . .

This is how the exodus from Egypt was achieved: mitzrayim *("Egypt") is the concept of narrow straits* (meitsar) *and boundaries—as in the finiteness of the physical world . . . When was revealed to them the King of all Kings of Kings, "He and His name alone," which is higher than the* hishtalshelut *of all the worlds, the very self and essence of God—then there was the Exodus from* mitzrayim.

In order for this revelation to be, they had to eat matzah. The concept of matzah is along the lines of what our Sages have said: "The infant does not know to call

---

53. Song of Songs 2:8–9.
54. The leap refers to the reduction of the Exodus out of love. Abraham was told that the Exodus would last 400 years, but it was reduced to 210.

'father' or 'mother' until he tastes the taste of grain,"[55] i.e., there is something in "grain" that enables the infant to recognize his father and mother. Similarly, it was by the means of the matzah that they recognized the Divine, the very self and essence of God [in a manner of] "Know the God of your fathers,"[56] [the word know] implying a recognition and sensing, etc.

There are two aspects of matzah. The first is [the matzah] which was [eaten] before midnight. This matzah needs watching over [that it should not ferment, as the Torah instructs] "you shall safeguard the matzot."[57] The second is [the matzah which achieved that the King of all Kings of Kings] revealed Himself to them"[58] . . . regarding which it is said, "the dough of our ancestors did not have time to ferment."[59] This matzah is not susceptible to fermentation at all.

But first we must understand the concepts of hametz[60] and matzah. Hametz rises and inflates itself and has a taste. Matzah does not rise and self-inflate, and has no taste[61] at all; as our Sages rule, "One who swallows matzah [whole], has fulfilled the obligation [of eating matzah on Passover]."[62] So, too, in man's service of God, matzah is the element of self-abnegation. This was the quality of the first matzah, which the Israelites ate before midnight—the "arousal from below" through

---

55. Babylonian Talmud, Tractate *Berakhot* 40a.
56. Chronicles 1, 28:9.
57. Exodus 12:17.
58. From the Passover *Haggadah.*
59. Ibid.
60. Leavened bread.
61. The word *ta'am* means both "taste" and "reason." Matzah has no taste and thus represents supra-rationality.
62. Babylonian Talmud, Tractate *Pesachim* 115b.

"nullify your will [before His]"[63] *. . . As is known, pride is the progenitor of all profanities, the source of all lusts. Thus through the quality of "nullify your will," one achieves self-conquest* (itkafia), *and as it is written: "and you shall eliminate the evil [from within you.]"*[64]

Likkutei Torah, Song of Songs 14c–d

Josy Eisenberg: Egpyt is Israel's first exile, the archetype for all future exiles. Pesah, the Jewish Passover that commemorates the exodus from Egypt, is above all a time to meditate on slavery and alienation. We focused on this in the previous chapter. But this is only part of the Exodus. The main theme of the holiday is, of course, freedom, and the many Passover rituals combine allusions to exile with symbols of redemption. For example, during the Passover meal, a plate containing a variety of foods is placed on the table. Some of these foods, like the bitter herbs, remind us of slavery. Others, such as the "shank bone" that represents the Passover lamb, stand for freedom. The most characteristic food of Passover is the matzah, the unleavened bread, which represents both of these features.

Matzah is the key feature of the Passover celebration. Unleavened bread is the only bread Jews are permitted to eat during the seven days of the holiday.[65] Eating leavened bread on Passover not only is strictly forbidden but is viewed as one of the gravest transgressions in Jewish observance. The Bible goes so far as to say: "*For whoever eats leavened bread from the first day to the seventh day, that person shall be cut off from Israel.*"[66]

---

63. *Pirkei Avot* 2:4.
64. Deuteronomy 13:6, and elsewhere.
65. In Israel. In the diaspora, the holiday lasts one day longer.
66. Exodus 12:15.

By contrast, every Jew's duty to eat matzah, and the precept: "*Seven days you shall eat unleavened bread,*"[67] is repeated no less than ten times in the Torah. This emphasis calls for two comments. First of all, matzah has such importance that the Passover holiday is often called by this name. In the Torah, although the holiday is sometimes called Pesaḥ, the most common name used to designate the exodus from Egypt is "*ḥag haMatzot,*" "the holiday of unleavened bread." On the other hand, it is surprising to find a dietary obligation rather than a prohibition, although such prohibitions are much more common in the Bible. Because an obligation to eat is so rare, there must be a reason why we are commanded to eat matzah. After all, it is only food.

Adin Steinsaltz: Only food? First of all, eating is important. It is what keeps us alive. Without food there would be no life. We sometimes forget how important eating is in a well-nourished, if not over-nourished, culture. In addition, we primarily eat highly standardized, manufactured products, and we tend to forget the importance of foods, what they are like, and how they are prepared. Nevertheless, what we are allowed to eat, just like what we are forbidden to eat on Passover, is not related to sustenance. These dietary rules go beyond commemoration or a social ritual. They are our way of personally taking part in the exodus from Egypt; it is more than recollection. We do not commemorate the exodus from Egypt, because it is constantly in our minds.

J.E.: We recall the Exodus several times a day in prayer. On Friday night and holidays, when we recite the *Kiddush* over a cup of wine, we proclaim that the Sabbath and the holidays are memories of the departure from Egypt. There are many

---

67. The first mention is in Exodus 12:15.

laws in the Torah commanding Israel to accomplish positive acts or certain rituals *"because I brought you out of the land of Egypt."*[68] If we only ate matzah as a remembrance of Passover, it would be superfluous, because the memory is strong enough to haunt the Jewish mind.

A.S.: This is why the Passover *seder*[69] is not simply a remembrance or a theatrical reenactment of the Exodus; it is, in fact, a personal reliving of the entire process of Exodus. Eating matzah reproduces the internal process of the departure from Egypt, and eating leavened bread would be returning to slavery and exile.

To Eat Is to Know

J.E.: In other words, in our everyday lives, we need food to live, whereas on Pesah we need to eat to achieve an awareness of our identity. This is what the Alter Rebbe states in a very original theory of knowledge, which expands upon the Talmud. I suggest we devote this chapter to this theory.

Before doing so, however, it should be said that the Alter Rebbe never viewed eating as an exclusively biological act. Although it is commonplace in Western cultures to differentiate earthly nourishment from spiritual nourishment, this type of concept is rare in Kabbalah and *Hasidut*, because it contradicts the Jewish idea of the unity of the person, his relationship to what is holy, and the true meaning of life. There is no real dichotomy between physiological functions

---

68. Exodus 20:2, and elsewhere.

69. The first night of Passover, in which there are rituals and dietary observances that re-create the history of the Israelites in Egypt. This ritual is called the *seder*, literally, "order."

and man's inner life. Rather, the physiological underlies all forms of mental life, including the intellectual and spiritual. The energy we obtain from food enables the brain to function, and the physical and mental are intertwined. Eating is the first step for the body and for the mind. It is the most ordinary of actions, yet it is already the first stage of knowledge.

A.S.: The concept of food as the basis for knowledge goes back to the Fall and the dissemination of the Divine sparks, which we talked about in the last chapter. The Divine is present in the world because it is not merely a pure essence that is located above and beyond all reality. Divine forces insufflate reality, combine with it, and enable it to live. The reality of the physical world, as we perceive it, is nothing more than the Divine, which is simultaneously concealed and revealed. It expresses itself in many forms. In a certain way, the "lower" the form of life, such as animals, plants, or food, the more they in fact contain Divine energy.

J.E.: You are alluding to a classic kabbalistic theory. Contrary to Western thought, which tends to situate the Divine very high and matter very low, and to believe that a chasm separates them, the kabbalists developed a concept whereby the highest point is connected to the lowest point. The highest level of reality corresponds to the first degree of the spirit. The more things appear to be weighty and far removed from the spiritual, the more thought is needed to conceive them. The more things appear to be material, the more spiritual energy they need to subsist. To make a trivial comparison, the world is like a car. The heavier the chassis, the stronger the motor needs to be. All physical reality is hence composite. Its apparent structure is raw matter. However, this matter only exists because of the hidden sparks that fell into the world when the "vessels shattered."[70] This is the case in particular for food. It is clearly something more than a simple combination of calories.

A.S.: This is why eating is a dual process. The first process is purely biological. We eat in order to live, since on a zoological level, we are primates who must eat. Here it makes little difference whether it is bread or matzah. We eat because we belong to the animal kingdom, and we are living beings.

However, we do not define ourselves exclusively by the fact that we belong to the world of the living. As Jews, when we eat, we are simultaneously nourishing the biological function and another function. Our being, which has a conscience, is united with an organic element that we ingest and that lacks a conscience. Nevertheless, even if it lacks a conscience, the food that I eat comes from God, just as I do. It has its part of holiness, and ingesting it consists precisely of fusing that part with myself.

This is why what I eat and how I eat is an issue that goes far beyond the biological framework, and even the purely religious framework of human dietetics. It in fact consists of uniting man with inner nature, the Divine essence of what he is eating.

Tell Me What You Eat

J.E.: It was important to begin our discussion of Passover with exile. We saw that our world is in exile and that matter is cut off from God by the lack of awareness that forms its shell. However, matter conceals (or imprisons, suffocates, destroys)

---

70. According to Kabbalah, when the universe was created, the "vessels" destined to hold the Divine light could not bear the intensity and broke. As a result, part of this light—the sparks—fell into matter.

sparks of holiness, and it is man's mission to free them. Nourishment is the most ordinary and most spectacular case of this quest for holiness in the heart of the mundane. Eating connects me to the earth through the body of the things I eat, and to the heavens through their souls if I know how to find and free it in my relationship to nourishment. Thus, eating is a paradoxical act, which can generate either total atheism or total faith. On the one hand, the biological or zoological function of eating points, often cruelly, to my limitations, my finitude, my fleeting ties to history and geography. On the other hand, if I analyze the whole process of the gift of nourishment, if I bless God for my daily bread, the bread itself becomes a permanent and irrefutable testimony of my faith.

A.S.: Man operates like a recycling plant. He transforms and grinds up nourishment, and absorbs some of it (some is not used) as his "fuel." At the same time he also absorbs "spiritual calories," the sparks of holiness. This is the meaning of the Ba'al Shem Tov's[71] interpretation of the famous verse, "*Man does not live by bread alone, but on all utterance from the mouth of the Lord does man live.*"[72]

In other words, man does not only live from the calories provided by bread, but from Divine energy. This is what the Torah calls the "*utterance from the mouth of the Lord.*" It makes the bread "live" and forms its true essence. In other words, although superficially I am only eating matter, in fact I am ingesting language, because the raw material of bread is the Divine word. Thus eating is simultaneously living and knowing.

---

71. Israel Ba'al Shem Tov (1700–1760), the founder of Ḥasidut.
72. Deuteronomy 8:3.

J.E.: The world was created by the Divine word. To be more precise, it was created by "ten utterances," since in the story of Creation God speaks ten times. *"God said, Let there be light, . . . God said, Let the waters below the sky be gathered,"*[73] and so on. Creation is the concretization of Divine discourse. Life is materialized language. All relationships to life—and above all, this necessarily intimate relationship of eating—remove the shell of matter in order to reach and absorb its kernel of the word, and hence, knowledge.

Throughout his works, the Alter Rebbe draws subtle connections between faith and knowledge. For instance, the existence of God is a question not of faith, but rather of knowledge, since clear thought and meditation lead straight there. God's presence in the world is on the level of reality, feelings, and perceptions, and is hence intelligible. Faith, by contrast, covers what cannot be perceived directly and rationally, such as the eschatological.

The Alter Rebbe considers the use of the intellect to be an indispensable tool for spiritual life. This is why eating or, in other words, nourishing the brain, is the beginning of any process of knowledge. However, there are two types of nourishment, or daily bread. There is ordinary bread that we eat all year-round and the unleavened bread that replaces it during the Passover week. What are their respective functions? The function of matzah, special bread, needs to be defined in the framework of the function of our daily bread.

According to the Talmud, it plays a prime role in a specific and fundamental form of knowledge, the father–son relationship. *"The child does not know to call 'father,' until he tastes grain."*[74]

The Alter Rebbe comments numerous times on this text,

---

73. Genesis 1.
74. Babylonian Talmud, Tractate *Berakhot* 40a.

which also appears in the *Zohar*. In Kabbalah, the father and mother—*abba* and *imma*—appear in two *sefirot*, Ḥokhmah (wisdom) and *Binah* (understanding). By eating bread, the child acquires the bases of thought and the premises of knowledge.

In the Zohar, matzah is also called the "food of faith" . . . since this quality is infused in the soul through the mitzvah of eating matzah.

This is along the same lines of the above-mentioned analogy of the bread which vitalizes the person, and in accordance with the saying of the Sages, "The child does not know to call, 'Father,' until he tastes [grain]." Now this knowledge of the child to call "Father," which has been infused and accomplished in him through his tasting the taste of bread, is not a true understanding, knowledge, and comprehension, for he does not know why this man is his father or why he must love him; nevertheless, he calls him "Father." Hence this call expresses a bond to his father which is not known and understood by him, but is merely a "recognition," which is a much lesser level than knowledge and understanding. Nevertheless, that bond is very strong, to the extent that his soul is very much bound to the soul of his father. This is because the knowledge that has been accomplished in the child through the taste of bread has its source in the world of Tohu ("Chaos"), which is higher than comprehensible knowledge, higher than Ḥokhmah, which is why it comes down as a faculty that is lower than comprehensible knowledge. This is why the bond is very strong.

So, too, is it in regard to the eating mitzvah of matzah, which the Zohar calls "food of faith." Faith is the recognition and knowledge of God and the bond with Him, and all Jews believe that He is exclusively Himself just as He was before the world was created. . . .[75]

. . . Thus the Zohar says that matzah is called the "food of faith," meaning that matzah infuses the community of Israel with faith on the level of the very essence of the Infinite Light, Blessed be He, which is higher than the manifestation and revelation of the light, as discussed above.

The reason that this is achieved specifically through this mitzvah can be understood by prefacing the saying of the Sages, "The child does not know to call, 'Father,' until he tastes grain." This is a wondrous thing: why should the cause of knowledge in the child be his tasting the taste of grain? But the explanation of the matter is that, as the saying implies, the only thing the child knows is to call "Father," but he has no true knowledge and comprehension of the concept of "father" itself—that this person has fathered him, the quality of his compassion and love toward him, that he sustains him and nourishes him, and so on. The small child recognizes none of this; nevertheless, at age three, or even before, he calls him "Father! Father!" as is commonly known.

So this that he knows to "call" is not a knowledge deriving from comprehension itself, but a knowledge deriving from a place higher than reason. It is not completely beyond reason, for he does know to call— that is, he recognizes [his father] with a true cognition—he won't call someone else "father." One must therefore say that this knowledge and recognition is drawn down from a place higher than reason into reason and cognizance. Yet this knowledge is not in the expansive state in which it exists in a place higher than reason,

---

75. *Likkutei Torah,* Leviticus 13d.

but has been lowered and clothed within the "lesser mind" to assume the form of mere "recognition."[76]

B-A-Ba: Abba

A.S.: From a linguistic standpoint, as much as from an anthropological or cultural one, bread can be defined as man's most staple food. It is the food that makes and proves that man is man. Meat, vegetables, or fruits are natural foods. But bread represents the first step toward civilization, the initial form of culture. This is why the child starts to speak when he or she eats bread.

In a certain way, the question of the type of bread is connected to the question of the tree of knowledge. What kind of tree was it? In the Talmud there are several theories. Some say it was a fig tree; others say it was a grapevine. The third theory is that it was grain or, in other words, bread. Regardless of the moral implications of Adam's eating of the "fruit of the tree of knowledge," if this tree is a "grain tree," there is a tight connection between eating bread and knowledge.

J.E.: Infancy is a period of total lack of knowledge, and the onset of language is clearly the first sign of awareness. Thus, the time a child starts to speak corresponds to weaning and the transition to a new type of food. It may seem strange that in Jewish tradition, language acquisition—when the child is able to say "father" and "mother"—is solely related to grain. The word *abba* (father) is formed by the first two letters of the Hebrew alphabet, the *a-b-ab*, which any child can learn. However, isn't a child's first identification to his or her

---

76. *Siddur Admor haZaken, Sha'ar Ḥag haMatzot*, p. 284b.

mother, in the womb, at birth, and through nursing? It seems more logical to have milk mentioned before bread.

A.S.: Naturally, the relationship to the father, to bread, is not the child's first experience with the outside world. But there is an enormous difference between the way a child perceives his mother and the way he perceives his father. The nonverbal relationship with the mother is a natural, biological relationship. In cultures where mothers nurse their infants, the mother is the first object in his discovery of the world. This is immediate knowledge. However, naming the father and the mother represents the transition from an almost instinctive form of knowledge to a higher form, which is unrelated to natural necessity, although it is still not true intellectual knowledge.

J.E.: Recognizing one's mother is thus an instinctive function, and here man is no different from animals. Recognizing one's father is not a natural reflex and calls for a more sophisticated process. The Alter Rebbe thus differentiates reflex from reflection. He bases his argument on the theory of the *sefirot*. The first three (of the ten) *sefirot* correspond to the thought processes. The seven remaining *sefirot* are called *midot*. One of the features of *midot* is that they typify development, in particular as regards the developmental order of functions or natural instincts. The Alter Rebbe refers to these categories when he says that the newborn possesses the *midot* before his intellectual abilities, called *moḥin*, develop. In other words, the transition from milk to bread corresponds to the stage when the *midot* begin to be controlled by the *moḥin*. The Alter Rebbe explains this through a striking comparison between digestion in the stomach and intellectual "digestion" of information.

We see that the infant is born very small, and that, through the mother's milk that it nurses, it grows in all its limbs in much greater proportion than its growth after nursing. For after the two years of nursing, it grows only in small amounts each year; although it eats a lot, this food does not cause it to grow as much as the mother's milk does in the first two years . . . This must be because it is the milk's nature to cause growth more than other foods . . . The reason for this is that the milk is from the breasts, the place of Binah (understanding) in the heart . . . for the blood of birth curdles and becomes milk . . . this milk is of the quality of "intellect"—only it has descended and materialized . . .[77]

When you said that the ability to call one's father represents intellectual progress but still does not constitute true knowledge, you are referring to another text by the Alter Rebbe, which I would like to reproduce here in its entirety because it sheds so much light on our discussion.

The Sages said that the child did not know how to say "father" and "mother" before he knew the taste of grain. This proves that even when he knows how to call them, he does not have real knowledge. This is because he does not know why his father is his father; he only knows how to call him without having a reason. This is because it is exclusively the back and the immaturity[78] of thought which is invested in grain, and not its essence and its substance; thus he only knows how to "call." The same thing is true for matzah: it is on the level of the "infancy

---

77. *Torah Ohr*, Exodus 106c.
78. The most elementary levels of thought.

of abba"[79] *which is invested there, and only by eating matzah can he recognize his Creator, the Father Who is in Heaven, and proclaim his own nothingness, although he does not know the real reason why; in other words, [he does not] know the reality of God, how He created everything, and that He considers everything (that exists) to be nothing.*[80]

A.S.: It is not enough to say "father." When a child says the word, he naturally feels something, but he is far from understanding all the implications of this concept. He does not know who his father is, he does not know what a father is. He merely has an inkling of something that prompts him to speak. He has access to words and to speech on that inner dimension that the kabbalists call *Malkhut*, Kingdom, and that is represented by the mouth.

J.E.: *Malkhut*, the tenth *sefirah*, represents the kingdom of God and reflects the ability to communicate, primarily through language.

The Leap into the Unknown

A.S.: In fact, the child experiences two things. First, the child discovers language. Then he makes what many texts call the first "leap" toward knowledge. We discover the world through our senses first. To know God, however, requires a leap on the ladder of knowledge. This leap, this emotional response, enables us to say and to recognize "daddy" or

---

79. *Abba* (father) is the symbol of the second *sefirah*, *Hokhmah* (wisdom).

80. *Maamarei Admor HaZaken, Taksah* (5668), 1808, p. 430.

"mommy." We are not fully conscious of this transition from the senses to the intellectual, because it goes beyond the senses in a process that is not entirely within our grasp. Someone can be sixty and still not have grasped what "daddy" or "mommy" means. Even people who think they have understood, still make the leap.

J.E.: The nature of this leap is hard to understand, unless we associate it with one of the major theories in Kabbalah. According to this theory, the intellectual development of the child (a microcosm) follows the pattern of the general process of Creation (the macrocosm) in four stages. The kabbalists call these stages *'ibbur, yenikah, katnut,* and *gadlut;* respectively, fecundation, nursing, infancy of the brain, and maturity of the brain. All forms of life are thought to adhere to this pattern. All matters go through a state of *'ibbur,* where they are "hidden" in the "belly" of what will "give birth" to them. They then receive sustenance from others, in a state of total dependency corresponding to nursing. In the third stage they gain some independence, or have "a small brain," before they reach maturity.

In terms of the *sefirot* it is said, for example, that the child first lives *midot,* his or her emotional life, but that *mohin,* the intellectual life that arises from the *sefirot* of thought, are only unveiled gradually. However, the first two intellectual *sefirot, Hokhmah* and *Binah,* are traditionally called *abba* and *imma,* father and mother. Thus, all concepts and all "conceptions" derive from an encounter between the "father" and the "mother," between the general ability to "conceive" (the father) and the ability to give consistency (the mother).

In a series of texts, of which we unfortunately cannot quote all, Alter Rebbe explains that speech cannot be linked to the tenth *sefirah, Malkhut* (the mouth), unless the ability to think (from the *abba*) is completed, enhanced, and exterior-

155

ized by the *imma*. Thus, it is no accident that the Talmud refers to "naming one's father and mother." The newborn possesses *midot*, which correspond to desire. Knowledge, however, is still in a state of *katnut*, or immaturity. A child is called "*katan*" (young) up to the age of puberty because, as the Alter Rebbe also points out, he or she cannot "conceive" before this.

"And the voice of the dove is heard in our land."[81] *"The voice of the dove" is the infusion of the "five constrictors"—[represented by the letters] MaNeTZe-PaKH*[82]*—of* Binah *to* Malkhut, *which is called "our land."*

The "letters of thought" are drawn forth from Binah *by means of the "five constrictors"—MaNeTZePaKH—of* Binah, *which distinguish and define [abstract thoughts into the "letters" of definitive thoughts]. From there they are drawn down into "five constrictors"—Ma-NeTZePaKH—that are in the "five speech-generators of the mouth," which distinguish and definitize the breath of speech [into the letters and words of language].*

On the face of it, it seems amazing that an infant of less than two years cannot formulate the letters of speech [into cohesive language]. In the realm of thought, he does not lack the ability to formulate "letters" . . . He can contemplate in his thoughts the desirability of something—such as a beautiful object—and request, by

---

81. Song of Songs 2:12.
82. Five letters of the Hebrew alphabet—מנצפ״ך, *mem, nun, tzadi, pe,* and *kaf*—which have two different forms, depending on their position in the word. They are connected to the left side, the side of delimitation and rigor, two necessary conditions for the emergence of language. The "five constrictors" are the *hei gevurot*.

means of gestures, that it be given to him to play with, and the like. So if he possesses the "five constrictors" that define thought, why cannot he translate his thoughts into speech by formulating the breath of speech in the same way he has formulated the very same combination of letters in his thought? In truth, however, the infant does not have the same capacity to formulate the "language" of thought as does the adult. He has the capacity for "imagination" . . . but not the distinct formulations achieved by the mind of an adult contemplating an intellectual matter. . . . The point at which a mind can achieve this degree of definition in thought, that is the point at which it can formulate the combination of [sounds of] speech—this occurs approximately at the age of two years—because at this point the "five constrictors"—MaNeTZePaKH—are drawn forth from Binah into the letters of thought to define them.[83]

J.E.: This text draws on kabbalistic categories to show how rationality, or in any case how the child's ability to think rationally, develops. There can be no true rationality without language, the logos, which is both words and logic. The process, however, is irrational. What enables me suddenly to grasp something that I did not understand before? The transition from the irrational to the rational takes place, according to the kabbalists, through a mysterious "leap," or discontinuity. One of the purposes of consciousness is to establish relationships, and a leap enables me to recognize my father and mother, and hence God. Can we say that the difference between bread and matzah is that the former enables me recognize my earthly parents, whereas the latter is an initiation to knowledge of God?

83. *Maamarei Admor HaZaken, Taksah* (5668), 1808, p. 488.

A.S.: There is clearly a difference between bread and matzah. Matzah is the most primitive form of bread. Leavened bread implies a societal order. Bread making is a cultural act that calls for availability, time, and some technique. A culture that makes bread is already an advanced culture. Matzah is an unadulterated food. It is scarcely more than a bit of wheat that has undergone a slight transformation. It is the simplest of foods. It has no salt or spices, it has no taste. It does not appeal to the refinement of our senses. The only thing that can be said about it is that it is bread.

From an intellectual point of view, the primeval or primordial situation where people ate matzah is represented by the Israelites in Egypt. This marks the birth of knowledge, its initial stage when the child learns to say "daddy" and "mommy." This awareness is not the outcome of a specific intellectual process but rather derives from the mysterious leap that is the essence of Passover. This explains the allusion in the Song of Songs to the leap of the beloved: "*Hark My beloved! There he comes, leaping over mountains, bounding over hills.*"[84]

J.E.: Indeed, the word *Passover* literally means "leap." According to the Bible, God leaps over the houses of the Israelites and spares them during the tenth plague. This leap gave the name to this holiday. It is a manifestation of Divine Will that surpasses reason. It is an act of love. It is easy to see why so many passages in the Song of Songs are related in Jewish tradition to the Passover. God enters into the history of the Israelites in a way that is beyond causality. It is gratuitous, like love. The Alter Rebbe deals with this topic at length and discusses the leap, the entry of God, bread and matzah, in the following sections.

---

84. Song of Songs 2:8.

The Leap

"The sound of my beloved, here he comes, leaping over the mountains, skipping over the hills. My beloved is like a deer."[85] *This verse refers to the exodus from Egypt, at which time the redemption came about in a manner of "leaping" [the* galut *having been reduced] from 400 to 210 years, as explained in* Midrash Shir Hashirim *(Song of Songs) in this verse.*

To understand all this [we must first explain what] we say in the Haggadah, *"Why do we eat this matzah? Because the dough of our ancestors did not have time to ferment before God, King of all Kings of Kings, revealed Himself to them and redeemed them." . . . Why do we say "the King of all Kings of Kings," instead of "the King," as we usually do?*

The King Is Causality

The Divine force that vitalizes all the worlds is referred to as "light," expressing the concept that it has no relevance whatsoever to the essence of God. . . . For the same reason, it is also referred to as [God's] name . . . and the concept of [God as] "king." The analogy is of a king's relationship with his country: the king's very self and essence is not apprehended by and disseminated throughout the country; only his name is—the fact that He is called "king" above them. Thus it is Above: that with which the Divine vitalizes all the worlds is merely the

---

85. Idem.

Divine "Kingship"—with that He is King over them, He vitalizes them and brings them into existence. That is to say, only His name [relates to the worlds]. But His very self and essence is beyond the very concepts of revelation and immanence, for He is one alone, exalted and aloof.

The King of All Kings of Kings Is beyond Causality

This is also the concept that "God, King of all Kings of Kings revealed Himself to them and redeemed them." "King" refers to the "Kingship of all the worlds," which vitalizes all the worlds as a mere "effulgence" and "name"; "King of all Kings of Kings" is the Divine Kingship as it exists [in purely potential form] within His essence [in a manner of] "He and His name alone." . . . This is what was revealed to [Israel at the time of the Exodus]—the Divine Kingship is above the hishtalshelut, on the level of the very self and essence of God.

This is how the exodus from Egypt was achieved: mitzrayim ("Egypt") is the concept of narrow straits (meitsar) and boundaries—as in the finiteness of the physical world . . . When was revealed to them the King of all Kings of Kings, "He and His name alone," which is higher than the hishtalshelut of the worlds, the very self and essence of God—then there was the exodus from mitzrayim. In order for there to be this revelation, they had to eat matzah.

The Bread with No Taste

The concept of matzah is along the lines of what our Sages have said: "The infant does not know to call 'father' or 'mother' until he tastes the taste of grain," i.e., there is something in "grain" that enables the infant to recognize his father and mother. Similarly, it was by the means of the matzah that they recognized the Divine, the very self and essence of God [in a manner of] "Know the God of your fathers," [the word know] implying a recognition and sensing, etc.

There are two aspects of matzah. The first is [the matzah] which was [eaten] before midnight. This matzah needs watching over [that it should not ferment, as the Torah instructs] "you shall safeguard the matzot." The second is [the matzah which achieved that "the King of all Kings of Kings] revealed Himself to them," . . . regarding which it is said, "the dough of our ancestors did not have time to ferment." This matzah is not susceptible to fermentation at all.

But first we must understand the concepts of ḥametz and matzah. Ḥametz rises and inflates itself and has a taste. Matzah does not rise and self-inflate, and has no taste at all; as our Sages rule, "One who swallows matzah [whole], has fulfilled the obligation [of eating matzah on Passover]." So, too, in man's service of God, matzah is the element of self-abnegation. This was the quality of the first matzah, which they ate before midnight—the "arousal from below" through "nullify your will [before His]" . . . As is known, pride is the progenitor of all profanities, the source of all lusts. Thus through the quality of "nullify your will," one achieves self-conquest

161

(itkafia) and as it is written "and you shall eliminate the evil [from within you.]"[86]

A.S.: In this passage the Alter Rebbe presents a certain number of ideas that I will discuss one by one. First is the leap, which, from various points of view, forms the essence of Passover. As is the case for all the holidays, Passover has two dimensions. The first dimension extends from "above to below," from God to man. The second extends from "below to above," from man toward God. From above to below, the King of Kings reveals Himself, in a form of absolute transcendence. This revelation is directed to a people who do not yet have the necessary maturity to draw all the conclusions from this revelation. The "below to above" dimension of the Exodus is the leap of faith. Despite its state of immaturity, Israel is able, in some mysterious way, to reach a certain level of knowledge. This knowledge is special in that it unites what is beyond reason and precedes all logic, something that is beyond all human perception. The most elementary stage of knowledge unites with the most advanced stage. Israel is simultaneously capable of perceiving what it does not understand and what is impossible to understand.

J.E.: Israel is in bondage. It may have some vague understanding of a special tie that united its ancestors, the three Patriarchs, with God, and the promise made to them. After so many years of slavery, all of this is distant. Israel is like a child who has some awareness that he has a father but cannot express what he feels. He will only be able to do so when God reveals Himself through the ten plagues. The knowledge process is always dual. I first go from the un-

---

86. *Likkutei Torah,* Song of Songs 14c–d.

known to the known, and I discover the existence of someone or something. Later, as an outcome of this process, I realize that I did not know, or may not yet know, or may never know something. The Greek philosophers, just like the talmudic Sages, concur in saying, "Know what you do not know."

Just like the child who learns to know his father and his mother by eating bread, entering into the cycle of knowledge also means entering into ignorance. By eating matzah the Israelites discover the existence of their "heavenly father" and the impossibility of knowing His essence.

The Child and the Sage

A.S.: In fact, the matzah eaten by the Israelites in Egypt has a dual meaning, as is clearly demonstrated by the *Haggadah* ritual. On the one hand, it is the symbol of flight and powerlessness. The dough prepared for the Exodus did not have enough time to rise, because the Israelites had to leave Egypt in haste. On the other hand, the Israelites were instructed to eat matzah on the evening of Passover to accompany the Passover lamb. "*They shall eat the flesh that same night; they shall eat it roasted over the fire with unleavened bread and with bitter herbs.*"[87] We are commanded to eat matzah although we eat bread the rest of the year and have apparently reached a higher level of knowledge. One of the basic features of Jewish existence, both on the personal level and on the level of collective history, is that there is no possible beginning without a return to the roots of faith, to a state of pure knowledge free of all rationalization. The rest is only construction, superstructure, and embellishment. The primary meaning of eating matzah is the return to the

---

87. Exodus 12:8.

starting point. This return is necessary even when I have "eaten" more sophisticated nourishment.

J.E.: Precisely because that is what I eat all year long. We have seen that Jewish tradition views the polarity between leavened and unleavened bread in a moral light. Leavened bread, our daily bread, represents all artificial forms of expansion, pride, and unchecked growth. Matzah, on the other hand, expresses the return to simplicity. This is, in fact, what the Alter Rebbe says.

But first we must understand the concepts of ḥametz and matzah. Ḥametz rises and inflates itself and has a taste. Matzah does not rise and self-inflate, and has no taste at all; as our Sages rule, "One who swallows matzah [whole], has fulfilled the obligation [of eating matzah on Passover]." So, too, in man's service of God, matzah is the element of self-abnegation. This was the quality of the first matzah, which the Israelites ate before midnight—the "arousal from below" through "nullify your will [before His]" . . . As is known, pride is the progenitor of all profanities, the source of all lusts. Thus through the quality of "nullify your will" one achieves self-conquest (itkafia), and as it is written "and you shall eliminate the evil [from within you.]"

A.S.: The important point here is not the moral point of view, although it is edifying. What is important is the basic fact of eating matzah, if we want a renewal and to leave Egypt.

J.E.: Hasidism says that through our limitations, we are always prisoners of "our own Egypt."

A.S.: We need to repeat the leap that initiated our history and become the child that we were in Egypt. In this way we start the cycle of knowledge and ignorance over again. There are two ways of saying, "I don't know." The child opens his eyes wide with astonishment at the world and says, "I don't know." The individual who has studied extensively, who knows a great deal, who "knows everything," suddenly finds himself facing a vast ocean of unknowns that a child could not even begin to imagine. There, once again, he must say, "I don't know," because the purpose of knowledge is to know what we do not know.

Here matzah represents one of the most basic dimensions of exile and the exodus from Egypt. The manifestation and revelation of God is so enormous that it crushes man and flattens his being and culture. All his knowledge, which had swelled like leavened bread over the course of the year or the last thousand years, suddenly collapses with God's revelation. This is why the *Haggadah* places so much emphasis on the fact that the King of Kings of Kings was revealed. To make this clearer, the *Haggadah* says:

I myself and not an angel, I myself and not a seraph, I myself and not a messenger, I am the Lord I am He, and no other.

When the Holy One, Blessed be He, reveals Himself so directly, without intermediaries, it matters little what level of knowledge man has reached; for he is brought back to his starting point.

J.E.: It is said that a little science distances someone from God, whereas a lot of science brings one closer. Thought, knowledge, and culture can reveal God, just as they can also lead to atheism. The fundamental freedom of the intellect is suspended in Egypt, because in Egypt there is no doubt as to the existence of God. There the revelation is total, absolute, and irrefutable.

A.S.: This is why matzah represents both the point of departure of all knowledge and its end point. It is the bread of slaves who are only just capable of opening their eyes and articulating "father"; it is also the bread of the Sages described in the *Haggadah.*

Even if we were all, wise all of us men of knowledge and understanding the law, it nevertheless is incumbent upon us to narrate the exodus from Egypt, and all those who relate more and more of the narrative of the exodus from Egypt are to be praised.

J.E.: One of the most remarkable features of the Passover holiday is that it is addressed to both the ignorant and to the wise. Customarily, the child's role, the role of the ignorant, receives greater emphasis. Most of the *Haggadah* is based on questions a child is supposed to ask. However, the wise are also under the same obligation. On Passover, the child and the wise man are on an equal footing.

A.S.: In fact, the whole Passover ritual could be summarized in a single commandment: "*You shall tell your son.*"[88] This is why at the beginning of the *Haggadah* the child asks four questions: "*Why is this night different from all other nights? Why do we only eat matzah?*" and so forth.

---

88. A commandment repeated four times in the Torah, e.g., Exodus 13:8.

According to the law, if there is no child present, or if an adult celebrates Passover alone, he must ask the questions, even though he is supposed to "know" the answers. It is customary in certain communities for adults to ask the questions, because on Passover we should, in a sense, become children. This is also why in the Bible, Passover is called the "spring holiday." On Passover, nature as a whole begins to blossom and man's renewal coincides with that of nature. The Sages have pointed to the parallel between the word *nitsan*, "bud," and *Nisan*, the month in which Passover takes place. It is a true renaissance. We become children once again, and all we can do is ask questions. Why should we, after all we have learned?

The Bread of Healing

J.E.: Matzah, the unadulterated bread, represents the unadulterated nature of the spirit and our willingness to learn regardless of our "knowledge." Leavened bread represents the state our knowledge has reached, with its advantages and disadvantages. Living means eating this kind of bread. It is good to alternate with another kind of bread. This is the significance of the strict rules of Passover. It is time to realize that we need to return to matzah. However, matzah is not only reserved for Passover. The sacrifices at the Temple in Jerusalem were accompanied by bread, and the Bible stipulates that this bread must be unleavened. In other words, the bread eaten in the Temple should be matzah. Why?

A.S.: Because matzah is a guarded bread. The Bible says: "*You will guard your matzot.*"[89] Jewish law has deduced a

---

89. Exodus 12:17.

large number of manufacturing rules to prevent bread from rising. On the first night of Passover we eat matzah known as "guarded matzah." This teaches us an important lesson. The beginning deserves particular care, and the slightest impurity in the first phase of a process can spread and corrupt. King Solomon said, *"More than all you guard, guard your heart."*[90] In other words, the heart, as the core of all things, must be protected from all injury. This concept of preservation is found in the Temple. Everything that came into contact with the Holy of Holies needed to be free of all knowledge and sophistication, and be in its primary, natural state. This is why meal offerings at the Temple were strictly supervised. Except in special cases, leavened bread was not placed near the altar, because the concept represented by leavened bread is incompatible with the concept the offering stands for. Leavened bread stands for intelligence and civilization. It is what develops over the course of history. Even its shape demonstrates what it is. Materially, leavened bread does not have any more substance than matzah, but it has more volume. It is thick, it is full, it has a smell, it can be seen, it has a taste; it has all the trappings of culture.

In our everyday lives we can, and we should, eat this kind of bread. It is necessary for our development. This kind of bread gives us the strength to go to the Temple. But in the Temple itself, a holy place, we must be completely pure, like the garments of the high priest that are pure white linen. In special circumstances, we eat only matzah, the simplest of breads.

Just as the temple is a place where we eat only matzah, Passover is the holy period when we eat only matzah. During Passover, new foundations are laid. During Passover I only

---

90. Proverbs 4:23.

eat matzah, as is said in the *Haggadah*: "*On all other nights we eat* hametz *and matzah, but on this night we only eat matzah.*"

The rest of the year, when we are involved in a constructive process, we can eat leavened bread. Before having eaten matzah, this would not be good for us; but once we have eaten matzah, leavened bread is once again permissible.

J.E.: In other words, there is the first matzah, a preparatory matzah, which clears the path to knowledge. This is the matzah our ancestors ate in Egypt before they ate leavened bread. The second kind of matzah is the one we eat every year on Passover, which "rectifies" the excess of "daily bread" of our knowledge.

A.S.: The Alter Rebbe makes an interesting point. He observes that in Egypt, the Israelites were only commanded to eat matzah on the first night, whereas we are commanded to eat matzah for a whole week. In his opinion, this is because our ancestors witnessed the King of Kings of Kings and did not need more than one day to know God. We, in contrast, need more time to rediscover the meaning of matzah. The *Zohar* has several names for matzah. It is known as the "bread of faith" and as the "bread of healing." This dual definition corresponds to the first day's matzah (yesterday's matzah), and the seven-day matzah (today's matzah). When we eat matzah on the first day of Passover, we recapture the feeling of when faith was born. I eat the bread of faith. But the other six days, I eat the bread of healing in order to rid myself of the leaven of the rest of the year. I need to be cured of everything I have forgotten and, perhaps more important, of everything I know. To do this, I need the other six days of Passover.

A PATH IN THE SEA

---

*Then Moses held out his hand over the sea and the Lord
drove back the sea with a strong east wind all that night,
and turned the sea into dry land. The waters were split
and the Israelites went into the sea on dry land, the
waters forming a wall for them on their right and on their
left. The Egyptians came in pursuit after them into the
sea, all of Pharaoh's horses, chariots, and horsemen. At
the morning watch the Lord looked down upon the
Egyptian army from a pillar of fire and cloud, and threw
the Egyptian army into panic. He locked the wheels of the
chariots so that they moved forward with difficulty. And
the Egyptians said, "Let us flee from the Israelites, for
the Lord is fighting for them against Egypt."*

Exodus 14:21–25

*It is written, "And Moses extended [his hand] . . . and
God caused the sea to go back by a strong east
wind . . . and He made the sea into dry land."*[91]

*It needs to be understood: Why does it say [that the sea
was transformed] specifically into "dry land" (ḥaravah),
which is a state of utter dryness to the extent that there
remains no moisture whatsoever?*

*It is known that the Sages have said, "All that is to be
found on dry land is to be found in the sea."*[92] *It is also
known that, in the supernal worlds, "sea" and "dry land"
refer to the "hidden world" and the "revealed world."*

*The explanation of the matter is as follows. It is written,
"Let the waters gather . . . and the dry land be re-*

---

91. Exodus 14:21.
92. Babylonian Talmud, Tractate Ḥullin 127a.

vealed."[93] *From dry land are derived all existences— mineral, vegetable, animal, and human—as it is written,* "Let the earth bring forth [living creatures],"[94] *and* "Let the earth sprout forth [vegetation]";[95] *also man was created from soil; hence it is written,* "Everything came from the soil."[96] *This is because, as the* Zohar *says, the earth begets and makes fruits. Not so the sea, which does not actually produce minerals, vegetables, animals, or humans out of the four elements. Yet the sea contains all creatures that exist on dry land—in a concealed, rather than a revealed state, as per the Sages' saying,* "All that is to be found [on dry land is to be found in the sea]." *And in order that they should become revealed, God said,* "Let the waters under the heavens gather, and may the dry land be revealed"; *meaning that the concealment should be diminished and withdrawn, so that the "dry land" may be revealed and produce the mineral, vegetable, animal, and human existences.*

A similar thing occurred in the supernal worlds with the supernal "sea" and "dry land." The supernal waters of the "hidden world" gathered to a side, as in the verse, "Let the waters gather," *and then,* "God said: Let there be light . . . Let there be a firmament . . ." *which is the quality of "speech," also called "revealed world" and "land" in the supernal realm. This is the significance of* "May the dry land be revealed."

And so it is on all levels, up to the highest of levels— everything comes as concealment and revelation, sea and dry land, as is known. In general, the above- mentioned "concealment of will" is the hidden world,

---

93. Genesis 1:9.
94. Ibid., v. 24.
95. Ibid., v. 11.
96. Ecclesiastes 3:20.

being the divine name HaVaYaH in Keter ("Crown"), as per above; and the revealed world—i.e., the divine name HaVaYaH as it brings the worlds into being—is "dry land" relative to the "sea."

Now, at the moment when God transformed the sea into dry land and the Children of Israel passed through "in the midst of the sea, on dry land" (although this event occurred here below in the physical sense—the physical sea was transformed into dry land—still, the physical sea and land derive from the supernal sea and land, all the way up to the highest levels) at that moment, the sea was transformed into dry land all the way up to the highest level, meaning that the quality of concealment came into revelation all the way up to the highest levels.
Maamrei Admor haZaken Taksav (1806), pp. 145–146

Josy Eisenberg: Passover is set between what are probably the two most astonishing and spectacular miracles in the Bible, the Exodus and the splitting of the Red Sea. The Exodus takes place on the first day of Passover and the splitting of the Red Sea on the seventh. Passover thus starts and ends with a miracle. These two events have had such an impact on Jewish thought that all Jews are commanded to recall them every day. They are mentioned several times in daily prayers. On a superficial level they can be interpreted as two stages in the liberation of Israel, as though the Exodus were a game with two half-times. First Pharaoh is forced to let the Israelites leave Egypt; and then, when he changes his mind and sets out in pursuit of his former slaves, he sees his army swallowed up in the sea. The miracle of what in Jewish tradition is known as "the renting of the Sea of Reeds" is apparently the final chapter in Egyptian oppression.

However, the unique event of the splitting of the Red Sea prompts a number of questions. Was it really necessary to perform such an amazing miracle as the "renting" of the waters of the Red Sea to save Israel? If the Egyptians needed a demonstration of Divine omnipotence, the ten plagues were amply sufficient. In addition, the Egyptians were all drowned and thus could not bear witness.[97] According to the Alter Rebbe, the "renting" of the Red Sea was not a lesson for Egypt but rather for the Israelites. The biblical text strongly suggests that Israel was not only the beneficiary of the miracle but also the recipient of the message, and that the event was designed to inspire faith.

And when the Israel saw the wondrous power which the Lord had wielded against the Egyptians, the people feared the Lord; they had faith in the Lord and His servant Moses.[98]

Thus, even though the first reading appears to restrict the "renting"[99] to a miracle of salvation, the second reading suggests that it is really a stage in the acquisition of faith. This is consistent with the fact that on the eve of Passover, when eating matzah, the Israelites reached the first stage of knowledge of God. What occurs one week later is a confirmation and reinforcement of this faith through the miracle of the Red Sea.

However, Jewish mystical tradition views the splitting of the Red Sea from a totally different perspective. This tradition emphasizes the interplay of two elements, sea and land,

---

97. In Jewish tradition, the only one not to drown was Pharaoh.
98. Exodus 14:31.
99. Or parting of the Red Sea, "renting" here to abbreviate.

because the sea becomes land to let the Israelites pass. Land and sea are important not only in our daily lives, but also in the imagination. They are also crucial features of the symbolic language of the Kabbalah. By drawing on the Kabbalah, the Alter Rebbe adds a third dimension to Passover. In addition to freedom and faith, Passover becomes a highpoint of knowledge.

Adin Steinsaltz: The essence of this event is indeed the transformation of the sea into dry land. The sea becomes a place where people can walk. Furthermore, the sea itself becomes dry. There is a qualitative difference between sea and land. Although both sea and land are characteristics of our planet, they represent radically different forms of existence, both because of their physical features and because of man's relationships to each. The land is the place where things live and grow in a way we can see. The sea, on the other hand, is populated by things that are concealed and hidden. Internal events take place in the sea, whereas external events characterize land.

Men are basically land creatures. Our entire lives are in the visible realm. Our modes of existence and our relationships with others take place in a universe that can be seen with the naked eye. In a sense, what we cannot see does not exist for us. The complementarity between land and sea thus mirrors the visible and invisible worlds.

In the Beginning Was the Sea

J.E.: One comment needs to be made at this juncture. The word *land* is used here for simplicity's sake. In fact, the Bible uses a different word to describe the crossing of the Red Sea: *yabbashah*, which literally means "dryness" or "dry land."

Yabbashah is used in Genesis, when God creates the world: "*Let the water below the sky be gathered into one area, that the dry land (yabbashah) may appear.*"[100] The term was as important to the commentators as was the fact that the Red Sea in the Bible is called *Yam Suf,* which is generally translated as the "Sea of Reeds." Significantly, *Yam Suf* can also be translated as the "the sea of extremes"; we will see later how significant this term, too, is. However, what is abundantly clear is that, as is the case with the beginnings of life, there is a tight bond between land and sea, a bond that is both complementary and conflictual.

It is written, "And Moses extended [his hand] . . . and God caused the sea to go back by a strong east wind . . . and He made the sea into dry land."[101]

It needs to be understood: Why does it say [that the sea was transformed] specifically into "dry land" (ḥaravah), which is a state of utter dryness to the extent that there remains no moisture whatsoever?

It is known that the Sages have said, "All that is to be found on dry land is to be found in the sea."[102] *It is also known that, in the supernal worlds, "sea" and "dry land" refer to the "hidden world" and the "revealed world."*

The explanation of the matter is as follows. It is written, "Let the waters gather . . . and the dry land be revealed."[103] *From dry land are derived all existences— mineral, vegetable, animal, and human—as it is written,*

---

100. Genesis 1:9.
101. Exodus 14:21.
102. Babylonian Talmud, Tractate *Hullin* 127a.
103. Genesis 1:9.

"Let the earth bring forth [living creatures],"[104] *and* "Let the earth sprout forth [vegetation]";[105] *also man was created from soil; hence it is written,* "Everything came from the soil."[106] *This is because, as the* Zohar *says, the earth begets and makes fruits. Not so the sea, which does not actually produce minerals, vegetables, animals, or humans out of the four elements. Yet the sea contains all creatures that exist on dry land—in a concealed, rather than a revealed state, as per the Sages' saying,* "All that is to be found [on dry land is to be found in the sea]." *And in order that they should become revealed, God said,* "Let the waters under the heavens gather, and may the dry land be revealed"; *meaning that the concealment should be diminished and withdrawn, so that the* "dry land" *may be revealed and produce the mineral, vegetable, animal, and human existences.*

A similar thing occurred in the supernal worlds with the supernal "sea" *and* "dry land." *The supernal waters of the* "hidden world" *gathered to a side, as in the verse,* "Let the waters gather," *and then,* "God said: Let there be light . . . Let there be a firmament . . ." *which is the quality of* "speech," *also called* "revealed world" *and* "land" *in the supernal realm. This is the significance of* "May the dry land be revealed."

And so it is on all levels, up to the highest of levels— everything comes as concealment and revelation, sea and dry land, as is known. In general, the above- mentioned "concealment of will" *is the hidden world, being the divine name HaVaYaH in Keter (*"Crown"*), as per above; and the revealed world—that is, the divine*

---

104. Ibid., v. 24.
105. Ibid., v. 11.
106. Ecclesiastes 3:20.

name HaVaYaH *as it brings the worlds into being—is "dry land" relative to the "sea."*

Now, at the moment when God transformed the sea into dry land and the Children of Israel passed through "in the midst of the sea, on dry land" (although this event occurred here below in the physical sense—the physical sea was transformed into dry land—still, the physical sea and land derive from the supernal sea and land, all the way up to the highest levels) at that moment, the sea was transformed into dry land all the way up to the highest level, meaning that the quality of concealment came into revelation all the way up to the highest levels.[107]

A.S.: The sea has always been one of man's greatest mysteries. We can only see the surface of this vast universe. Replete with life, it is called *'alma de-itkasya*, the "world of the hidden things." The mystery of the sea is none other than the mystery of life, which, we know, emerged from the sea. When the Bible describes the creation of the world, the first elements are aquatic. "*When God began to create the heaven and earth— the earth being unformed and void, with darkness over the surface of the deep and a wind from God sweeping over the water.*"[108] The initial source of life is the sea, but in the sea life remains hidden and mysterious. Life needs to come up onto the land to become visible.

J.E.: Physically, the world comes from the waters that were gathered in, leaving the land in the open. Man can also be

---

107. *Maamrei Admor HaZaken Taksav* (5566), pp. 145–146.
108. Genesis 1:1–2.

described in terms of water and dry land, since "*The Lord God formed man from the dust of the earth.*"[109] This only refers to man's body, because his soul comes from the sea (not the ocean), from what the Kabbalah calls the Supernal Sea or Sea of *Atzilut.*

Atzilut is the first of the four universes that structure all reality. It is the first emanation of the Will and creative thought of the Infinite God—*En Sof.* It is a spiritual reality from which the essence of all life derives, and is the first habitation of the life of the soul. This vast, unstructured "place," the supreme source of the souls, is itself "close" to its source (this is the basic meaning of the word *Atzilut*), the sea of *Atzilut.*

In one sense, man is a false earthling, an extraterrestrial. His body is from here, but his soul comes from somewhere else. Typically, this "elsewhere" is referred to as the heavens; we say that souls come from heaven and return to heaven. This "heaven" is what the Kabbalah calls "the sea."

A.S.: We are amphibian beings. Like frogs, we live partially on land and partially in the sea, partially in the world of matter and partially in the world of the spirit. Despite this duality, our daily lives are played out in the visible world. Although mystery is part of our lives, it is part of the unknown. Because this mystery is within us, we can seek it out. It is not really foreign to us. When we reach the heart of the "sea," we are home.

J.E.: Man's real personality is like the sea: It is concealed. We are like icebergs.

---

109. Genesis 2:7.

A.S.: Yes, but with one basic difference. The visible part of the iceberg is its tip. In man, it is the lower part. The Alter Rebbe says that what is hidden is not below, but rather beyond, consciousness. In other words, man's real nature reaches up to the heavens, but we only perceive the lower part located on earth. Man's head is plunged into a vast sea, and only the soles of his feet are showing.

J.E.: Let us clarify this picture of the "upside-down man." In many of his texts dealing with the splitting of the Red Sea, the Alter Rebbe gives a highly specific definition of the true nature of man according to his very original reading of the *Zohar*'s interpretation of the story of Creation. The *Zohar* states that although the Bible appears to be describing events that take place in the world below, these events refer to similar phenomena occurring in the worlds above. Actually, these events first took place in the world of Divine thought, in the conception of essences. The existence of things is only a copy, or a reproduction in the finite world of what originally happened in the infinite world of God's creative Will. The biblical statement that in the beginning there were the waters, and the waters gathered in to let the continents emerge, refers to something that first took place in the world above.

It is written, "And Moses extended [his hand] . . . and God caused the sea to go back by a strong east wind . . . and He made the sea into dry land."[110]

It needs to be understood: Why does it say [that the sea was transformed] specifically into "dry land" (ḥaravah), which is a state of utter dryness to the extent that there remains no moisture whatsoever?

---

110. Exodus 14:21.

179

It is known that the Sages have said, "All that is to be found on dry land is to be found in the sea."[111] It is also known that, in the supernal worlds, "sea" and "dry land" refer to the "hidden world" and the "revealed world."

The explanation of the matter is as follows. It is written, "Let the waters gather . . . and the dry land be revealed."[112] From dry land are derived all existences— mineral, vegetable, animal, and human—as it is written, "Let the earth bring forth [living creatures],"[113] and "Let the earth sprout forth [vegetation]";[114] also man was created from soil; hence it is written, "Everything came from the soil."[115] This is because, as the Zohar *says, the earth begets and makes fruits. Not so the sea, which does not actually produce minerals, vegetables, animals, or humans out of the four elements. Yet the sea contains all creatures that exist on dry land—in a concealed, rather than a revealed state, as per the Sages' saying, "All that is to be found [on dry land is to be found in the sea]." And in order that they should become revealed, God said, "Let the waters under the heavens gather, and may the dry land be revealed"; meaning that the concealment should be diminished and withdrawn, so that the "dry land" may be revealed and produce the mineral, vegetable, animal, and human existences.[116]*

The Alter Rebbe employs kabbalistic categories to say that the sea represents the infinite Will (*Keter*, the first *sefirah*)

---

111. Babylonian Talmud, Tractate *Hullin* 127a.
112. Genesis 1:9.
113. Ibid., v. 24.
114. Ibid., v. 11.
115. Ecclesiastes 3:20.
116. *Maamrei Admor haZaken Taksav* (5566), pp. 145–146.

and Divine thoughts (*Hokhmah,* the second *sefirah*), which are hidden and inaccessible as long as they are not concretized in the world Above (*Malkhut,* the tenth *sefirah*)—the "mouth" or "speech." The relationship between the sea and the land is mirrored in the relationship between concealed thought and speech, the first form of revelation. The relationship between the concealed and the revealed, found in the creation of the world, is also found in man's own complex nature, since the individual is made up of the concealed cloaked by the visible. The world can only exist when Divine speech emerges from the unfathomable sea of Divine thought. Speech turns the potentialities of the infinite essences into finite realities. This is why in the Bible, the story of Creation is made up of a series of utterances: Ten times God spoke, and things came into being. This is the real meaning of the gathering in of the waters at the time of Creation, an event that takes place a second time during the splitting of the Red Sea.

A.S.: Indeed, the two events appear to be similar. In both cases the sea turns into dry land. A liturgical Passover poem says this explicitly: "*On the day in which the deeps became dry land . . .*"[117] At the time of the Creation, the land emerges from the sea, and dryness is born of the waters. When the Red Sea parts, the sea opens in order for the land, the seabed, to become visible.

Free as Water

J.E.: These two events are only superficially similar, and their respective revelations are opposites. The emergence of

---

117. Poem for circumcision, by Rabbi Yehudah HaLevi, recited also on *Shabbat Beshallah* and on the seventh day of Passover.

181

the land during Creation is more a concealment than a revelation. The land we perceive in the physical world, the word we hear in the world of the spirit, is only the tip of the iceberg. There is land above the waters: the revealed world. There is also land under the waters: the concealed world. The splitting of the Red Sea is the direct opposite of the gathering in of the waters during Creation, because the land is in fact concealed by the waters during Creation and revealed when the Red Sea parts. The waters were gathered in because this was necessary for life, and as such it was not a real revelation (although people might be led to believe that this is the sole reality). By retracting just enough to let the tip of reality emerge from the waters, the sea hid much more than it revealed.

A.S.: When they crossed the Red Sea, the Israelites returned to the beginnings of life and could see into the depths of reality. In this case, man returned to the sea from which he emerged, but he moved forward on dry land, in his own element, and could see everything in all the universes.

A similar thing occurred in the supernal worlds with the supernal "sea" and "dry land." The supernal waters of the "hidden world" gathered to a side, as in the verse, "Let the waters gather," and then, "God said: Let there be light . . . Let there be a firmament . . ." which is the quality of "speech," also called "revealed world" and "land" in the supernal realm. This is the significance of "May the dry land be revealed."

And so it is on all levels, up to the highest of levels— everything comes as concealment and revelation, sea and dry land, as is known. In general, the above- mentioned "concealment of will" is the hidden world, being the divine name HaVaYaH in Keter ("Crown"), as

> *per above; and the revealed world—i.e., the divine name*
> *HaVaYaH as it brings the worlds into being—is "dry land"*
> *relative to the "sea."*[118]

J.E.: The parting of the Red Sea is a historical event. Above all, however, it is a spiritual act that can only be explained through kabbalistic categories. According to Kabbalah, from the infinite to the finite, from God to matter, everything related to conception or creation passes through four worlds. The first world, *Atzilut,* represents pure potentiality and is beyond all causality. *Atzilut* is the world, the time, and the phase where anything and everything is possible. On Yom Kippur we strive to attain *Atzilut* in order to obtain Divine forgiveness.[119] The three other worlds[120] are governed by determinism and causality: a causality of the spirit, where one idea leads to another, a cause produces an effect, a given value implies another, and so on. Generally, the human mind can only perceive this causal universe because these three worlds are characterized by finitude.

In other words, there is a spiritual reality, the template, the root of all things, which is called the Earth Above; earth being the prime example of a place governed by causality. In addition, there is a world, *Atzilut,* that is beyond all causality, where the Divine Will is boundless. This world is called the "Supernal Sea," the concealed world, because the human mind in its finitude cannot grasp it.

At the time of Creation—the quintessential creative act—

---

118. *Maamrei Admor haZaken Taksav* (5566), pp. 145–146.

119. See the chapter on *Yom Kippur,* for the meanings of *before God.*

120. *Beriah* (Creation), *Yetzirah* (Formation), and *'Asiyyah* (Action).

God instructs the world of *Atzilut* to gather itself in, so that the perceptual world and causality can operate. As land emerges, so does rationality. When the Red Sea parts, man's spirituality must retrace this process. When the waters of *Atzilut* part, they reveal the upper bound of spiritual reality. The bottom of the sea is the basis of all things.

A.S.: This is a time of revelation in which the mind sees what is impossible to perceive through reason alone. This is why the Sages say: "*A maidservant saw at the [splitting of the] sea, what was not seen [even] by the prophet Ezekiel.*"[121] It is as though suddenly the heavens open. The veil of mystery is torn away, the infinite world can be glimpsed, and in a single glance I can contemplate all the levels of reality.

J.E.: Contemplating means entering into the world of the infinite light of the Divine Will. The chart below helps clarify the Alter Rebbe's framework. On the left is the hidden world and its manifestations. On the right is the visible world.

INFINITE	FINITE
THOUGHT	SPEECH
DARKNESS	LIGHT
SEA	LAND

Each time man rises above the world of pure reason to the world that only revelation enables him to glimpse, he goes from darkness to light, from the land to the sea, and so forth. Reciprocally, each time a pure potentiality becomes an act, it follows the return route. This is why it is written at the beginning of Genesis that God "separated the light from the darkness," and then, the land from the waters. It is practi-

---

121. *Midrash Mekhilta, Beshallah* 3.

cally the same process.[122] In fact, all these categories are manifest in the parting of the Red Sea. First of all, light replaced the darkness, which in kabbalistic terms is an act of revelation.

The angel of God, who had been going ahead of the Israelite army, now moved and followed behind them, and the pillar of cloud shifted from in front of them and took up a place behind them, and it came between the army of the Egyptians and the army of Israel. Thus there was the cloud with the darkness and it illuminated the night so that the one could not come near the other all through the night.[123]

A.S.: The Alter Rebbe places a great deal of emphasis on the final part of this text: It is darkness that lights the night. In other words, the "obscurity" of the Infinite becomes light. Second, just before the parting of the Red Sea, Moses says to the Israelites: "*God will fight for you and you shall be silent.*" "*God said to Moses: 'Why do you cry out to me? Tell the Israelites to go forward.'*"[124] The Alter Rebbe suggests that Israel is asked to be silent because it is about to enter into a world beyond speech. The Red Sea signifies the world of silence, the sea above, and thought. The Red Sea not only splits, but also rises up to form two walls. Walls and stones symbolize silence, a sign of awe, stupefaction, and humility, what the Alter Rebbe calls the "abnegation of the spirit." This

---

122. Except that there are several levels of light, and its separation from the darkness enters into very complex processes.
123. Exodus 14:19.
124. Exodus 14:14–15.

explains the Sages' statement as regards the Prophet Ezekiel. In a famous vision, the Prophet sees the four sides of the heavenly chariot. This is the world of causality; the eye of the Prophet cannot go any further. In contrast, during the parting of the Red Sea, the lowliest of servants could see the root of all spiritual realities, since she asked to look and not to understand.

As explained above, at the time of the splitting of the Red Sea there was an emanation of light from the level of 'atik,[125] which is above the entire hishtalshelut (evolution of the worlds). This is why the quality of "abnegation of existence"[126] (bittul bi-metziut) was found in all the worlds, as it is written, "and you shall be silent." This is also why the supernal "sea" was transformed into "dry land"—that is, the bestower was transformed into a recipient. This is the significance of what is written, "they stood as a wall"—that the sea became (dry land), silent and unmoving as dry land.

Thus is understood the saying of our Sages, "A maidservant saw at the [splitting of the] sea what was not seen by Ezekiel."[127] For the prophesies of Ezekiel were only of the "chariot" (merkavah) . . . which is the world of Yetzirah, or in the world of Beriah; as is known, the "face of the lion," the "face of the ox," etc., connote the divi-

---

125. *'Atik:* one of the terms designating the effulgence of the Infinite and unknowable will.

126. In Hebrew, *bittul,* one of the basic concepts in the thought of the Alter Rebbe, signifies annulment, annihilation. It refers to the intellectual and moral situation of the individual, who is in fact nothing compared to the Divine Infinite and who acknowledges the nothingness of his or her own existence.

127. *Midrash Mekhilta, Beshallah* 3.

sion of the Divine attribute into benevolence, judgment, and compassion, etc.— "the face of the lion to the right . . . the face of the ox [to the left]. . . ."[128] But the Supernal Crown (Keter 'Elyon) *is above even the source of the division between "right" and "left."*[129]

Our Mother the Sea

J.E.: In my opinion, the Sages deliberately referred to a maidservant. A maidservant is on the lowest rung of the social ladder and experiences the most extreme form of alienation. Who is subjected to more determinism than a slave? Who is the least likely to think about the Infinite? The most sublime revelation occurs on that very level where man is unable or can no longer think.

A.S.: This is what the Alter Rebbe terms the "unification of impossibilities." The theme is a very common one, and the parting of the Red Sea is used by the Sages to describe paradoxical situations. The most well-known example is probably marriage. It is said, "It is as difficult (for God) to mate a couple as to split the Red Sea."[130] This is because marriage consists of uniting two elements, a man and a

---

128. Ezekiel 1:10.

129. *Sefer HaMaaramin, Taksah* (1808), p. 175. In the three worlds of Creation, Formation, and Action, there are scales of value. All things are situated to the right (grace), to the left (rigor), or in the center (compassion), and are hence defined. In *Keter*, the Supreme Will, the equivalent of the first world of *Atzilut*, no specific location defines things.

130. Midrash, *Bereshit Rabbah;* see *Tanya* 2.

woman, who form two dissimilar worlds. A special force must intervene to hold them together. The real miracle is that man could remain man while in the "sea," and that the finite could combine with the Infinite and continue to exist as the finite.

J.E.: And that the Israelites did not die or go crazy!

A.S.: The paradox is being land and sea at the same time. The supernal world, symbolized by the sea, is a fusional state. In *Atzilut*, where there is total indifferentiation, everything is of a piece, homogeneous, and integrated. The opposite is true for the earth, in the visible world, where everything is disintegrated. We do not live in *Atzilut*, because man could never survive in an integrated world; in fact, he would dissolve into it.

J.E.: He would drown.

A.S.: Nevertheless, man is never entirely cut off from *Atzilut*, because his soul originates in the integrated world. Man is the lower extremity of *Atzilut*, the *Malkhut* of *Atzilut*, this great source from which all emanates and toward which all strives to return.

J.E.: *Malkhut*, Kingship, is the tenth *sefirah*, the lowest degree of *Atzilut*, or the smallest "quantity" of Infinity; the passageway, according to the Kabbalah, from *Atzilut* to the three finite worlds. Our soul is born there and begins to detach itself there. *Malkhut* and the sea of *Atzilut* are represented as a mother. The belly of the sea is also the mother's belly.

"The sea saw and fled . . . the mountains danced like rams."[131]

The Shelah[132] *explains that "fleeing" is the service of God out of awe, and "dancing," the service of God out of love. This corresponds to the levels of "minister" and "slave" [in the service of the Almighty]. When the king reveals himself, the minister, whose service is with joy, experiences an increase in his joyfulness; these are the "mountains," the attributes of Atzilut, from which stem the souls that are referred to as "brothers" to God. The slave, whose service is with awe, is overcome with great fear and terror when the king reveals himself; this is the "sea," which is the source of the quality of [relationship with God] as a slave before a king.*

In Pri Etz Ḥayyim[133] *it is explained that the splitting of the sea also represents the concept of the "birth of the souls." This is the meaning of the verse "And the children of Israel went on dry land in the midst of the sea."*[134]

The meaning of this is as follows:

The souls of Israel "arose in the mind [of God]."[135] *It is on this level that they are called "brothers" and "fellows" of*

131. Psalms 114:3.
132. Isaiah haLevi Hurwitz, famous commentator (1565–1630), called so after his major work, the *Shelah*—acronym for *Shnei Luḥut haBrit* ("The Two Tablets of the Law").
133. Kabbalistic treatise by Rabbi Ḥayyim Vital (1543–1620).
134. Exodus 14:29.
135. One of the basic beliefs of Jewish mysticism is that the idea of Israel was the starting point, and hence the final goal, of the plan of creation.

the Holy One, Blessed be He; "brothers" and "fellows" because "The Holy One Blessed be He" connotes the infinite light of the Blessed[136] as it is enclothed within the attributes of Atzilut. So the 600,000 souls of Israel, which derive from the 600,000 letters of [Divine] thought, are "brothers" to the Holy One Blessed be He, which is the attribute [of Atzilut] just as, for example, in an intellectual thought, the letters [of the thought] are as of a piece with the essence of the idea implicit in them, and likewise an emotional thought with the emotion, etc. Thus, on this level, [the souls of Israel] are Divinity itself.

In order that the soul should materialize as a being (yesh),[137] as a "creature" that is distinct from the abso-lute nullity (ayin) . . . this is achieved through the Divine attribute of Kingship (Malkhut), which is a "garment" that conceals and hides.

For this is the general rule: the attribute of Kingship is the cause of beingness. That is why it is called the "lower mother" and "matron."[138]

A.S.: All of creation is like delivery. What is hidden in the mother's womb becomes visible, and what was fusional becomes autonomous. All individuals arise from a fusional state, in that they were united with their mothers until they were born. Afterward, a person can never return to this state of integration or absolute fusion. It can be fantasized but never re-created. Our soul has an identical history. In *Atzilut*

---

136. Infinite God, *En Sof.*

137. Have an autonomous life and conscience, and hence bring the initial fusional state to an end.

138. The Lower Mother, the one who gave birth to the World Below. *Binah* is the Upper Mother. *Likkutei Torah, Tzav,* 16b–c.

it lived in a fusional state with the Divine and then was separated from it. What happens during the splitting of the Red Sea is the miraculous recreation of this primordial fusional state. Israel discovers *Atzilut*, its source, its profound identity.

J.E.: It is somewhat like imagining an operation in which you cut open the body and x-ray the soul.

A.S.: While preserving the individual's identity. The real meaning of the splitting of the Red Sea is being able to see the Infinite, in order to discover that there is another reality, while at the same time remaining in the finite.

J.E.: Having your feet on the ground and your head in the sky. It is almost impossible. There is a story in the Talmud about four rabbis who tried to enter the "Orchard." Three out of four succumbed: one died, the second went crazy, the third became a heretic.[139] This could have happened to Israel had God Himself, through an act of total grace, not opened the "sea."

A.S.: The splitting was an absolute necessity. It was a necessary phase for Israel, which enabled it to live out the rest of its history. It was a time of initiation.

Israel: A Pilot Fish

J.E.: We need to specify what kind of initiation was involved. Clearly, God first wanted to show Israel the root of its soul, its

---

139. Babylonian Talmud, Tractate *Ḥagigah* 14b–15a.

191

spiritual family tree, so that each individual could see that his source is in *Atzilut*. To understand this, each individual needed to cross the sea and become a fish. The *Zohar* compares the soul to a fish. Before the soul is incarnated, it lives in the Sea of *Atzilut*. It also describes Israel as a "fish living on dry land."[140]

A.S.: What characterizes a fish and distinguishes it from a man is, first of all, its mode of existence. Man lives on, and not in, the land, whereas a fish lives in its element. This is one integrative factor. Second, men live in a highly structured and lateralized world, with an up, a down, a right, and a left. In the sea, these distinctions are meaningless. A fish simply lives in the water. It is so much a part of its natural element that in Jewish law a fish is no different from water. Fish are considered to be solidified water.

J.E.: This is why Jewish law and mysticism consider fish to be particularly pure in essence. Fish live in an environment of total purity, and no ritual slaughter is required before eating them. A fish is part of *Atzilut*, as all souls are.

A.S.: There are impure fish, too, because even in the world of *Atzilut* some essences may not be entirely pure. However, pure or impure, fish are always considered to be an integral part of the sea. It is interesting to note that amphibians, which can live on land and in the sea, are not considered to be fish by Jewish law. The definition of a fish is an animal able to live only in the water. The same is true for the soul in *Atzilut*. It does not just pass through it; it is an integral part of it. One

---

140. *Zohar* 3:42a.

of the basic tenets of Jewish mysticism is that the soul is "*part of God, that comes from the world above.*"[141]

J.E.: We should take the expression literally. The soul is Divine in essence, and when it is incarnated it is necessarily separated, as is the case in delivery, from its heavenly mother. However, the umbilical cord is never completely severed, because the soul would be like a fish out of water and could not survive.

A.S.: The basic question for man is how the soul, although not cut off, can exist so far removed from its source. The Alter Rebbe replies with a poetic expression. He refers to a silver thread[142] that unites the "navel" of the soul to God. This cord is the thread of life.

J.E.: A kind of backbone.

A.S.: As long as the soul remains attached to God, it is still an integral part of the supernal sea from which life emanates. Once created, man tends to see things differently. He considers himself to be a *yesh*, a self, which not only possesses self-awareness but also sees itself as an autonomous being.

J.E.: The main purpose of the splitting of the Red Sea is to set the priorities straight. It reminds man where he comes from and that his intimacy with God constitutes the true reality of his existence, even though daily life—the sea—too often conceals this reality and obliterates it. As a step toward knowledge, the splitting of the Red Sea is a presage and a

---

141. Job 19:26. This verse is the traditional phrasing used in Jewish mysticism to define the Divine nature of the human soul.

142. Based on Ecclesiastes 12:6.

premonitory sign. When the Prophet Isaiah announces the coming of the messianic age, when the knowledge of God will reach all men, he refers to the sea:

They shall not hurt nor destroy in all my holy mountain, for the earth shall be full of the knowledge of the Lord as the waters cover the sea.[143]

The messianic era is the time when the knowledge of God will cover the land. Land will be the natural element of man, and will be as homogeneous, total, and unchanging as water in the ocean. Israel glimpsed this reality only once. By commemorating it every day, every Jew makes the personal connection. The nations will discover it at the end of days. Somehow, by becoming a fish, by rediscovering for an instant their fish-soul in the sea of *Atzilut*, the Israelites were the pilot fish for humanity as a whole. This miracle had a major impact on Israel's mentality, and I suggest we deal with this next.

---

143. Isaiah 11:9.

MOSES, THE HUMAN FISH

"And Israel saw the great hand that the Lord (HaVaYaH) wrought upon Egypt; and the people feared HaVaYaH, and they believed in HaVaYaH, and in Moses His servant."[144]

There are two levels of the Divine name "HaVaYaH." One is the "lower HaVaYaH," which generates all the worlds out of naught into being . . . through the constriction (tzimtzum) of the Divine light. There is also an "upper HaVaYaH," which is the will that arose in the Divine mind . . .

Thus Pharaoh said, "Who is HaVaYaH?" as he did not believe in the upper HaVaYaH, though he certainly knew the lower HaVaYaH, which brings all the worlds into being . . .

But the people of Israel, upon seeing how God transformed the sea into dry land, and dried the sea so that there remained no moisture whatsoever—in the manner of "Let the waters gather . . . and the dry land be revealed"[145]—believed in HaVaYaH, that there can be a revelation of the upper HaVaYaH . . . This is the meaning of the verse, "And the people feared HaVaYaH, and they believed in HaVaYaH."

Torah Ohr, Beshallaḥ 61d–62a

Josy Eisenberg: Up to now, the Alter Rebbe has suggested we view the crossing of the Red Sea on dry land as a kind of

---

144. Exodus 14:30–31.
145. Genesis 1:9.

biblical *eureka*. Israel realizes that there is more to life than life. Israel is like the commoner who suddenly discovers the secret of his royal birth; he simultaneously learns that there is a mystery and that he can decode it. The Bible, however, does not define the outcome of this event in terms of knowledge but rather in two categories closely related to it—fear and faith.

"And Israel saw the great hand that HaVaYaH wrought upon Egypt; and the people feared HaVaYaH, and they believed in HaVaYaH, and in Moses His servant."[146]

The two themes I would like to discuss in this chapter are the emergence of faith and the astounding association of Moses to God as an object of faith.

Adin Steinsaltz: The splitting of the Red Sea is part of an unfolding revelation that takes place gradually, in three stages, in the fifty days that separate Passover from Shavuot.[147] The first stage takes place in Egypt. There, during the tenth plague, on the eve of the Exodus, it is said that the *"King of Kings of Kings revealed Himself to them."* We have commented extensively on this phrase.[148] Then the miracle of the Red Sea took place. This was the second stage. The third stage takes place on Mount Sinai, when the Ten Commandments are handed down.

During each of these three stages, a forceful revelation takes place, like a tidal wave. Each stage has its own particular features. Let us take the case of the Red Sea. Religious

---

146. Exodus 14:31.
147. The Feast of Weeks.
148. See previous section, "A Path in the Sea."

feeling is classically defined as an "oceanic feeling." Crossing the sea on dry land is a very singular form of revelation. It is not a typical revelation; it is not a revelation of the Other. Although the splitting of the Red Sea is in some ways a revelation of transcendence, this is not the most important feature. Its essence is less to reveal God than to reveal my own infinity to myself. This revelation brings the individual to the depths of his own self. It is a preparation and a tool for the third stage, the revelation of the Other.

J.E.: *The* revelation is when God reveals Himself. A revelation is when I reveal myself. Naturally, the former requires the latter. In the same way that I cannot love others if I do not love myself, I cannot know God if I do not know myself.

A.S.: It is a preparatory stage that goes further than the Socratic instruction "Know thyself." It is the sea, not the heavens, that opened. I descend to that ultimate point where my reality is entirely laid open to me. From this point, I will be able to receive other forms of knowledge. In other words, I need to know what I am capable of doing before, for example, receiving the Torah. The goal of the parting of the Red Sea is to reveal my own existence to myself. Everything opens, the curtain is torn open, and I see. Everything takes place through vision. *"Israel saw . . . a mere maidservant saw."* It is written that *"the people had faith in the Lord and in Moses His servant"*—not because they had witnessed an amazing miracle, for they had already seen amazing miracles, but because they saw what reality was like.

J.E.: *Reality* is a term you use often, and I am afraid it might be misconstrued. In everyday language, the word *reality* apparently designates concrete, physical, material things; the "realities of life." In Judaism, spiritual values and essences are as real as visible entities, but they are more difficult to apprehend because they are beyond perceptual experience. Who can challenge the "reality" of the mind, ideas, or even fantasies? The soul has as much reality as the mind or the body.

It seems to me that there are three types of revelation. The first is the existence of God and His transcendence; we are not dealing with this here. The second is self-knowledge, Socratic knowledge, or the unconscious in psychoanalysis. Judaism adds a third dimension to these two classical ones. Beyond all thought and all introspection we have an inner self, our soul, whose roots can be traced to the inception of all beings and which runs deep into the complex terrain of the Infinite. Alone, I cannot make this voyage to the center of myself, located beyond all rationality and normal experience. I need someone to "rent" the veil that, according to the Kabbalah, separates the Infinite (*Atzilut*) from the three finite worlds in which we live.

This is what happened during the crossing of the Red Sea. The Israelites discovered the inner nature of their souls. This was the indispensable preparation for the awe-inspiring encounter with God that was to take place at the foot of Mount Sinai. What is the relationship between the splitting of the Red Sea (which a fleeting lesson in metaphysical epistemology) and the birth of faith that begins here, in the middle of the sea? It is written: *"they saw . . . and they believed."*[149]

It's Him, I Recognize Him

A.S.: The relationship is the following. At each of the major stages of the revelation—the Exodus, the parting of the Red Sea, and Sinai—the concept of faith comes to the fore. What is Moses doing in Egypt? He publicly reveals the miraculous

---

149. Exodus 14:31.

powers that God gave to him at the burning bush. And how do the people react? "*And the people believed, when they heard that the Lord had visited the Children of Israel and that He had looked upon their affliction.*"[150]

J.E.: This first use of the verb *believe* is even more important, because it responds to Moses' primary concern. At the burning bush, he keeps repeating to God: "and what if they don't believe me?"

A.S.: During the parting of the Red Sea, it is said a second time, that "the people believed." Finally, at Sinai, God says to Moses: "*I will come to you in a thick cloud, in order that the people may hear when I speak with you and so believe you ever after.*"[151] This again involves bringing Israel to faith. But the approaches are different. When Moses performs the miracles in Egypt, they elicit trust, the most elementary form of faith; in other words, I do not really know what or who it is, but I feel that something exists.

J.E.: It is still a mystery.

A.S.: The second form of faith is reflected in the Hebrew etymology of the root *AMN*, from which come the words *emunah*[152] and *emet*.[153] During the parting of the Red Sea, faith is an apprehending of truth that receives verification. When it is said that Israel "*saw the powerful hand . . . and believed in the Lord and in Moses,*"[154] it means that they knew it was true. In other words, now I have experienced all

---

150. Exodus 4:31.
151. Exodus 19:9.
152. Faith. The term is derived from *amen*.
153. Truth.
154. Exodus 14:31.

the things that I only believed in before. I knew, but only through hearsay; I heard about it for generations. Now I really see it and have a personal vision of it.

J.E.: Science is often contrasted with faith; however, the two stages you describe in the sequence of faith are similar to the field of science. First the scientist has an intuition of a theory. He believes in it, often before he is able to test it. Then the laboratory will confirm or disprove it—what he believed, he now knows. In a similar way, Israel in Egypt had the intuition of Divine existence and of its own mission. During the parting of the Red Sea, it felt this intuition in the most concrete way, by experiencing it.

The basic difference between the three stages of faith is the channel of communication. In Egypt, the message is auditory; in the Red Sea it is visual. In the first case it is said, "*The people heard that the Lord had remembered their plight.*"[155] At this stage, a revelation by hearsay takes place. Note that God only reveals Himself to Moses. The Israelites hear about it and accept it, but this is once removed from hearing the message themselves. During the splitting of the Red Sea, the people see.

The Sages have written extensively on the differences between hearing and vision. Vision is always presented as a personal and immediate relationship that is higher (in terms of certainty) than hearing, which by definition is mediated. In order to believe what I hear, I need not only to decode the utterance but also to trust the person speaking to me. This is why in the Bible, vision is used by the Prophets. It is full and accurate revelation. It leaves no room for doubt. When God appears to Job at the end of the story, Job's cry is magnifi-

---

155. Exodus 4:31.

cent: "*I had heard you with my ears but now I see You with my eye.*"[156]

Job obviously did not see God; but because he really heard Him, he possesses that knowledge with the absolute certainty that the Hebrew language calls "vision." Just like Job, the Israelites had heard of God, and now they see Him. We are progressively increasing our certainty. In the third stage, on Mount Sinai, Israel sees and hears at the same time. This is the apotheosis: "*And the people saw voices.*"[157] But let us return to the parting of the Red Sea.

A.S.: Moses best summarizes the nature of the event at the start of the song of the Red Sea:

> *Then Moses and the Israelites sang this song to the Lord.*
> *   They said:*
> *I will sing to the Lord for He has triumphed gloriously,*
> *Horse and driver he has hurled into the sea.*
> *The Lord is my strength and might,*
> *He has become my deliverance.*
> *This is my God and I will enshrine Him,*
> *The God of my father, and I will exalt Him.*[158]

The key word here is the word *ze*, which means "this." If the Bible had said "that," God would have remained distant. But the word *ze* always designates something that you can point to. A very poetic midrash says that the mothers of Israel crossed the Red Sea while nursing their infants. Suddenly, the babies stopped nursing and cried out, pointing: "*This is*

---

156. Job 42:5.

157. Exodus 20:18. This verse will be commented upon in the section "Seeing Voices," concerning Shavuot.

158. Exodus 15:1.

201

my God!"[159] The infant, like the adult, suddenly sees the Other, that God, coming closer, like someone we do not think we know, until we realize, "It is him, I recognize him!" This is a new step forward in faith; in one unique moment, I see.

J.E.: This event is indeed unique. The sea parted, and the Israelites saw. When the sea returned, what remained of this experience?

A.S.: What remained is memory. The parting of the Red Sea is destined to be inscribed in our memory. All the Jewish holidays etch a historical event in our memories and are more than archetypes: They create a genetic mutation in the Jewish people. We cannot perceive the parting of the Red Sea. It occurred once and for all, and will not repeat itself. The memory of this event, however, is engraved in the holiday, and hence in our collective experience.

J.E.: The high points of our history are a kind of genetic inheritance.

A.S.: They are indeed. A true mutation was created, as though we had seen it with our own eyes. However, we also forget this special moment of direct vision.

J.E.: The "sea" returns to its place.

A.S.: Yes, but the moment continues to live in my unconscious. It is a foundation on which I can build at any time. I can forget and even deny it. Nevertheless, it exists in me and

---

159. Babylonian Talmud, Tractate *Sotah* 30b–31a; based on Exodus 15:2.

cries out from my chromosomes: *"This is my God and I exalt him."*[160] I can reject it, but it remains within me.

J.E.: We do forget. The Alter Rebbe points this out and answers my initial question as to how the Egyptians could be witnesses, since they all drowned. The answer is that we are all Egyptians.

It is written, "And Egypt shall know that I am God."[161] *This requires explanation, since it is written, "the waters covered up their enemies; not a single one of them was left."*[162]

But there exists an "Egypt" in every man, at all times. Thus it is said, "In every generation a person must regard himself as if he went out of Egypt."[163] *And it is written,* "In order that you remember the day you went out of Egypt, all the days of your life."[164] *And the Tosefta*[165] *adds that one must also remember the splitting of the Red Sea.*[166]

Moses: You Will Always Cherish the Sea

J.E.: The hasidic masters have a saying: "Learn to leave your Egypt." Slavery, alienation, and anxiety are for all ages, and

---

160. Exodus 15:2.
161. Exodus 14:18.
162. Exodus 14:28.
163. From the Passover *Haggadah.*
164. The exodus from Egypt did not stop with the Exodus; the parting of the Red Sea is an integral part of it.
165. *Tosefta, Berakhot* 2:4.
166. *Torah Ohr, Beshallaḥ* 62b.

above all—for every day. The first outcome of Israel's ability to see (as represented by the splitting of the Red Sea) is the emergence of faith. It is part of a complex process; the people see, then fear, then believe. "*Israel saw the powerful hand . . . the people feared the Lord and they believed in the Lord and His servant Moses.*"[167]

The Alter Rebbe analyzes this process by asking a good question. Because they saw, they were in the realm of the intelligible and rational. But since faith involves something that is beyond human reason, what is faith doing here? The answer is that these two dimensions of consciousness complement each other.

There are two levels of the Divine name "HaVaYaH." One is the "lower HaVaYaH," which generates all the worlds out of nothingness into being . . . through the constriction (tzimtzum) of the Divine light. There is also an "upper HaVaYaH," which is the will that arose in the Divine mind . . .

Thus Pharaoh said, "Who is HaVaYaH?" as he did not believe in the upper HaVaYaH, though he certainly knew the lower HaVaYaH, which brings all the worlds into being. . . .

But the people of Israel, upon seeing how God transformed the sea into dry land, and dried the sea so that there remained no moisture whatsoever—in the manner of "Let the waters gather . . . and the dry land be revealed"—believed in HaVaYaH, that there can be a revelation of the upper HaVaYaH. . . . This is the mean-

---

167. Exodus 14:31.

ing of the verse "And the people feared HaVaYaH, and they believed in HaVaYaH."[168]

The Tetragrammaton,[169] which we translate as "Lord," in fact connotes two facets of Divinity. The Alter Rebbe explains that there is a Tetragrammaton of the world below, which corresponds to the perception of the Divine Presence in the visible world. Then there is the Tetragrammaton of the world above, which is the necessarily concealed essence of the Divine Will. The latter is distant, and the former is close. Israel only "saw" the Tetragrammaton of the world below, and this explains why there was fear and the need for faith.

"Sight" only applies to things that are revealed and perceivable to all. Thus, the verse "and they saw God" (Exodus 14:31) refers to the lower HaVaYah, which brings all worlds into existence; for this [Divine name] is of the "revealed world," and the concept of sight is therefore applicable to it, for it can be apprehended through contemplation and comprehension. For this HaVaYah is near [to our existence], because it is the Divine force that acts [within creation].

By way of analogy, a person who stands before a king of flesh and blood, the nearer he stands, the greater his awe. The primary awe is an inner awe, an "awe of shame"—one is ashamed and one's existence is completely nullified. And the closer one is, the greater is this "awe of shame." This comes specifically from a revelation from near; from afar, one does not experience this "awe of shame." Thus the word yir'ah *("awe") is com-*

---

168. *Torah Ohr, Beshallaḥ* 61d–62a.
169. See previous section, "A Path in the Sea."

*prised of the same letters as re'iyah ("sight"), as sight
and awe are related—one who sees attains awe. Thus,
the above-quoted verse says vayir'u (which can be read
both as "and they feared" as well as "and they saw")—
they experienced an "awe of shame" from the revealed
HaVaYah.*

*But on the level of the hidden HaVaYah, which is the
HaVaYah within the hidden will (as explained above),
there cannot be awe, since there is no perception and
comprehension at all, as it is hidden and concealed, being
above and beyond comprehension, and it is not seen and
understood at all. This is why it is called "the hidden
world." Regarding this level of the Divine name, the
verse says, "And they believed in HAVAYAH." This is to
say that in this, hidden name HaVaYah they had only faith,
faith being beyond comprehension and intellect.*[170]

J.E.: In other words, the parting of the Red Sea allowed
Israel to "see" the presence of God in the world but only to
glimpse everything this Presence implies, which is the real
basis for faith. Believing in God, or even in a concealed God,
is not crucial at this point. The Torah adds that they also
believed in Moses: "*And they believed in HaVaYaH and in
Moses His servant.*"[171] Does that mean that they believed in a
man? Jewish tradition rejects this entirely. However, Moses is
a special case. If seeing is believing, the discovery that there
is something at the bottom of the sea can only be made
through Moses, because he is a man of the sea: the Sea
Above.

The Alter Rebbe comments on passages in the *Zohar* that

170. *Maamrei Admor haZaken, Taksav* (1806), pp. 146–147.
171. Exodus 14:31.

teach that Moses' soul came from the Sea of *Atzilut*. Not all souls originate in the same place. Moses is, in fact, a kind of extraterrestrial. In Jewish mysticism, the verse describing how Moses was saved by Pharaoh's daughter is interpreted in this way: *"And she called him Moses because she drew him out of the waters."*[172] According to the *Zohar*, Moses was drawn out of the Waters Above. For this reason, the parting of the sea, which opens the Waters Above, is dependent on Moses' actions, and it is his rod that parts the sea. The sea is his natural element.

Land of Men

A.S.: In the *Zohar*, some men are described as "fish of the sea that walk on dry land." A man like Moses never really left the "Sea Above." He lives in the visible world as though he were still in the concealed world. This world is not really the "visible" world for him. Crossing the Red Sea is the most natural thing for Moses to do. Living in this specific dimension is both the greatness and the specificity of Moses, and his personal tragedy. He can hardly speak the same language as his people, and they scarcely understand one another. There is a dual problem of communication between the man of the sea (the man of the absolute) and men of the land. Moses has trouble speaking to Israel. This is the real meaning of Moses' exclamation: *"I am heavy of the mouth and heavy of tongue."*[173] "Heavy of tongue" is his difficulty in transmitting the written law; "heavy of mouth" is his difficulty with oral law, called the Torah of the mouth: *Torah she-be'al peh.*[174]

---

172. Exodus 2:10.
173. Erroneously translated as "stuttering." Exodus 4:10.
174. See *Likkutei Torah*, Deuteronomy 85c.

J.E.: Moses' difficulty arises from the fact that the words he uses do not have the same meaning for those listening to him.

A.S.: In contrast, when Moses needs to understand the concerns and demands of men, the same misunderstandings arise. When the Israelites whine for meat, Moses complains to God: *"Where am I to get meat to give to all this people!"*[175] According to the Alter Rebbe, Moses is asking, "Is this men's problem, eating? Are they really revolting over meat?"

J.E.: Moses himself does not eat for forty days when he receives the Torah. Clearly, he does not have this problem. The Alter Rebbe also points out that Moses talks about giving fish to his people. This is bizarre, because the sea is far away. *"Could enough flocks and herds be slaughtered to suffice them? Or could all the fish of the sea be gathered for them to suffice them?"*[176] The Alter Rebbe explains that eating meat signifies entering into the world of matter, something Moses is far removed from. Traditionally, only the Sages have the right to eat meat. Therefore, Moses asks whether it would not be better to give Israel fish, which is healthier. This is the real meaning of his exclamation. In other words, we should appeal to the concealed world (the fish in the sea) to reach the visible world (the flocks of the earth). The Alter Rebbe says that this is why we eat fish before meat on the Sabbath.[177]

A.S.: This is why Moses always needs a go-between, a mouthpiece, who translates what he receives from the world above to the world below. Moses is a "man of the sea" who

---

175. Numbers 11:13.
176. Numbers 11:22.
177. *Likkutei Torah*, Numbers 33b.

never went onto the land. This explains the dual statement: *"They believed in the Lord and in Moses His servant."*[178]

For the first time, the Israelites not only understand God; they can understand Moses and his universe, because they have just entered it. This is also what happens during the revelation of the Law on Mount Sinai. Once again the Israelites can understand Moses, because they are in the same universe as he is.

J.E.: There are a number of symbols for that world, including the sea, knowledge (*Hokhmah*, the second *sefirah*), and silence. It is the world of pure, undifferentiated Divine thought, the world of One. Multiples only appear in the third *sefirah*, *Binah*. This undifferentiation, represented by the sea, this Divine knowledge in its original state, is called "the world of silence." What the kabbalists call "silence" is precisely that state where everything is still possible. It is the place where no word, no formulation has been uttered. This is the world of the Torah Above. The Torah Below is the Torah of language, values, differentiation, and hierarchies. When the Israelites enter the sea, they are asked to enter into the world of silence. Moses calls to them and says, *"God will fight for you and you, will remain silent."*[179]

According to the Alter Rebbe, Moses' call is much more than a simple instruction to trust in God. It prepares Israel to enter the silence of the sea (the real world of silence), Divine wisdom, the Torah Above, the "place" of pure essences. This is the real purpose of the parting of the Red Sea. Moses' soul is truly "a fish of the sea walking on land," because the sea is the world of unity that Moses never left, and land is the world of multiplicity.

---

178. Exodus 14:31.
179. Exodus 14:14.

Like a Fish on Land

J.E.: Moses is asking Israel to become a fish, as he is. This should help clarify one of the most paradoxical verses in the Bible. This is not the first time that men are compared to fish. Shortly before his death, Jacob blesses his grandchildren, saying, "*and let them multiply like fish in the midst of the earth.*"[180] What a strange blessing! Would it not be more appropriate to want Israel to be like a fish in the sea? The fish-people, Israel is called upon to live outside of its natural element, the Holy Land, for extended periods of time. Living like a fish on land is practically a normal feature of Jewish existence.

A.S.: It is doubly miraculous, because it involves not only surviving but also not being asphyxiated, like a fish out of water forced to live on dry land. "Remaining a fish" implies bringing one's own world along, while living on land.

J.E.: In contrast to the laws of evolution, mutation is not the goal; Israel remains a fish.

A.S.: And despite this exile, Israel will not only survive and remain in keeping with itself, but it will multiply (as in Egypt) like fish, which are the symbol of blessing and fruitfulness. Fish on land, on all the lands of the diaspora; this is the true originality of Jewish existence.

J.E.: We now understand why Moses is both the archetype of the Jew and the guide for the revelation. Moses, the amphib-

---

180. Genesis 48:16. The Hebrew term is *ve-yidgu*, related to the word *dag*, "fish." The paradox can be resolved easily. The Alter Rebbe explains that Jacob is referring to exile.

ian being whose head always touches the heavens (the sea), is in exile on this earth, which is so unsuited to him. The Alter Rebbe says that this was the real reason why Moses was prevented from entering into the promised land and could only see it from afar: "*You may view the land from a distance, but you shall not enter it.*"[181]

Moses could share his world with his people for an instant, when the Red Sea parted. He still needs to make them see what they had only glimpsed; and to do so, Israel must cross the desert after having crossed the sea.

---

181. Deuteronomy 32:52.

FOURTH GATE

Shavuot
and the
Giving of the Torah

SEEING VOICES

On the third new moon after the Israelites had gone forth from the land of Egypt, on this very day, they entered the wilderness of Sinai. Having journeyed from Rephidim, they entered the wilderness of Sinai and encamped in the wilderness, and Israel encamped there in front of the mountain. And Moses went up to God; and the Lord called to him from the mountain saying, "Thus shall you say to the house of Jacob and declare to the children of Israel: You have seen what I did to the Egyptians, how I bore you on eagles' wings and brought you to Me. Now then, if you will obey Me faithfully and keep My covenant, you shall be My treasured possession among all the peoples. Indeed all the earth is Mine but you shall be to Me a kingdom of priests and a holy nation. These are the words that you shall speak to the children of Israel" . . .

Moses came and summoned the elders of the people and put before them all that the Lord had commanded him. All the people answered as one, saying "All that the Lord has spoken we will do!"

The Lord said to Moses: "Go to the people and warn them to stay pure today and tomorrow. Let them wash their clothes. Let them be ready for the third day for on the third day the Lord will come down in the sight of all the people on Mount Sinai" . . .

On the third day as morning dawned there was thunder and lightning and a dense cloud upon the mountain and a very loud blast of the horn; all the people who were in the camp trembled. Moses led the people out of the camp toward God and they took their places at the foot of the mountain. Now Mount Sinai was all in smoke . . . the whole mountain trembled violently. The blare of the horn

grew louder and louder. As Moses spoke, God answered
him in thunder.

Exodus 19:1–10 and 16–19

Josy Eisenberg: This passage from the book of Exodus is the prelude to the revelation of the Ten Commandments. It describes the setting and paints a majestic and impressive picture of the scene, full of thunder, lightning, and the sound of a mysterious *shofar*. Crowning it all is the Voice of God promulgating the Ten Commandments.

There are many ways of approaching this high point of the revelation. Occurring fifty days after the miracle of the "parting" of the Red Sea, the other high point in the knowledge of God, the event at Sinai is undoubtedly the ultimate stage and the crowning moment in the unveiling of the Divine. This is the sole and unique time in the history of humanity that men heard God speak to them directly.

What makes this face-to-face encounter even more remarkable is that it has no equivalent in other religious traditions. In almost all faiths, the founders of the religion, or a select few, receive personal revelations, but there is never reference to a collective revelation. Moses himself comments before he dies: *Has any people heard the voice of a god speaking out of a fire, as you have, and survived?*[1]

For Judah Halevy,[2] the public nature of revelation is irrefutable proof of its historicity. You can fool one man, it can be a figment of his imagination, but you cannot fool an entire nation.

This facet of the revelation at Sinai is clearly important, as is, of course, the content of this revelation, which is univer-

---

1. Deuteronomy 4:33.
2. Jewish philosopher and poet, author of the *Kuzari* (1075–1141).

sally recognized (although not always implemented) as the ethical charter of humanity. The fact that God speaks to men is so unique, extraordinary, amazing, and fundamental that most commentaries focus on it alone. The Sages share the same fascination. However, they tend to stress the complementary dimension of the revelation; namely, the attitude of the Children of Israel. This is the topic I would like to discuss with you in this chapter.

We tend to forget that revelation is not unilateral. It is neither a monologue nor a lecture. For there to be a revelation, there must be a transmitter of the revelation and a listener who accepts it. The right recipient of the message must be there, or at least a recipient who is willing to listen. This is the case of Israel at the foot of Mount Sinai.

In other words, it is not enough for God to want to speak: Man must be willing to listen. For the Sages, Israel's acceptance is just as important as the Divine intent. They comment in length on the terms Israel uses to declare itself ready to enter into the Covenant: "*All that the Lord has spoken we will do!*"[3]

A little later on, this commitment is detailed in the terms that have become fundamental for Jewish thought: *Then he took record of the covenant and read it aloud to the people. And they said, "All that the Lord has spoken we will do and we will hear!*"[4]

Na'ase Venishma'—"We will do and we will hear"—this heartfelt cry has always been interpreted in Judaism as being the prime merit of the children of Israel and an affirmation of absolute unconditionality.

It would be erroneous, however, to interpret these words as a sign of obedience. "We will do, we will hear." According to

---

3. Exodus 19:18.
4. Exodus 24:7.

the Sages, the real meaning of the combination of "do" and "hear" is the following. Everything that God requires, we will do without knowing its content beforehand; and now we are ready to hear, "we hear" these requirements.

It is clearly an act of faith to enter into a contract without knowing the terms or to give someone such latitude. It is also a paradoxical attitude, and I would like to begin by examining the cart of faith and commitment before the horse of reason, which has garnered such praise for Israel.

The Secret of the Angels

Adin Steinsaltz: It is paradoxical, but do not forget that paradoxes are part and parcel of reality. I mean that it is not contrary to the nature of things. It is unusual, rare, but still in the domain of the possible. This said, the statement *na'ase venishma'*—"we will do and we will hear"—can be interpreted on various levels.

The first meaning, of course, is willingness. I accept the yoke of Kingship without hesitation, I accept it consummately. This is what *na'ase*, "we will do," means. The second statement, *nishma'*, "we will hear," means that after having accepted the Law in general, I am now ready to hear it presented point by point.

This dual statement basically corresponds to the two types of behavior we typically engage in when we have a decision to make. We either make decisions analytically or through a synthesis. In an analytical decision we examine the features of a situation, and by combining them, we gradually develop a picture of a complex reality whose final shape will influence the decision we make.

On the other hand, we can accept a fundamental principle right away. Here, we are not called upon to act immediately but rather to agree to a principle and then see which obligations derive from it. This is the psychological side. This decision, however, also has an ontological side, because it sheds light on the nature, or the essence, of the children of Israel. According to the Talmud, when the people cried *"We will do and we will hear,"* God exclaimed:

> *Who revealed the secret of the angels to My children? For it is written, "Bless the Lord O His angels, mighty creatures who do His bidding, to hear the voice of His word."[5] First it is said that they carry out His bidding and only then that they hear it.[6]*

J.E.: At the time of the revelation of the Torah, the angels were very aggressive toward man. There are many *midrashim*[7] telling how the angels criticized giving the Law to weak "creatures of flesh and blood," and Moses had to convince them that despite the absolute transcendence of its Divine origin, the Torah was indeed intended for men. Men need the Law precisely because they are not angels. The Law is no less holy because of this, and the angels are its guardians. Why do men deserve the Torah? This is apparently the secret of the angels that men need to discover to become the legitimate recipients of the Torah. What is this secret?

A.S.: This secret has to do with instinct. Israel's "we will do and we will hear" parallels the angels' "who do His bidding

---

5. Psalms 103:20.

6. Babylonian Talmud, Tractate *Shabbat* 88a.

7. Classic homiletic commentaries by the Sages of the talmudic and post-talmudic periods.

and then hear it." These two modes of behavior correspond to intellectual and instinctive behaviors. Sometimes we do things because we have thought about them and we understand them. At other times, with no prior reflection, our instinct dictates our behavior. There are things that we instinctively see are right and necessary. At Sinai, instinct superseded reason.

J.E.: You say reason and not intelligence, because instinct is not the opposite of intelligence.

A.S.: Of course not. In fact, the most basic things in life are not dictated by reason but rather by instinct. Our vital functions, such as heartbeat and respiration, are not governed by reason or will but by natural instinct. I breathe instinctively, and it makes no difference whether or not someone proved to me that it was right. Instinctively, I know that this is the right way to act.

J.E.: The angels have no free will. They obey blindly, not because they are stupid and programmed, but because they feel instantaneously that this is what should be done. Some things are so obvious that any thought, which will by nature be critical, is superfluous.

The End of Amnesia

A.S.: This is what happens during the Giving of the Torah. At some point, we feel it is no longer foreign or forced upon us from the outside, like a constraint, but rather obvious, like an instinctive function. To say *"we will do and we will hear"* comes down to saying, "We know that this is what we must do." This attitude can be compared to the attitude of an artist.

A painter knows instinctively what color he wants, and a musician knows that a particular note is the right one, the effect he wants to create.

J.E.: The Israelites at Sinai experienced a moment of grace, a *eureka*, and had the instinctive knowledge that had been the exclusive property of the angels. You mentioned ontology. This means that the Children of Israel have an innate, natural, instinctive relationship with the Torah and that they are the Torah's soulmate. There is instant recognition.

This is what can be termed an instinctive reaction. I wonder, however, if it would not be more appropriate to speak of intuition rather than instinct, since Judaism, like other religions, is fairly reticent as regards manifestations of instinct.

A.S.: We need to know what kind of instinct we are talking about. Too often, people link instinct with the body and consider it to be primitive.

J.E.: And demean it.

A.S.: In Judaism, there is a postulate that states that man's most primitive features are his purest. If we remove all the trappings of human behavior, we reach a solid core of truth that is the essence of the soul itself. This view is based on the following idea: The soul is a Divine spark, it is a "part" of God and, as such, does not discover anything exterior, only the Divine within it. This is why the return to instinct, to the primeval, to the foundation of being, is a return to the essence of the soul itself, unadulterated by creation, time, and space. In Jewish tradition, the soul was originally under God's throne of glory. There it knew exactly what it had to do. Once incarnated in the body, it forgets who it is—as does Israel, at

221

times, in exile. Thus, the *"we will do"* spoken at the foot of Sinai, which we associated with instinct and intuition, is in fact related to Plato's definition of memory. Memory is recall. This exclamation simply means: *I knew it, but I forgot it!*

J.E.: Exile is a form of amnesia. At the foot of Sinai the collective soul of Israel recovers its memory or, in other words, the Torah. This is not an ethical choice, consisting of the decision to accept the Law; it is an epistemological process. The Alter Rebbe places the events at Sinai on a level of knowledge. Leaving the traditional redundancies of simple faith and unconditionality far behind, he places Israel's acceptance on an entirely different register. He views Sinai in terms of the workings of human knowledge and thought, whose source is in the structure of Divine thought, and focuses us on the process of creation of the world.

To draw down the light of the Infinite, Blessed be He, requires Torah, which is the Divine wisdom and will . . . and is thus a revelation of the light of the Infinite, Blessed be He. This level is called av *("father"), and is the root and source of the entire* hishtalshelut *("chain" of creation).*[8]

. . . as it is written, "You made them all with Ḥokhmah."[9] *For all of existence is drawn forth from concealment into revelation from the attribute of* Ḥokhmah. . . .

When it arose in His will to create the worlds, all the worlds were created, in the general sense, with a single thought. Thus the Targum Yonatan *translates, "In the*

---

8. *Likkutei Torah*, Song of Songs 32a.
9. Psalms 104:24.

> *beginning God created"* as *"With* Ḥokhmah *God created."*[10]
>
> *In relation to the light of the Infinite, Blessed be He, even when the "constriction" (tzimtzum) takes place and the light departs leaving only a "residue," there is no true concealment as far as the essence of the light is concerned. . . .*
>
> *Also at the time that the world was created, and He constricted His light and there manifestly remained only a "residue"—in truth, as regards God Himself, the light shines within the residue as it did before the constriction. . . .*[11]
>
> *The Lord by wisdom [Ḥokhmah] founded the earth; by understanding [Binah] He established the heavens.*[12]

What is this passage about? According to the Kabbalah, the first three *sefirot* are *Keter,* or will; *Ḥokhmah,* or thought; and *Binah,* or intelligence. God wills the world and then directs His thoughts to it. Divine thought is made up of two inseparable parts. The first is *Ḥokhmah,* which represents global thought, an idea as a whole, and the capacity for thought. The second is *Binah,* defined as the mental ability to analyze. *Ḥokhmah* is the implicit and undifferentiated components of intelligence. *Binah* is analytical, and *Ḥokhmah* synthesizes.

These are the general categories of Divine thought. The human mind, however, operates in exactly the same way, and

10. *Likkutei Torah,* Numbers 32a.
11. *Likkutei Torah* 53d.
12. Proverbs 3:19.

the notion that man was created in the image of God reflects this. The Alter Rebbe uses kabbalistic concepts to go beyond traditional interpretations of the Revelation. He shows that *"we will do and we will hear"* corresponds to the dual concept of thought. *"We will do"* is Ḥokhmah, global intuition, and the immediate and instinctive recognition of truth. *"We will hear"* is understanding, and the upsurge of *Binah*, where things become intelligible because they are differentiated. The Torah is Ḥokhmah, and the 613 commandments are *Binah*.

Hear What I See

A.S.: It seems perplexing that *"We will do"* should designate Ḥokhmah. However, in Kabbalah, there is a close connection between thought and action. Although it is the initial source of perception, Ḥokhmah is not intrinsically rational. This leads to an additional paradox—reason does not originate in the sphere of the rational. The kabbalistic meaning is easier to grasp if we know that these two *sefirot*, these two categories, are represented and expressed by vision and hearing. Ḥokhmah is the initial perception; *Binah* is the intellectual and rational development of this perception. Similarly, vision is immediate; I see something as it is. In contrast, hearing is indirect perception, since I need to decode the message.

There is another distinction between vision and hearing. When we see, we see a whole, or what philosophers call a *gestalt*, a general shape. Hearing, however, requires analysis. The process requires rationality to assemble the pieces of reality into a coherent form.

Consequently, what is specific to Ḥokhmah, regardless of any a-posteriori explanations I may give to myself or to others, is that I see something as it is. I discover its essence, what Kant called *Insicht*. At this point I need to develop an

224

intellectual system to reveal the details. Thus, *na'ase* corresponds to instantaneous, immediate knowledge of things as they are. It leads to *nishma'*, when I understand how things happen.

J.E.: We should not translate *na'ase venishma'* as "We will do and we will hear" but rather as "We know that it is the truth and we want to know the terms, the conditions involved." At Sinai, Israel consolidated and unified general and specific knowledge. In Hebrew and in English, these two verbs both refer to knowledge. In English you can say "I see," or "Do you see," to refer to a level of understanding. This is also true for "I hear you," meaning "I grasp your meaning." The biblical text provides a perfect illustration of these two forms of intelligence, since it says that the Israelites "saw voices": "*All the people saw the thunder and lightning, the blare of the horn.*"[13]

A.S.: What does "seeing voices" mean? Normally, I hear and understand something, but I cannot "see" understanding. To see what I hear is a unique situation. It refers to the ability to apprehend something that I normally would perceive indirectly, immediately, and in its totality.

Know-How

J.E.: Kabbalah, which often seems so obtuse, gives us a simple lesson here in epistemology and psychology. Earlier, however, you alluded to the relationships between thought and action. These are also basic concepts in Jewish thought, in particular in Hasidism, which state that men's lives are

---

13. Exodus 20:15.

lived out in terms of thought, speech, and action. Further-more, things exist exclusively via these three dimensions. By translating *na'ase* as *Ḥokhmah*, and not as "we will do," the Alter Rebbe shows that the first level, thought, and the last level, action, are identical. This is surprising, because we are accustomed to differentiating the world of thought from the world of action.

A.S.: Kabbalah frequently makes comparisons between *Ḥokhmah* (intelligence) and action. These relationships are based on the notion of the great circle, where the beginning and the end meet. All beginnings are the end of a process and all ends begin another. Thought is the start, and action is the end. Their proximity is expressed in a well-known saying: "Last in creation, first in God's plan."[14]

There is no better way to define to what extent thought and action belong categorically to the same universe. The kabbalists expressed this through a very compelling image. Thought is *Ḥokhmah*, the second *sefirah*; action is the world of *Malkhut*, kingdom, the tenth and last *sefirah*. In kabbalis-tic symbolism, *Ḥokhmah* is called *abba*, father, and *Malkhut* is commonly called *berata*, or "daughter" in Aramaic. To define the relationships between thought and action, the kabbalists use the following expression: "the father founded the daughter."[15]

J.E.: Thought produces action. This is a real truism. I think, however, that the kabbalists were trying to teach a dual lesson. First and foremost, thought and action belong to the same family, the same essence. The father is not superior to the daughter; simply—and this is the second lesson—he

---

14. *Lekhah Dodi*, Friday Night liturgy.
15. *Zohar, Ra'aya Meheimna* 258a.

antedates her. Between thought and action, there is an ontological equality, but a hierarchical chronology.

A.S.: The originality of this theory is easier to appreciate if we compare it to Western thought. There is a familiar postulate that action is inferior to intelligence. This postulate is based on a purely rational or rationalistic view of the universe. This is particularly true for Aristotelian or Scholastic philosophy, which posit a world-theory where reality is rational.

J.E.: This implies that reality is merely the inferior expression of reason.

A.S.: According to the kabbalists, there is a completely different relationship in the Divine plan between the world of ideas and the world of action. Matter, which forms the substrate of the world of action and identifies with it, is considered to be the deepest expression of authentic existence. This existence may not necessarily be rational. The material world is not an inferior world that has no real existence but rather a closed world with a special shape.

The real opposition is not between rational and irrational, but between empirical and logical. These two categories also stand for *Hokhmah* and *Binah*. Modern science is clearly moving in the direction of the Kabbalah. There is a growing tendency to reject the notion that logic determines reality. In fact, the prime and determinant datum is reality. Logic is constructed from this reality afterward. Science, like the Kabbalah, tends to consider that the beginning and the end of all things lie in the empirical. The empirical is the world of action. This is why the *na'ase* and the *nishma'*, the "doing" and the "understanding," are tightly connected. There are many things that words are unable to express or explain.

Sometimes, an action or a gesture is much more meaningful than language, and experience prevails over rationality.

J.E.: You can only demonstrate motion by moving.

A.S.: This is why the outcome of Ḥokhmah, or its materialization, is directed toward the world of action. This accounts for the close relationship between Ḥokhmah, the father, and *Malkhut*, the kingdom, the daughter.

My Kingdom for a Mitzvah

J.E.: Let us talk a little about this kingdom. In the cosmology of the Kabbalah, the first *sefirah* is *Keter* (Will), and the second *sefirah* is Ḥokhmah (Thought). At the end is the tenth *sefirah*, *Malkhut*. In other words, what God wills and thinks is the Kingdom. This is the meaning of the saying we quoted earlier: *"Last in creation, first in God's plan."*

God thinks first of all about accomplishing His plan. Thus, reality is synonymous with fulfillment. This fulfillment is what the kabbalists call the Kingdom, simply because the Kingdom of God is truly of this world. Our world is basically a world of action; living is acting. In addition, the term *Kingdom* defines our lower world, because the purpose of our actions is to establish on earth a place where God can be present. The world becomes a Kingdom when men proclaim God's Presence there by obeying His law. The classic sociological transition from a state of nature to a state of culture is captured in religious terminology by the transition from polytheism to monotheism, or from the world of *tohu* to this world of *tikkun*, which we discussed as regards Exodus.

The ultimate end of God's Will is to make this world of action and to have this world become His Kingdom. He desires recognition and respect. This clarifies why Judaism places so much emphasis on the fulfillment of the commandments, the mitzvot, and why ethics and rituals are far more pivotal than a way of life and the acceptance of certain values. A Jewish life takes on meaning through a person's ability to act according to the Divine Will.

A.S.: In contrast to Western ideas, matter, where things take place, is higher than reason. A Sage once said that all the higher worlds, all the transcendent and abstract things, have no value compared to the world of action. The world of action is the most perfect form of the Revelation of God. It is said, *"The existence of the material is the substance of the Divine."*

In other words, the highest values are found within matter, in the material world. The world of matter is both the lowest world, because it is mute, and the highest, because it is the supreme expression of God's Ḥokhmah. Ḥokhmah and Malkhut meet in Divine thought, but the principle of action itself preceded the principle of rationality. What God wants is the outcome; this will determine the beginning.

J.E.: Paradoxically, the end, the outcome, preceded the beginning. In many areas of life as well, the goal I set for myself is the impetus for the intellectual and emotional processes that will enable me to achieve this goal.

A.S.: This is what happened on Mount Sinai. The Israelites say "do" before they speak, and "hear" before they understand, because they immediately grasp that the essence of the revelation is action. Afterward, we can move on to the *nishma'*, and everything involved in theory, commentary, and details. The Children of Israel realized that theory only serves to explain reality. This was their great merit. They understood that action was not the outcome of a theory—

229

J.E.: —in which case they would have needed to study the theory before they agreed to act—

A.S.: —but on the contrary, they realized that the supreme world in Divine thought is the world of action. By saying, "we will do" they attained the first *sefirah*, of which *Hokhmah* itself is but a form of expression: namely *Keter*, Divine Will. This is called *kabbalat 'ol Malkhut Shamayim*, "accepting the yoke of Heavenly Kingship." This implies union, the fusion of human will with the general Will of God.[16]

Hear O Israel

J.E.: We reaffirm this acceptance every day. Sinai was not merely a historical, one-time event, but rather a prototype. The way the Israelites understood and heard the revelation is something we must relive daily in our relationship to God. The talmudic Sages pointed out that the promulgation of the Ten Commandments is preceded by the verse: "*On the third new moon after the Israelites had gone forth from the land of Egypt, on this very day, they entered the wilderness of Sinai. Having journeyed from Rephidim, they entered the wilderness of Sinai.*"[17] "This very day," the Sages say, is today. And the comment:

It is to teach you that these words must be as new to your eyes as though they had been given today.[18]

---

16. The daily profession of faith involves a dual acceptance: of Kingship and of the commandments.
17. Exodus 19:1.
18. Midrash, *Tanhuma Yashan, Yitro* 7.

What happened during the *na'ase venishma'* at Sinai? By saying *na'ase*, the Israelites associated themselves with God's overall plan. By saying *nishma'* they accepted the commandments. All Jews repeat this process every day in the key passage of the liturgy called the *Shema' Israel*, "Hear O Israel," which begins with the verse: *"Hear O Israel the Lord your God the Lord is One."*[19]

This prayer is made up of three paragraphs taken from the Torah. The Sages call the first paragraph "acceptance of the yoke of Heavenly Kingship" and the second, "acceptance of the yoke of the commandments." In other words, every day we relive the experience at Sinai, and we accept the Divine Kingship before we accept the commandments. The word governing all is *hear*, "Hear O Israel," which so strongly marks the event at Sinai.

A.S.: The *Shema' Israel* is our way of carrying out the *na'ase venishma'*. We state our complete willingness to open ourselves to pure Divine Will. It is a special moment of knowledge. It is the Divine Oneness that beacons me, not just a facet of the Divine. I say, "the Lord is One," and I acknowledge Him. Afterward I can ask questions, such as, What? How? In what way? I state my relationship to the essence of the sacred before the details, before I have heard the voice of God.

J.E.: Do Jews still express this willingness, which was demonstrated so forcefully at Sinai?

A.S.: This is one of the problems facing this generation. We have perhaps become too "intelligent," too knowledgeable, or too rationalistic, to be able to experience the total and spontaneous allegiance of our ancestors. Worse still, we tend

---

19. Deuteronomy 6:4.

to forget that there is something beyond reason. Jews need to face this question both as individuals and as a nation. How can we recover this ability to transcend the particular and seize reality in its totality, without performing fancy calculations beforehand, without asking, "Do I understand?" "Do I want this?" "Am I ready?" This is why the Sages say that every day we need to place ourselves at the foot of Mount Sinai. This can take place on Shavuot or on any day of the year. The face-to-face encounter at Sinai involves an encounter with Oneness and willingness to accept things that are beyond our faculties of comprehension.

AWE YES, FEAR NO

All the people saw the thunder and lightning, the blare of the horn and the mountain smoking; and when the people saw it they fell back and stood at a distance. "You speak to us," they said to Moses, "and we will hear, but let not God speak to us, lest we die." Moses answered the people, "Be not afraid; for God has come only in order to test you, and in order that the fear of Him may be ever with you, so that you do not go astray."[20]

Josy Eisenberg: The promulgation of the Ten Commandments is like a play in three acts: Before, During, and After. Act One was the theme of the last chapter. Israel prepared itself to receive the Law through a profound intuition of the essence of Divine Will and its correspondence to the Jewish soul. There is nothing to think over or hesitate about; this is what needs to be done. Israel has the floor.

In Act Two, God is center stage and promulgates the Ten Commandments. So much has been written on the Ten Commandments that we will not comment on them here, although not everything about the how and why of this revelation is clear. We will return to some of the less-known features of this event. In Act Three, Israel speaks again. All of a sudden, the atmosphere changes, as though this instant of fusion and total openness to God is as fleeting as a rose in bloom. God utters several short sentences from the mountaintop, and Israel retreats, literally and figuratively, and begins an astounding dialogue with Moses. The mountain suddenly generates a totally unexpected response: fear.

---

20. Exodus 20:18–19.

"You speak to us," they said to Moses, "and we will hear, but let not God speak to us, lest we die." Moses answered the people, "Be not afraid; for God has come only in order to test you, and in order that the fear of Him may be ever with you, so that you do not go astray."[21]

It looks like a love story gone sour. The honeymoon starts out as a perfect idyll, with total availability, and suddenly turns into fear, flight, and separation. What fear? Why this fear? This chapter is devoted to seeking answers to these questions.

Once again, we discover a series of paradoxes. Immediately after having given itself totally to God, Israel steps back. Moses first tells the people not to be afraid but then immediately adds that God revealed Himself for the people to fear Him. At best, this is disconcerting. Is the purpose of the revelation the fear of God? Should it not be love?

Adin Steinsaltz: Let me say first of all that fear (or awe) is not a very popular concept in the modern world. We prefer love, even those who do not like to talk about it. Love is the latest fad. Fear is something we avoid talking about. It is a devalued term and, in fact, is hard to understand. Nevertheless, fear is a basic concept in Judaism. It is so specifically Jewish that it has always been a stumbling block for other religions or philosophies. For example, in antiquity, the Greeks never grasped what the Jews meant by fear of God. The proof is that the pagans who converted to Judaism, and in particular the "semi-proselytes," were called "the God-fearing" ones. The concept of fear was very novel to them.

---

21. Exodus 20:18–19.

J.E.: Let me make a short historical digression, because you mentioned Jewish proselytism, and the subject is still a touchy one. In antiquity there were many pagans who were afraid to take the leap and convert to Judaism. However, they adopted many Jewish rituals and beliefs. In particular, they rejected idol worship. The Jews called them the "threshold proselytes," which was a good definition of their situation, or the "God-fearing." In Greek they were called *sebomenoi*, and in Latin the *metuentes*: "those who fear." Historians believe that the "God-fearers" were the most responsive to Paul's preachings. These semi-Jews were naturally the most attracted to what at that time was simply a variant on Jewish teaching. This shows to what extent the fear of God was, from the outset, a difficult idea to grasp, which makes it all the more crucial for us to define.

Suddenly, So Close

A.S.: Let us begin with a terminological clarification. *Yir'ah* is not fear but awe. In Hebrew, the word for "fear" is *pahad*, and is different from *yir'ah*, "awe." We know what fear is: fear of being hit, of being punished, of being sent to hell. Awe is something else. Strange as it may seem, it is a feeling that is part of the process of unification with God.

A famous example sheds light on this idea and concerns an event that is both very similar and very different from what happened at Sinai, namely, the sacrifice of Isaac. Abraham is always described as being full of the love of God. In the Bible, the Prophet calls Israel "*Seed of Abraham, who loved Me.*"[22] When the episode of the sacrifice of Isaac ends, what does the angel who stayed Abraham's arm say? "*For now I know that*

---

22. Isaiah 41:8.

you fear God."[23] Traditionally, this is described as the last of the ten trials of Abraham. In other words, the final test of faith is awe.

The dialectic between love and awe is one of the major themes in Jewish religious thought. The Bible commands us to love and to fear God. How are these two concepts related? Which precedes or conditions the other? The Sages make a number of distinctions, all of which would require lengthy discussion. Overall, the impression is that the goal is love. However, the story of Abraham lends tremendous weight to fear.

A.S.: Awe is something that can be experienced on a number of levels. The first level of awe is a feeling of distance. This is part of a complex process that is characterized by man's distance from God, while justifying man's love of God in this way. This is the inner contradiction that governs Jewish philosophy. God is both near and far from everything. Let us examine proximity first. It creates a series of problems. First of all, intimacy may breed familiarity. The real danger is that it may destroy the attraction.

J.E.: In other words, love of God, if there is only love, could destroy the relationship.

A.S.: I may reach such a degree of intimacy that I may have nothing left to desire. I have no more aspirations, I have no further goal to attain. This is where what we call "awe" intervenes. Its prime function is to set a breakpoint and to make manifest what separates me from my object of love. This involves recalling the distance, and the abyss, that separates me from God. In the language of the Bible and in

---

23. Genesis 22:12.

prayer, God is called *Nora*, the One Who is feared. It is generally translated as "awe-inspiring." The true meaning of the word is the perception of transcendence. Once I am aware of this transcendence, the chasm separating creature from Creator, I can consider the means at my disposal to bridge the gap and approach God. This paradox, that only distance can create desire, is an apparent one.

J.E.: This fear has nothing in common with the fear that the sky is falling. In Hebrew there is an expression *yirat shamayim*, or "fear of the heavens," but this is related to the feeling of transcendence that forces men to place themselves before God. This is sometimes translated as a feeling of respect. The Torah uses the term "fear of the father,"[24] which is a reverential fear.

We can now try to grasp what the Israelites felt at Sinai. In fact, they found themselves in a complex situation. They are in great intimacy with God, because this God Who speaks to them is suddenly very close. Simultaneously, they are aware of Divine majesty. Everything suggests that this intimacy created a real shock and brought the Israelites back to a feeling of distance, and hence—awe.

A.S.: This is what is termed "reverential fear" and it is the highest form of fear. What happened at Sinai can be compared to the feeling one can have when looking at a skyscraper. When I am far away, I can see it perfectly; when I get closer, I cease to see it as it really is, and it seems smaller and smaller. But when I am very close to it, I have a feeling of being crushed. This is exactly what happened at the foot of Sinai. First God was far away. Then He seemed to be infinitely close, and then, at the moment of greatest proximity, the

---

24. Leviticus 19:3, and elsewhere.

Israelites became aware of the infinite distance separating them from God.

J.E.: We say that the exodus of Israel from Egypt to Sinai is punctuated by a series of revelations through which God gradually comes closer to Israel. The first stage is the miracles in Egypt. God manifests Himself from a great distance through prodigious events that make Him seem to be a *deus ex machina*. We are in the realm of hearsay. Then, in the second stage during the parting of the Red Sea, Israel sees, anticipates, understands, and enters the concealed. Sinai, however, is the *nec plus ultra* of revelation, for there is no greater proximity than speech. At Sinai, the giving of the Torah implies a permanence of the Presence. There are no longer ten plagues or the parting of the Red Sea, which are unique events. The Law implies a covenant and daily obligations. We understand why this proximity elicited such reverential fear.

This said, the tree of the Torah can, at times, hide the forest of the revelation. The content of the Ten Commandments has played such a fundamental role in the history of humanity that their content generally receives greater importance than He Who said them. This fear that overwhelmed the Israelites was not prompted by the terms of the Ten Commandments but by the encounter with God.

I, *Anokhi*

A.S.: At Sinai, God reveals Himself in His Infinity. He reveals His Being. He says *I*: "*I am the Lord your God.*"[25] By saying the word *I* at the start of the Ten Commandments, God reveals

---

25. Exodus 20:2.

the Being Who is above all the worlds. What matters is not the content of the speech, which we call the Ten Utterances, but rather that God expressed Himself personally. Furthermore, as you said, do we really know which words were said at Sinai? There are at least four opinions on this in the Talmud. The first is that the Israelites heard all Ten Commandments. The second is that they only heard the first two.

J.E.: I would like to develop this point. If you read the Ten Commandments, you will see that only the first two Commandments are expressed in the first person. The first Commandment is "*I am the Lord your God.*" The second Commandment is "*You shall have no other gods before Me.*"[26] However, starting with the third Commandment, God speaks in the third person. This leads to the hypothesis that from this point, it was Moses rather than God who spoke to Israel, and that the people, for reasons we will discuss in detail later, could not bear to hear God speak to them directly.

A.S.: This is the most common explanation. But there are two other hypotheses. The first is that they only heard the first two words: " I am the Lord."[27] The second is that they only heard the first word—*anokhi,* "I." In other words, hearing God speak was unbearable.

J.E.: The Bible clearly says that the Israelites pleaded with Moses: "*You speak to us, and we will obey, but let not God speak to us, lest we die.*"[28] This passage suggests that they spoke after having heard the Ten Commandments; but the Israelites could have said this while the Commandments were being spoken. Furthermore, the issue of death is raised.

---

26. Ibid.
27. Only two words in Hebrew.
28. Exodus 20:19.

A.S.: The issue is raised in a very particular way. According to the Talmud, "*Their soul flew out of them each time a word was said.*"[29]

J.E.: A soul that departs sometimes designates death. Here, it seems to refer more to fainting or ecstasy.

A.S.: God reveals Himself at a greater degree of proximity than had ever existed before. The weight of the revelation is enormous and undoubtedly impossible for man to bear in his natural state.

J.E.: When, later on, Moses asks God to reveal His glory, God replies: "*You cannot see my Face, for man may not see me and live.*"[30] How did they survive this encounter?

A.S.: This is the shock the Israelites experienced. They encountered the Infinite, the absolute, and nevertheless they lived. Time and time again their souls left them, reaching the heavens and the heavens of the heavens, but they remained human beings before their Creator. This extraordinary combination of Divine, Infinite Presence, and human, finite presence accounts for the Israelites' awe.

J.E.: They lived through it in a kind of trance.

A.S.: There is a text that says that Moses heard the Divine voice from every direction: up, down, right, left. It is even said that the Israelites heard with their toes. In other words, at Sinai the Israelites became the amplifiers of the Infinite. While remaining human, they ceased to be separate. They

---

29. Babylonian Talmud, Tractate *Shabbat* 88b.
30. Exodus 33:20.

heard the voice of God not from the outside but from the inside, from within their own beings. This is the core meaning of the phrase: "*And all the people saw the voices.*"[31] When I perceive a sensation that comes from the outside, I hear it or I see it. But here, the Divine penetrates man's being. To say that God "descended" on Mount Sinai is to state that the Divine engulfed the material.

J.E.: Is the most remarkable thing about this revelation this ecstatic state, in which I am no longer myself—while remaining so myself?

A.S.: This is the true dimension of the giving of the Torah. The Torah was not given to us to reveal the existence of the Divine somewhere in the absolute, but rather that the Transcendent manifest itself in the here-and-now, in our own reality. We can reach it through this reality. If not, why would we need the Torah?

J.E.: Perhaps for ethics?

A.S.: I do not think so. If you look at the Ten Commandments, you will see that there is nothing really original in them. Overall, they are laws that cultures the world over have accepted. I do not need the Torah to tell me not to murder or not to commit adultery. What happens is that honoring your mother and father, which in itself is purely a social convention, becomes here the locus of revelation of the Infinite. Let me repeat myself: What characterizes the events on Sinai is the breakthrough of the Infinite in the finite. Material reality acquires a new dimension.

Israel encounters the Infinite in great intimacy. It causes

---

31. Exodus 20:14.

souls to expire and creates reverential fear because there is nowhere to hide. King David said, "*Where can I escape from Your spirit? Where can I flee from Your presence? If I ascend to heaven You are there; if I descend to Sheol, You are there too.*"[32] At Sinai, this feeling of not being able to escape the Infinite is even stronger. It is in me. I cannot even take refuge within myself, because He encompasses me.

A God Who Desires Me

J.E.: If the feeling of fear comes from the assessment of distance, it is easy to understand that the feeling is much stronger when this distance is suddenly abolished. I should be far away, keeping my distance, respectfully, maybe obsequiously, and here I am sitting on the steps of the royal throne, so close! Nevertheless, I wonder whether the feeling the Israelites had derives from another source. By stating the Ten Commandments, God reveals His Will. According to the talmudic saying, man's will should annihilate itself before the Divine Will. Being filled with the Divine being, with the Presence, and then by His Will—the Law—may make me doubly depersonalized.

A.S.: Yes, indeed. In Kabbalah the word *anokhi,* "I," connotes the first *sefirah, Keter,* referring to the Crown and Will. Kabbalists point out that the numerical value of the word *Keter* is 620, and that there are 620 letters in the Ten Commandments.[33] The revealing of will is, to a certain

---

32. Psalms 139:7–8.

33. According to the Talmud, this figure corresponds to the 613 commandments in the Torah, plus the 7 commandments promulgated by the Sages.

extent, the revealing of the essence of the individual. God is will. In this sense, the Torah is the place where God manifests not only what He expects of me, but simply, what He wants.

J.E.: The revelation of the Torah and the revelation of God are one and the same. By understanding the essence of the Torah, I perceive what the essence of God is—or, in any case, His immanence. The only thing I can know of God is His Will; hence, knowing His Will is to know Him. I cannot go beyond this.

A.S.: When two people know each other, they know a certain number of things about each other. Sometimes they say what they expect from one another. All of a sudden, however, they discover the other person's personality, and at this point each perceives who the other person is intrinsically, as clearly as they perceive themselves. At Sinai Israel perceived God's "ego," if I dare use the term. By revealing His Will, God made man His associate in a certain way. From now on a tie binds them, a direct relationship without go-betweens. The others do not speak to me of God, I am not satisfied to know that He exists or that He commands. For once, I am entirely engulfed by the situation. I said earlier that according to one opinion, the Israelites only heard one word of the Ten Commandments: *anokhi*, "I." The Talmud suggests we read this word as an abbreviation:

Ana	I	אנא
Nafshi	Myself	נפשי
Ketavit	Wrote	כתבית
Yehavit	[and] Gave	יהבית

This sentence can be read in two ways. The literal meaning is "I Myself wrote and gave (the Torah)." In other words, just as in Egypt, I did not have recourse to an intermediary: I wrote this Torah. Yet there is a deeper interpretation: I inscribed and gave Myself.

J.E.: This interpretation is remarkable. God gave Himself by writing the Torah, the way a writer reveals himself in a novel. Here, the Torah becomes the autobiography of God, above all because by giving the Torah to men, God gave them Himself. The covenant is irreversible. Note that the word *nafshi,* which we translate as meaning "myself," literally means "my soul" and also means "my desire." We could thus translate it as "I wrote my desire, my will."

A.S.: The Torah is clearly the place where God's will and desire are anchored. I would like to illustrate this with a personal example. I had a friend who tried to find himself for twenty years. One day he told me he had decided to become an observant Jew and to accept, as they say, the yoke of heavenly Kingship. When I asked him what had made him decide, he answered, "There is a verse in the book of Job that has always obsessed me. Job says to God, *'You desire the work of Your hands.'*[34] I could not sleep because of this verse. Finally, I said to myself, If God desires me, how can I say 'No?'"

At Sinai, the Israelites experienced the same feeling when God said, "I want." God wants you, God wants us to be together. This face-to-face encounter, this desire and union, are a unique yet instant moment. This is the specificity of the event of Sinai.

J.E.: It is permanent because we can hear it every day, and because in Jewish tradition, the person who studies and

---

34. Job 14:15.

teaches the Torah is constantly at the foot of Mount Sinai. We said that Sinai was the highpoint of faith.

To conclude, I would like to situate it in the progression from the Exodus to the Ten Commandments.

A.S.: There is indeed a progression. I would define it in the following way. In Egypt, Israel learns that heaven exists. At the Red Sea the Israelites discover that they can enter it and reach it. In both cases these are relationships between heaven and earth, which unite the Divine to the human. At Sinai I stop being interested in this relationship: I find myself directly before God. It is said that the Alter Rebbe was once heard to say in his prayers: "*I do not want Your paradise, I do not want Your World to Come, I want only You.*"

FIFTH GATE

Sukkot

THE STATE OF GRACE

You shall live in booths seven days; all citizens of Israel shall live in booths in order that future generations may know that I made the Israelite people live in booths when I brought them out of the land of Egypt, I the Lord your God.

Leviticus 23:42

All who survive of all those nations that came up against Jerusalem shall make a pilgrimage year by year to bow low to the King Lord of Hosts and to observe the Feast of Booths.

Zechariah 14:16

It is written, "For Israel is a youngster and I love him," and: "My precious boy Ephraim . . . a child of merriment." [1] *This is an analogy to a youngster or a small child who has not yet acquired knowledge and intelligence, so that his father might derive pleasure and joy from the good quality of his mind and intellect. [Instead], the father laughs, entertains, and plays with him, and from these games which the child plays with him, the father derives merriment and great pleasure. . . .*

In the spiritual realm, this is analogous to the communality of the souls of Israel, who are called "a child of merriment" in a reference to their state of "immaturity of mind" (katnut hamohin) on Rosh Hashanah and Yom Kippur, when they humiliate themselves, in the Ten Days of Repentance, with the confession, "We are guilty" to the extent that [they profess that] there is no good in them, in and of themselves, at all. They are then in a state of extreme "immaturity," as the child or youngster who

---

1. Hosea 11:1 and 3.

does not yet possess any intelligence at all. Thus, their "arousal from below" cannot awaken an "arousal from Above" [by the standard criteria of virtue and achievement], since they do not possess any good deeds. How, then, do they initiate an "arousal from Above"? By drawing down a supernal merriment, not by means of knowledge and comprehension, but as in the analogy of the father who indulges in merriment with his child by play alone, as per above. . . .

This [is revealed] on the festival of Sukkot, when the "encompassing lights" (makifim)[2] are drawn down . . . [Then God's] love comes in an "encompassing" manner, which is not [internally] understood in the vessel of its recipients, for the "arousal from below" cannot reach it at all [to evoke it]. This is the source of the great revelation of joy on the festival of Sukkot, which is called "the time of our rejoicing."

Sefer Taksav (1806), pp. 365–366

Josy Eisenberg: The cycle of the three pilgrimage festivals (Pesaḥ, Shavuot, and Sukkot) ends with Sukkot, which is generally translated as the "Feast of Tabernacles" or "Booths." "Booths" in my opinion is more accurate, because the *sukkah* is a kind of cabin or hut covered with the branches for which the *sukkah* is named. Briefly, Sukkot is a remembrance of the wanderings of the Israelites after the exodus from Egypt. During the forty years in the desert, the Israelites built huts to shield themselves from the sun. This gave rise to the biblical commandment to build a hut every year in the autumn, five days after Kippur, to recall the desert years.

---

2. These lights are total and unconditional. The term *makifim* is discussed further in this section.

> *You shall live in booths seven days; all citizens of Israel shall live in booths in order that future generations may know that I made the Israelite people live in booths when I brought them out of the land of Egypt, I the Lord your God.*[3]

We are instructed to live in the *sukkah*, to eat there, and, if possible, to sleep there for seven days. It is, of course, easier to sleep in a *sukkah* in Israel today than in Poland in the old days. Sukkot has two key features. First of all, Sukkot is a series of holidays. The last day of Sukkot is called Hosha'na Rabbah and has its own specific rituals and liturgy. The eighth day, which ends Sukkot, is considered to be a separate festival and is called Shemini 'Atzeret or Simhat Torah.[4] This is the day when we conclude the annual reading of the Torah and begin the cycle again, which is also commemorated by a specific ritual. Each of these deserves comment. However, we will restrict ourselves to the Sukkot holiday proper and the meaning of the *sukkah*.

The second specific feature of Sukkot is its originality. In contrast to Pesah or Shavuot, it has no equivalent in other religions. It could be termed the "most Jewish" of all the Jewish holidays, because it commemorates a purely historical event, which for this very reason should only involve those who lived through it. Paradoxically, however, Sukkot is the festival that is dedicated to humanity as a whole. During the seven days of the holiday, seventy sacrifices were brought to the Temple in Jerusalem in honor of the seventy nations of

---

3. Leviticus 23:42.

4. In Israel they take place on the same day. In the diaspora, Shemini 'Atzeret and Simhat *Torah* are celebrated on two consecutive days.

the Earth.[5] Sukkot rituals thus combine and unite the particular and the universal. In Jewish tradition Sukkot, the festival of Israel's intimate relationship with God, is also the day when all the peoples of the Earth will recognize the God of Israel as their Lord.

All who survive of all those nations that came up against Jerusalem shall make a pilgrimage year by year to bow low to the King Lord of Hosts and to observe the Feast of Booths.[6]

Adin Steinsaltz: This clearly shows that Sukkot only partially belongs to the Jewish world. Nothing that we commemorate on Sukkot is connected to a specific event. Pesaḥ recalls our freedom. Shavuot celebrates the giving of the Law. As a harvest festival, the essence of Sukkot is universal. It is celebrated when the seasons change, when the harvest is gathered in. The holiday is universal in nature, and so are its symbols.

Why do other religions not celebrate Sukkot? Our response is that they are waiting for the right time. Sukkot involves two types of relationships with the nations. As you said, seventy sacrifices were offered up in the name of peace for all the nations, for the seventy peoples of the earth. The Prophet Zechariah proclaimed in particularly strident terms

---

5. According to the Sages, there are seventy nations on Earth, reflecting the natural division of peoples. Division into states is considered to be more of a quirk of history. The seventy sacrifices were spread over the seven days of the festival. Thirteen were offered the first day, twelve the second, and so on, and seven on the last day.

6. Zechariah 14:16.

that at the end of time, all men would make the pilgrimage to Jerusalem on Sukkot. The world is waiting for the time when it can enter the *sukkah*. When we say *"sukkaht shalom,"* the *sukkah* of peace—

J.E.: It is a phrase we say every Sabbath in prayer: *"Spread over us Your* sukkah *of peace."*

A.S.: —this refers to the *makifim*, this outside influence we will discuss in depth further on. According to the kabbalists, we have not yet reached this stage. But at the end of time, everyone, Jews and non-Jews alike, will be able to enter into the *sukkah*, into the *makifim*.

God's Embrace

J.E.: You mentioned the *makifim*. To deal with this idea properly, we need to show how Sukkot fits into the sequence of festivals that take place during the month of Tishrei. Sukkot is the third pilgrimage festival and also the third festival of the month that starts with Rosh Hashanah, continues with Yom Kippur, and ends with Sukkot. The New Year and the Day of Atonement are transcendental holidays, where man is judged by his Creator. Sukkot is a holiday of immanence, presence, and intimacy. It is said that the Jew in the *sukkah* is like an infant in its mother's womb. In this tiny cabin we are in God. In Kabbalah, the word *makifim*, or "circles," designates the global influences and values surrounding man. This explains why Sukkot corresponds to one of those situations in which man lives entirely within a certain universe. Rather than saying that Jews live in the *sukkah*, we should say that the *sukkah* inhabits man.

253

A.S.: The classic metaphor used to describe the Tishrei festivals comes from a verse in the Song of Songs: "*His left hand under my head, his right arm embraces me.*"[7]

The customary explanation is that the left hand, which is the symbol of rigor and judgment, designates Rosh Hashanah and Yom Kippur. On Sukkot we are supported by God's right, the symbol of love.

God's two "arms" correspond to the architecture of the *sukkah.* The law requires that the *sukkah* have at least two walls, plus the beginning of the third. This is exactly the form of an embrace.

J.E.: In his work *Peri Etz Ḥayyim*, Rabbi Ḥayyim Vital[8] describes this image more fully. He shows that the two walls of the *sukkah,* plus the beginning of the third, are an exact match for the arm, the forearm, and the hand. When the arm is bent, we obtain the shape of two walls, plus the start of the third.

A.S.: This is God's embrace, *"His right embraces me."* Embraces are referred to frequently in Jewish symbolism but are considered to be external relationships. Although an embrace is an intimate gesture, the intimacy is not internal. The crux of all the kabbalistic commentary on the relationship called *makifim* deals with the issue of external and internal. There are many simple and concrete examples of a *makif,* something that surrounds us; basically, it is something that comes to us from the outside.

In fact, there is a strong resemblance to transcendence. In all languages, transcendence is what is beyond us; in other words, what is beyond the great circle that circumscribes all.

---

7. Song of Songs 2:6.

8. 1542–1620, the foremost disciple of the Ari (1534–1572), the greatest of the kabbalistic masters of Safed.

The basic issue as regards the *makif* is the following: What relates man (or any other creature) within the circle to transcendence (which surrounds this circle), and thus apparently cannot be internalized?

J.E.: A *makif* is a value or external force that surrounds me and hence influences me.

A.S.: How can we be influenced by something without internalizing it? Can something that we do not feel or absorb be an influence? If we look around us, we realize there are many examples of influences and outside forces of this type. In physics, if we take the concept of electromagnetic field, we see that the concept of "field" is exactly what defines the *makif.* I am subjected to forces outside of me simply by being in a place that fulfills certain criteria. An electromagnetic field is a force that is in no way connected to the object it affects. The object, however, alters the field in which it exerts its force, as well as everything in it.

To return to psychology: There is one kind of influence that people internalize from having an understanding of something. However, there is another kind of influence that affects people because they find themselves in a certain place at a certain psychological or physical time—for instance, a demonstration or a football game. Even though individuals cannot really hear in the crowd, they are caught up in the atmosphere. Actors in the theater, or anyone in a group, can be affected by it. This "encompassing" influence is what is termed *makif.*

Between Grace and Mercy

J.E.: You quoted a very beautiful line from the Song of Songs: *"His left hand under my head, his right arm embraces me."* It describes the relationship of intimacy in an embrace, which characterizes the Sukkot holiday but not its inner influence. You suggested that an external influence can be likened to a crowd phenomenon. However, being in a *sukkah* is a deliberate choice. If I go to a football game or to the synagogue, the choice reflects some kind of commitment. Even if I am not a wild supporter or deeply convinced, I have taken the first step, which can lead me in a new direction.

In other words, celebrating Sukkot, and entering into the encompassing influence of *sukkah* (the *makif*), is in itself an act of love. God responds to this love by embracing me. The Alter Rebbe says that embracing is a way of trying to keep someone. This is a little like what happens on Sukkot, because the eighth day, Shemini 'Atzeret, literally means "the eighth of detainment." There are numerous rabbinical commentaries on this topic, suggesting that Israel is close to God and lives in symbiosis with the Creator in the *sukkah*. When the holiday is over, the Jews return to their era, but God wants to detain them one day more.[9]

Sukkot is thus the festival of love. According to the Alter Rebbe, there are two forms of love: *Hesed*, the fourth *sefirah*, which represents grace or goodness; and *Rahamim*, the sixth *sefirah*, which represents mercy and compassion. *Rahamim* is more specific to the Day of Atonement. During the month of Tishrei we go from the rigor of Rosh Hashanah to the compassion of Yom Kippur, and finally to the love of Sukkot. What differentiates compassion from love?

A.S.: You are right to raise this question, because these two feelings are similar. Both imply proximity and intimacy. The fundamental difference is that the concept of *Rahamim*, or

---

9. The Sages explain that during the seven days of Sukkot, God takes care of the seventy nations and their children through the seventy sacrifices offered at the Temple, but that after these ceremonies He keeps Israel, His eldest son, for an intimate encounter.

compassion, necessarily involves a relationship between giver and receiver. To elicit compassion, others must be in need. Compassion is elicited by the fact that someone needs something and is suffering. In a certain way we feel compassion for others before we judge them, because they are in need.

J.E.: Pity is not an instinctive, spontaneous feeling, because I necessarily analyze the condition of others. This is why the *sefirah* of goodness is on the right side of the *sefirot* system, the *sefirah* of judgment on the left, and compassion in the center, because it is a complex feeling combining judgment and goodness. This is what differentiates it from *Hesed*, which is grace, freely given love, and unceasing goodness.

A.S.: *Rahamim* suggests *din*. In other words, compassion always implies judgment. It encompasses love and justice, but at the same time goes beyond them. All of our prayers for mercy on Rosh Hashanah and Yom Kippur are captured in the phrase: "*Our Father our King, be gracious to us and answer us though we have no merits, deal charitably and kindly with us and save us.*"[10] I possess nothing, I have nothing to give in exchange, we are not equal, and this is why I appeal to Your mercy.

J.E.: Furthermore, the prayer leader begins his personal prayer, which he recites before he starts praying in the name of the community, by the plea: "*I am one deprived of [good] deeds.*"[11]

---

10. *Avinu Malkenu,* "our Father, our King," a prayer recited during the Days of Awe and on fast days.

11. Prayer for the *Shaliah Tzibbur* (Prayer Leader) before *Musaf* of Yom Kippur.

The concept of mercy, which so strongly colors the Tishrei festivals, stems from the fact that we are abject creatures, devoid of merit. This is why Rosh Hashanah and Yom Kippur are both days of judgment and days of mercy. The plea for mercy is based on personal soul-searching that we share with God. Sukkot is different, because judgment and compassion are no longer mentioned, only Hesed.

A.S.: Let us define Hesed. Typically, the central value of this attribute is love. Hesed is spontaneous love, which comes more from the giver than from the receiver. It corresponds to the giver's need to give, his need to love. But what is love? Is the person who says, "I love you," addressing himself to the object of his desire or to his inner, personal concept of love? What makes love possible is the projection of this inner concept on others. This is why Hesed has no real connection to others' objective circumstances. This form of love is unrelated to the other's merits. The sole question is, Do I love him or not? Hesed, the Alter Rebbe would say, is as irrational as fatherly love. This is exactly what happens on Sukkot.

It is written, "For Israel is a youngster and I love him," and: "My precious boy Ephraim . . . a child of merriment."[12] This is an analogy for a youngster or a small child who has not yet acquired knowledge and intelligence, so that his father might derive pleasure and joy from the good quality of his mind and intellect. [Instead], the father laughs, entertains, and plays with him, and from these games that the child plays with him, the father derives merriment and great pleasure. . . .

In the spiritual realm, this is analogous to the communality of the souls of Israel, who are called "a child of

---

12. Jeremiah 31:19.

merriment" in a reference to their state of "immaturity of mind" (katnut hamoḥin) on Rosh Hashanah and Yom Kippur, when they humiliate themselves, in the Ten Days of Repentance, with the confession "We are guilty," to the extent that [they profess that] there is no good in them, in and of themselves, at all. They are then in a state of extreme "immaturity," as the child or youngster who does not yet possess any intelligence at all. Thus, their "arousal from below" cannot awaken an "arousal from Above" [by the standard criteria of virtue and achievement], since they do not possess any good deeds. How, then, do they arouse an "arousal from Above"? By drawing down a supernal merriment not by means of knowledge and comprehension, but as in the analogy of the father who indulges in merriment with his child by play alone, as per above. . . .

This [is revealed] on the festival of Sukkot, when the "encompassing lights" (makifim) are drawn down . . . [Then God's] love comes in an "encompassing" manner, which is not [internally] understood in the vessel of its recipients, for the "arousal from below" cannot reach it at all [to evoke it]. This is the source of the great revelation of joy on the festival of Sukkot, which is called "the time of our rejoicing."[13]

This brings us back to the issue of Jews and non-Jews, and *makif*, because there is giving that is unrelated to its recipient. For example, I can wear a custom-made suit or eat a meal that agrees with me. By contrast, the *sukkah* is open to all. Because the *sukkah* is on the level of *makif*, it is not dependent on a given place or a given individual. Unlike other holidays that correspond to specific events for the Jewish

---

13. *Sefer Taksav* (1806), pp. 365–366.

people, the *sukkah* is so encompassing that all individuals have their place. Everyone can come in: adults, children, the wise, the simple, those who know, and those who do not. Love eliminates all these differences, including those between Jews and non-Jews. The more this love grows, the more room there is for others. A *makif* of love encompasses all.

J.E.: The specificity of *Ḥesed* is that it can encompass all, because it is freely given, nonprovisional, irrational, and hence boundless love. *Raḥamim*, which derives from judgment and reason, is necessarily bounded. This is why the same relationship between *Raḥamim* and *Ḥesed* can be found between Rosh Hashanah and Yom Kippur, on the one hand, and Sukkot, on the other. On the first two holidays, God judges men as they are, with their pasts and their histories, and grants (or does not grant) atonement. On Sukkot, after Yom Kippur has cleansed us of our sins, love can be total and boundless because we are like newborns. Life begins anew; we are innocent.

A.S.: This is why God embraces us. The Sages emphasize the fact that Sukkot is the first day of the "New Year's accounts of our sins."

J.E.: On Yom Kippur the tally was set back to zero. On Sukkot it starts up again.

A.S.: A new world is beginning, as is described in the Psalms: "*like a weaned child with its mother; like a weaned child am I in my mind.*"[14] On Sukkot I feel like a child, because all is reciprocal love. The joy I feel during the holiday is

---

14. Psalms 131:2.

free-flowing.[15] This kind of joy also relates to the *makif,* in that I do not rejoice because I *have* but because I *am.*

J.E.: If someone brings me a present, that makes me happy. But if I love the person, my real pleasure is in the fact that the person has come to see me.

A.S.: It is the joy of living, the joy of being alive, something that is echoed in the water-drawing festival.[16] Sukkot is known as the holiday of our rejoicing; "*You shall rejoice during the festivals.*"[17]

Traditionally in the Ḥabad movement, the *sukkah* is not decorated, in an effort to derive joy from the simplest pleasures. I gathered in my harvest, I have my wheat, my wine, I have brought all the reasons for rejoicing into my house. Now that I am seated and I look around me, I feel the pure joy of living. The Alter Rebbe often mentions a form of love he calls *ahava beta'anugim:* love-pleasure.[18] My desires have been fulfilled, and very simply I am happy that we are together now.

The Dew and the Rain

J.E.: It is true that Sukkot is pure joy. After Kippur we are pardoned, and we feel relieved. A new life begins. However, we

---

15. Each festival has an associated name. Pesaḥ is called "the time of our freedom," Shavuot is called the "time of the giving of the Torah," but Sukkot is simply called "the time of our rejoicing."

16. The water libation festival. This was a great festivity at the Temple during Sukkot (Mishnah, Tractate *Sukkah* 5).

17. Deuteronomy 17:14.

18. The Alter Rebbe considers this to be the highest form of love of God: I am happy because He exists.

do ask for something else. On Sukkot there is at least one thing we pray for fervently—rain. The last day of Sukkot, *Hosh'ana Rabbah*, has a special liturgy, which includes processions in the synagogue. We pray for rain, without which no life is possible. The word for "rain," *geshem*, has given rise to the word *gashmiut*, which means "materiality." Water is the condition sine qua non for physical life. The earth receives water in the form of rain and in the form of dew. At Pesaḥ we pray for dew, just as we pray for rain on Sukkot. Paradoxically, the Alter Rebbe says that Sukkot is related to dew and that rain comes from the earth and dew from the sky. Isaac the Patriarch blessed Jacob by saying: "*May God give you of the dew of heaven and the fat of the Earth.*"[19] Nevertheless, dew seems to come from the earth. Is Sukkot the festival of rain or of dew?

A.S.: Let us first define the ways in which rain differs from dew. Rain implies temporality. For example, there is a rainy season. Furthermore, I only want rain at a specific time. I certainly do not want rain when I am harvesting or when I am sitting in my *sukkah*. The Sages say, "Sometimes you want it, sometimes you do not."[20] Dew is different. The Prophet Hosea was able to say, "*I will be to Israel like dew,*"[21] because the dew is always desirable.

J.E.: Dew is permanent, like God, whereas rain is sporadic. Rain can be a hindrance, but dew is never harmful.

A.S.: That is the first feature. Second, rain is part of a cycle. Waters rise from the earth, evaporate, and then fall again on

---

19. Genesis 27:28.

20. See, for example, Babylonian Talmud, Tractate *Rosh Hashanah* 27b, and elsewhere.

21. Hosea 14:6.

the earth. In contrast, dew is only dependent on the atmosphere. It is not connected in any way to a give-and-take cycle as rain is. In addition, rain is perceived as a response to men's needs and activities. Man does what he has to do, and then the rain makes his work flourish, whereas dew is a spontaneous gift of God.

J.E.: Rain is a reward, and dew is a present.

A.S.: In fact, during Sukkot we give thanks for dew. We only start to pray for rain after the festival ends. Summer is the time of interaction between God and man. When it is over, and when Sukkot comes, we start to ask for rain. Sukkot belongs to the world of dew. It is another facet of *makif*: a gift from Above, which is not connected to need.

J.E.: The dew is freely given, an unconditional blessing.

A.S.: The proof is that when the Prophet Elijah cursed the earth and predicted that there would be no rain and no dew the whole year,[22] there was still dew, because it is a spontaneous gift of God that cannot cease.

J.E.: Rain derives from *Rahamim*, Divine mercy. We appeal to Divine mercy in times of drought. The Talmud and the Bible are full of commentary on rain rituals. Dew, because it does not depend on our merits, and because it is a free gift, the expression of unconditional love, is connected to *Hesed*, which is pure love. This helps explain why the sources are reversed in the realm of values. Rain comes from the earth, in

---

22. 1 Kings 17:1. "As the Lord lives, the God of Israel whom I serve, there shall be no dew or rain except at my bidding." And see Babylonian Talmud, Tractate *Taanit* 3a–b.

that it comes from the needs and works of the land. Dew, as Isaac said to Jacob, really comes from the highest of the high, from the heavens, from the core of Divine love. This symbolism is very logical. The earth always represents the bounded and the finite, whereas the heavens represent those things that are beyond the laws of determinism, including the Infinite, God's love, and dew.

The Alter Rebbe discusses this topic in relationship to a verse in the Bible: "*And He will come to us like rain, Like latter rain that refreshes the earth,*"[23] a line amply commented upon by talmudic Sages. Israel asks for rain. But rain depends on man's work. It corresponds to what the kabbalists call the Arousal of the World Below; in other words, the ways in which men elicit and solicit Divine compassion. Rain falls if men deserve it. This explains why rain comes from the earth, that is, from men, and not from the heavens. God responds: "*I will be . . . like dew.*" The dew arises from the Arousal of the World Above and not from elicitation by the World Below.[24] This is an absolutely free gift and is on the level of *makif.* The Alter Rebbe concludes that dew falls during the night when men sleep. Sleep, because it is by definition a form of inactivity, is a period of time when men are without any merit. The survival of Israel itself in the night of exile is described by the Prophets as the expression of this mysterious and freely given salvation of Divine love.

The remnant of Jacob shall be, in the midst of the many peoples, like dew from the Lord, like droplets on the

---

23. Hosea 6:3.

24. According to the Alter Rebbe, there are two types of Arousal of the World Above. One is elicited by human actions and is therefore relative and conditional; the other is non-elicited Arousal, which is a gift, freely given.

grass—which do not look to any man nor place their hope in mortals.[25]

Rain comes from a "place" where there are reason, judgment, and sanctions. Dew comes from the absolute transcendence of God, the God Who preceded creation, the God Who "surrounds the worlds"; in short, the dimension of *makif*.[26] Sukkot is the time par excellence of *makif*, because the *sukkah*, with its roof and walls, forms a kind of concentric circle around men, representing what precedes determinism and what goes beyond it. Sukkot also hints at a time when the limits of materiality will be abolished. Sukkot captures two of the supernal moments that are central to Jewish belief; namely, the messianic era and the resurrection of the dead. Sukkot is the holiday during which, when the time comes, all the nations of the earth will come to celebrate in Jerusalem. Resurrection is often linked with dew, for instance, "the dew that raises the dead."[27] A gift from the heavens, dew has something of the supernal, and we can grasp why it is considered to be a sort of potion of resurrection.

A.S.: The idea of salvation and resurrection are central to the Sukkot liturgy, in particular in the prophetic passages that we read at the synagogue during the holiday. The dew of resurrection, like the dew that falls every day, is beyond

---

25. Micah 5:6.

26. This is a summary of a series of the Alter Rebbe's teachings in his commentary on Deuteronomy (page 72 *in extenso*) and on the Song of Songs (in particular 34d and 35d). This topic is also dealt with in length by the grandson of the Alter Rebbe, Menaḥem Mendel, known as the Zemaḥ Zedek (1789–1866), who was also the author of a discourse on the Song of Songs.

27. Babylonian Talmud, Tractate *Shabbat* 88b.

human experience. It is, once again, a spontaneous gift of God. It is written, "*O let Your dead revive, let corpses arise, awake and shout for joy you who dwell in the dust. For your dew is like the dew on fresh growth you make the land of shades come to life.*"[28] And in the Song of Songs: "*For my head was drenched with dew.*"[29]

This is how the true Messiah, the true lover, is described. The fact that his head is covered with dew is the sign of revealed love.

J.E.: There is no better way to conclude. Sukkot is the time of intimacy of man with God, in God. Sukkot is the promise of future intimacy of the nations and universal harmony. It is the time of love, as represented by each morning's dew. It is a time when men live in a special place, a place that also inhabits them. In Jewish tradition, men do not live alone.

The second part of this chapter deals with the very special guests who join us every year in the *sukkah.*

---

28. Isaiah 26:19.
29. Song of Songs 5:2.

SEVEN FIGURES IN SEARCH OF A *SUKKAH*

When Ashur[30] shall come into our land and when he shall tread in our palaces, then we shall raise against him seven shepherds, eight Princes of Man.

Micah 5:4

The lighting of the lamp that was in the Holy Temple— one lamp with seven branches—represents the seven general levels among those who serve God. There are those whose service is in the sphere of love, those whose service is in the sphere of awe, and so on. These [seven levels] derive from the Seven Shepherds (Ro'im)" . . . The eight lights of Ḥanukkah[31] represent the "Eight Princes of Man" as referred to in Micah . . . The Seven Shepherds are Abraham, Jacob, Moses, etc. And the Eight Princes of Man are Jesse, Saul . . . the Messiah, and Elijah . . .

The explanation of the matter is as follows. Ro'eh has two meanings:[32]

a) one who feeds and nourishes others (as in "nourish us (ro'einu), feed us");[33]

b) one who himself feeds, as in "the asses are feeding (ro'im) by their side."[34]

---

30. Assyria.
31. See the section "The Man-Light."
32. In Hebrew, the word *shepherd* is *ro'e*, and it is the present participle of the verb *to graze*. The shepherd is the one who makes the sheep graze.
33. In Grace after Meals, the blessing *Boneh Yerushalayim.*
34. Job 1:14.

Similarly, regarding the Seven Ro'im, *both these elements are present. [On the one hand] they nourish the community of Israel.*[35] *Abraham feeds them love, as it is written, "Abraham, who loves Me."*[36] *For his root is from the supernal attribute of* Ḥesed,[37] *which is the attribute of love, and he provides of this attribute to the community of Israel. Moses provides the attribute of* Da'at *(knowledge); he is thus called "the shepherd of faith" (*ra'aya meheimna*), for he nourishes the faith [of Israel] by providing knowledge of God. And Jacob provides [the attribute of]* Raḥamim *(compassion).*[38]

However, through that they nourish the community of Israel, they too are nourished. For it is known that En Sof, *be He Blessed, is exalted and aloof from the attribute of* Ḥokhmah *and of [all Divine] attributes,*[39] *as it is said, "He is not of any of these attributes (*midot*) at all."*[40] *In order that a revelation of the light of the* En Sof, *be He Blessed, should be drawn into the supernal attributes, this is in accordance with the deeds of man. When there is an "arousal from below" with love, then, "as water reflects the face"*[41] *there is also drawn down from Above a revelation of the light of* En Sof, *be He Blessed, into the attribute of love and* Ḥesed, *that it should be "I have*

---

35. The collective soul of the Jewish people.

36. Isaiah 41:8.

37. The *sefirah* of *Ḥesed*, the source of pure love.

38. See the commentary on this text in this section in "Substance and Subsistence."

39. Thought, the second *sefirah* and its values; in other words, the whole world of *sefirot*, the essence of the finite world.

40. *Petiḥat Eliyahu*, from the introduction to *Tikkunei Zohar*. The word *midot*, which is one of the terms used to designate the *sefirot*, means "measure"; the Infinite is not "measurable" or finite.

41. Proverbs 27:19.

shown you love, said the Lord."[42] *Thus when the Seven Shepherds provide love and awe to the souls of Israel, the love and awe that is aroused in the souls of Israel draw forth additional light and revelation from the* En Sof, *be He Blessed, to the supernal attributes, which are the root of Shepherds. So they themselves are nourished through this. This is [the meaning of the verse] "Eat, friends (re'im)"*[43] *—these are the Shepherds (ro'im) who are friends (re'im) to God.*

The same applies to the Supernal One, as it is said: "Israel provides sustenance for their Father in Heaven."[44]

Torah Ohr, Mikketz 33c–d

Josy Eisenberg: The *sukkah* is a special place where each of us can experience closeness to God. Because this is a love story, I would be tempted to say that the *sukkah* is the room we share with God. The image is not as daring as it may seem, since the Song of Songs makes the same reference when it says *"The king has brought me to His chambers."*[45] Nevertheless, as the passage from the Alter Rebbe we quoted at the beginning of this chapter shows, there is more to the *sukkah* than closeness with God. Living "with" God or "in" God can never be equated to living with the Infinite God *En Sof,* Who is unknowable and unapproachable; rather, it is a way to relate to Him through the various forms of His revelation, which are finite. One form is the Torah ("The Holy One Blessed be He

---

42. Malachi 1:2.
43. Song of Songs *Zouta* 5:1.
44. *Midrash Rabbah* on the Song of Songs 1:9.
45. Song of Songs 1:4.

and the Torah are one"),[46] another is through the mediation of the *sefirot*, through which, according to the kabbalists, the Infinite, ineffable One "splinters" into finite and knowable values. The Alter Rebbe's mention of the Seven Shepherds refers to this spectacular feature of the Sukkot holiday.

Traditionally, each of the seven days of the holiday is dedicated to one guest, one heavenly ruler, and on that day we ask for his blessing and help. These seven characters, the "exalted guests," are Abraham, Isaac, Jacob, Moses, Aaron, Joseph, and David, in that order. They are also called the Seven Shepherds. Each of these guests represents a Divine virtue, and through them we can speak of the presence of God and closeness to Him.

The Prophet Micah predicted that Israel would one day be protected by the Seven Shepherds and the Eight Princes of Man, eight prominent figures. What role do the Shepherds play? How do they differ from the Eight Princes? The Alter Rebbe comments at length on these questions in a passage that deals with both Sukkot and Ḥanukkah. The Eight Princes, he says, represent the eight days of Ḥanukkah, and the Seven Shepherds refer to Sukkot when we host them in the *sukkah*.

The lighting of the lamps that were in the Holy Temple— seven candles—represent the seven general levels among those who serve God. There are those whose service is in the sphere of love, those whose service is in the sphere of awe, and so on. These [seven levels] derive from the Seven Shepherds (Ro'im) . . . The eight lamps of Ḥanukkah represent the "Eight Princes of Man" as referred to in Micah . . . The Seven Shepherds are

---

46. See the *Zohar*, Leviticus 73a.

Abraham, Jacob, Moses, etc. And the Eight Princes of Man are Jesse, Samuel, Saul, Elijah, Zephania, Amos, Zedekaih, and the Messiah.[47]

Adin Steinsaltz: The Seven Shepherds mentioned by the Prophet are seven eminent figures in our history. Of course, they are also much more than that. They are personalities who continue to lead the Children of Israel, even in our times, in an invisible fashion. We invite them to our *sukkah* because we really feel that they are present among us and are not figments of the past. Men fall into two categories. The first is composed of men who act at one point in history. They belong to the past and their actions have come to a close. The Seven Shepherds, however, belong to the second category of men: those who have a permanent impact on the Jewish soul, an impact that has lasted up to this very day.

J.E.: This is not specifically Jewish. At all times and in all countries, men have continued to affect ideas and history after their deaths. What is somewhat different here is that these men are called "Shepherds." With the exception of Isaac and Aaron, they really were shepherds, but this is fairly secondary. What counts for the Alter Rebbe is the ambivalence of the word *shepherd*. In Hebrew, there is no noun form of *shepherd*. The present participle of the verb *to graze, ro'eh*, is used. This verb is both transitive and intransitive. In other words, it can mean "to graze"—when the shepherd takes his flock to pasture—and "to graze as a form of eating," as in animals grazing. So a shepherd is both the raiser of sheep and the consumer; or to put it another way, the one who gives

---

47. *Torah Ohr, Mikketz* 33c–d; Babylonian Talmud, Tractate *Sukkah* 52b.

and the one who receives. This is fairly straightforward when the shepherd is a man; by feeding his flock, the shepherd receives payment. It is a reciprocal relationship by which each provides sustenance for the other. How do we interpret this reciprocal relationship when the Shepherds are archetypal figures such as Abraham, Moses, and David?

Substance and Subsistence

A.S.: First, these Shepherds are more than archetypal figures. A more fitting description is that we, as their descendants, have undergone their influence and have integrated part of their personalities. The Seven Shepherds are not figures or role models, but rather seven facets, or seven fundamental features of our identity. These Shepherds do not roam the fields; they roam our souls. In a sense we are their descendents in the flesh—

J.E.: Which would be true for Abraham and Jacob—

A.S.: Or in spirit, as for Joseph or David. Regardless, they are our spiritual fathers, and we "carry" their genes. They are the building blocks of our heritage and our spiritual genetic background. This said, why are they called Shepherds? Some were indeed shepherds, and this was, at times, the primary reason they were chosen to lead. This is particularly true of Moses. The Midrash tells us that just before God appeared to Moses in the burning bush, Moses was chasing a lost sheep, and God said to him: "You will lead Israel because you have mercy over a flock."[48]

---

48. Midrash, *Exodus Rabbah* 2.

J.E.: Leaders of flocks who become leaders of men, and the search for lost sheep, are two of the most famous clichés in historical and religious literature the world over. If that were the whole story, it would be extremely banal. However, the Alter Rebbe suggests that the Seven Shepherds are not seven remarkable models but rather mediators who transmit messages, both from above to below and from below to above.

First of all, from above to below. Let us analyze the Alter Rebbe's comments on the Seven Shepherds point by point.

Ro'eh *(shepherd) has two meanings:*

a) One who feeds and nourishes others, as in "nourish us (ro'einu), feed us";[49]

b) One who himself feeds, as in "the asses are feeding (ro'im) by their side."

Similarly, regarding the seven Ro'im, *both these elements are present. [On the one hand] they nourish the Community of Israel. Abraham feeds them love, as it is written "Abraham, who loves Me." For his root is from the supernal attribute of* Ḥesed, *which is the attribute of love, and he provides of this attribute to the community of Israel. Moses provides the attribute of* Da'at *[knowledge]; he is thus called "the shepherd of faith"* (ra'aya meheimna), *for he nourishes the faith [of Israel] by providing knowledge of God. And Jacob provides [the attribute] of* Raḥamim *(compassion).*[50]

---

49. As in the Grace over Meals.
50. *Torah Ohr, Mikketz* 33c–d.

According to kabbalists, the infinite God, *En Sof*, is revealed through the ten *sefirot*. The first three *sefirot* involve the will and the intellect. The seven others, the *midot*—which means both "measures" and "virtues"—each represent a specific facet of the supreme values or virtues of God.

In history, each of the Seven Shepherds incarnates one of these supernal values. Abraham represents love; Isaac, fear; Jacob, mercy; Moses, knowledge; and so on. These figures are nourished, or fed, by the abstract values they keep alive on earth and for which they serve as the living model. Here the *sefirot* themselves play the role of shepherds. They provide subsistence for human virtues. They "feed" love, fear, and so forth, and they themselves receive nourishment.

However, through what they nourish the Community of Israel, they too are nourished. For it is known that the En Sof *be He Blessed is exalted and aloof of the attribute of* Ḥokhmah *and of [all Divine] attributes, as it is said: "He is not any of these attributes (*midot*) at all."*[51] *In order that a revelation of the light of the* En Sof, *be He Blessed, should be drawn down into the supernal attributes, this is in accordance with the deeds of man. When there is an "arousal from below" with love, then, "as water reflects the face,"*[52] *there is also drawn down from Above a revelation of the light of the* En Sof, *be He Blessed, into the attribute of love and* Ḥesed, *and awe, to the souls of Israel, the love and awe that is aroused in the souls of Israel draws forth additional light and revelation from the* En Sof, *be He Blessed, to the supernal attributes, which are the root of "Shepherds."*[53]

---

51. The infinite is incommensurable. *Midot* means "measure" and characterizes the defined and finite features of the *sefirot*.

52. Proverbs 27:19.

53. *Torah Ohr, Mikketz* 33d.

The straightforward idea is that God's love of men is nourished by the love of men for God. Through feedback, one of the basic principles of Kabbalah, men's actions are constitutive of Divine "behavior." Kabbalists often refer to a mirror image; in other words, God acts as the mirror of our actions. Human actions, according to a classic formulation, increase or decrease Divine potential. Moses said: *"You neglected the Rock that begot you, Forgot the God Who brought you forth."*[54]

God's Friends

A.S.: This is a highly original view of relationships to God. At times, the talmudic Sages go even further, with such astounding pronouncements such as *"Israel feeds his Father Who is in heaven."*[55]

This is the meaning of the verse "Eat, friends (re'im)"[56]*—these are the Shepherds (ro'im) who are friends (re'im) to God.*[57]

In the Song of Songs, the shepherd (God) says to the shepherdess (Israel): *"My sister, my friend, my dove, my innocent one."*[58] "My friend" should be translated as *"my shepherdess, my source of nourishment."* These examples confirm the saying from the Midrash that Israel feeds God. A definition of food helps make this statement less anthro-

---

54. Deuteronomy 32:18.
55. Midrash, *Song of Songs Rabbah* 1:7.
56. Song of Songs 5:1.
57. *Torah Ohr, Mikketz* 33c–d.
58. Song of Songs 5:2.

pomorphic. Taking nourishment unites body and soul. By nourishing the human body, I enable the soul to reside there. What is true for the individual is also true in universal terms. Assuming, as we do, that God is the soul of the universe, behaving in such a way that God will be present in the world is metaphorical "nourishment." Individuals who conduct their lives in such way that God will remain in the world, and not disengage Himself from it, can thus be called the shepherds of God, His nourishers.

J.E.: By nourishing the *sefirot*, which represent the immanence of God, we "nourish" the here-and-now Presence of God. We nourish God's desire to maintain and bless the world, which is neither automatic nor unconditional. God needs men, and our actions are like the shepherdess's response to the shepherd.

A.S.: The relationship is reciprocal. The Psalms often refer to God as the Shepherd of Israel, as in "*The Lord is my shepherd, I shall not want,*"[59] and there is no better way to say that God ensures us sustenance and life. We ensure His Presence on earth by "nourishing" Him. This is why He calls us "my brothers, my friends." A friend is one who nourishes. The Sages draw on this concept to make a somewhat audacious interpretation of the verse in Isaiah, "*So you are my witnesses, declares the Lord, and I am God,*"[60] which they reformulate as "*If you are my witnesses, I am God.*"[61]

The idea is that God is saying, "As long as you are my witnesses, I am God. If not, I am no longer God." Without us, without our efforts, if we do not serve Him, God certainly exists, but He is not present or visible in the world.

---

59. Psalms 23:1.
60. Isaiah 43:10.
61. Babylonian Talmud, Tractate Ḥagigah 16b.

J.E.: The Alter Rebbe often emphasized that Israel made the world aware of God. The term "God of Israel" does not mean that God belongs to Israel or that He is exclusively the God of Israel, which would be absurd. The God of Israel means God through Israel and that Israel is the revealer of God.

A.S.: This is the true definition of a witness. A witness is not only someone who is present at an event: It is also someone who can provide an account of it. This is one of the functions of Sukkot. In the *sukkah* we live in the shadow of God, in the palm of His hand, embraced by His arm, as is said *"And I sheltered you with My hand."*[62] The Seven Shepherds we invite to the *sukkah* are in fact none other than ourselves. We become the Shepherds of God; we discover our own ideal selves in the Patriarchs.

Reconstructed Man

J.E.: It is as though we were made up of parts of Abraham, Isaac, Moses, and David. When we welcome the Seven Shepherds each day of Sukkot, we reconstruct the building blocks of our being. In the Bible Sukkot is also known as the "harvest festival." The literal meaning of the word *assif,* "harvest," is "assembly." Just as we harvest our crops, so we harvest what the Shepherds have sown within us.

A.S.: Assembly, meeting, and re-unification characterize Sukkot. Within ourselves we unite the scattered fragments of our identity, and at the Temple in Jerusalem there were seventy sacrifices to unite the scattered nations. These were

---

62. Isaiah 51:16.

called peace sacrifices. Peace, *shalom,* is wholeness, or *shlemut.* The seventy sacrifices at the Temple were aimed at bringing men together, and restoring the wholeness of humankind in a broken, disunited world. Sukkot ends with another form of wholeness, since on Simḥat Torah we complete the Torah readings.

Fulfillment only comes with tranquillity and peace. Unbridled, unrestrained joy only comes in fulfillment. Sukkot is the only holiday that is called the "time of our rejoicing" because all the forms of fulfillment are granted simultaneously—earthly wealth, the concluding portion of the Torah, the uniting of the nations. We are filled with an extraordinary sense of well-being. Seated in the *sukkah,* we live in perfect harmony in the shadow of God, echoing the verse in the Song of Songs: "*I delight to sit in His shade.*"[63] When I welcome the Seven Shepherds in my *sukkah,* I attain supreme harmony.

An invitation implies a willingness to receive. By opening my door to the Shepherds, I open the door of my being and say that I am ready to receive that part of my being that is in them. I say to each, "Enter within me with all you have to give and receive, with all that there is of me in you."

J.E.: The Seven Shepherds make Sukkot a holiday of internalization. Yet Sukkot is both internal and external. Internalization only takes place because I leave home and live elsewhere. In the Talmud, the Sages stressed the need for a change of scene: "*Leave your residence and go live in a temporary home.*"[64] The Shepherds are in me, but I am also in the *sukkah.* Here as well, commentators have noted that the

---

63. Song of Songs 2:3.
64. Babylonian Talmud, Tractate *Sukkah* 2a.

sukkah is one of the rare commandments that is accomplished by being in a certain place, rather than by performing a certain deed. In Judaism there are only three precepts of this type: the *sukkah*, the ritual bath where I must immerse myself, and the Holy Land where I must live. The Alter Rebbe suggests that this contrast between internalization and externalization parallels the distinction the Prophet makes between the Seven Shepherds and the Eight Princes of Man. We have only mentioned the Shepherds up to now. Who are the Princes of Man? What role do they play? Before we answer this question, I suggest we look at another passage from the writings of the Alter Rebbe.

The Torah also provides nourishment to the soul, as it is written, "Your teaching is in my most innermost parts."[65] *The quality of the Shepherds is that they impart in an internal manner . . . like the understanding of Torah, that it should be apprehended and grasped in the [recipient's] mind . . . This is analogous to the shepherd who feeds and waters the sheep—that is, the imparting of vitality internally. In every generation, these are the leaders and teachers of Israel, who teach them Torah. As [Rav Safra] said [to Rava]: "Moses, is it correct what you said?"—Rava is referred to as "Moses," because he was a teacher of the Torah. Likewise, the nourishment that the "Shepherds" receive through this is also internally apprehended, as for example, the concept of "from my students [I learned] most of all."*[66]

---

65. Psalms 40:9.
66. *Torah Ohr, Mikketz* 33c–d. The last quotation is from the Babylonian Talmud, Tractate *Sukkah* 7a.

The anecdote is as follows. One day the famous talmudic Sage Rava[67] was called "Moses," suggesting that all teachers have the qualities of Moses. The reciprocal nature of the exchange between teacher and student parallels the reciprocal relationship between *sefirot* and men's deeds. The type of nourishment the Alter Rebbe is talking about is the Torah, the food of the soul. Thus, a shepherd is a teacher of the Torah.

But the quality of Princes of Man is not that they nourish and teach Israel, as Moses and the Patriarchs, but that they are wholly righteous, like Jesse, who "died only because of the serpent."[68] They too impart power to the souls of Israel in their service [of God], [but] in a transcendent and "encompassing" manner (makif),[69] unlike the Shepherds whose [contribution] is imparted internally and is called "food" as per above . . . [Thus they are called "Princes"], like the prince who possesses the quality of Kingship, which is an "encompassing" quality— the people of his country are called by his name—but there is no true inner influence. (For example, a person might be inspired by the prayer of a righteous man who prays with awe and love, thus affecting him as well. This is a radiance of an "encompassing" quality, since he did not receive from him an internal conception and wisdom via speech, which is [the medium] of internal influence, but was only affected by this person's righteousness.)[70]

---

67. End of the second century—beginning of the third century B.C.E.

68. In Jewish tradition, sin kills men. Wholly righteous people thus would not die, had it not been for the serpent that irrevocably introduced death in the human race.

69. *Makif*—a global influence—was defined earlier in this chapter.

70. *Torah Ohr, Mikketz* 33d.

The Shepherds are the Sages, the Princes of Man are the righteous.

The Princes of the Future

A.S.: The Prophet Micah refers to, but does not name, the Eight Princes of Man who will lead Israel to victory over Assyria. The Talmud contains several different lists of these Eight Princes. The most generally agreed upon list contains people who vary enormously in titles and functions: an ordinary man, Jesse, the father of David; two kings: Saul and Zedekiah; four Prophets: Samuel, Elijah, Amos, and Zephaniah; and finally, the Messiah. What do they have in common?

J.E.: The Alter Rebbe defines them as "the righteous."

A.S.: They are guides or spiritual leaders, as were the Shepherds, but on another level. The distinction the Alter Rebbe makes between internal influence (or, in other words, the Torah) and outside influence (i.e., righteousness and integrity) corresponds to two types of power. On the one hand, I can undergo an influence that I internalize, so that it becomes part of my being.

J.E.: Such as a message, a lesson, an idea, or values.

A.S.: There is, however, another type of influence, an external influence, where there is no direct message to my mind. The Shepherds who feed me directly represent intimate communication. The message is so profoundly integrated that there ceases to be a difference between the spiritual leader and the individual he leads. The Shepherd becomes part of the flock, and they become friends.

J.E.: This characterizes the student–teacher relationship. The Talmud often refers to the "student-friend," suggesting a sharing of knowledge. The concept is rational, and it serves to overcome hierarchical obstacles.

A.S.: An outside influence, a *makif,* acts on one not because it permeates one, but because it creates a climate, an atmosphere, or an environment that affects one in an overall fashion. We cited the example of the crowd. The Alter Rebbe mentions the righteous person, who in rabbinical tradition influences you and makes an impression on you not because of what he does, but because of who he is. Some of the Eight Princes had political power, in that they were kings. Others were prophets and sometimes, as in the case of Elijah, they were recluses. However, all belonged to a special race of men: men whom we may not even know exist and who yet have an indirect influence on the world. Because these men exist, the world is no longer the same. They have the ability to change the world simply by existing (something that is true not only for men but also for systems, and even for the laws of nature). Some exert a direct impact, whereas others, like the law of gravity, have an effect by their mere presence. This defines what the kabbalists call *makifim,* peripheral forces.

J.E.: There is a scientific basis for the kabbalistic distinction between peripheral and internal influences. Men are subjected to both centrifugal and centripetal forces. The nervous system recognizes the difference between what is internal, or central, and what is peripheral.

A.S.: The forces we call *makifim* are often very powerful. This is why the Eight Princes of Man do not necessarily need to have worldly power. The most striking example is the Messiah, which after all is only a belief. But belief in the Messiah has always been a major motivator for action, even though the action is not connected to a specific time. In other words, there are Princes of Man who are not princes of today, but rather princes of tomorrow.

J.E.: There is nothing more revolutionary, and thus more powerful, than ideas; but here, the distinction between Shepherds and the Princes of Man is more subtle. Both are spiritual leaders, but the former influence us by their teachings, while the latter do so by their charisma. They complement each other, since teaching is on a rational level and charisma on the irrational and can open the gates to the supernal. The Alter Rebbe presents a lengthy discussion of the respective values of these two types of influence. We need the Princes of Man because somewhere, the righteous affect systems that the Sages cannot touch. Because they are on the level of *makifim,* they are part of the absolute transcendence of God, which the kabbalists call *sovev kol 'almin,* "the One Who encompasses the worlds." The Sages act in the world of immanence, *memale kol 'almin,* "the One Who fills the worlds." The Princes are in a sense the vessels, which are immutable. The Shepherds are the contents, the values, which are more fragile.

In a long passage that I would like to summarize, the Alter Rebbe analyzes a story from the Talmud[71] to clarify this distinction. The greatest Sage of his time, Rabbi Yoḥanan Ben Zakkai, who lived during the time of the destruction of the Second Temple, went to see a righteous man who was famous for his piety and his power to pray for Divine mercy. This man, Ḥanina Ben Dosa, left no teachings. He was an ascetic and a holy man. The Sages say that the world was only created for a man like him. He lived, the Alter Rebbe says, in

---

71. Babylonian Talmud, Tractate *Berakhot* 34b.

the world of *makifim*, and the wisest Sage could not knock at the Heavenly gates as powerfully as this pure soul. In ordinary circumstances, the Seven Shepherds and their impact on us are sufficient. In times of crisis, we need the additional weight of the Eight Princes of Man, these souls untarnished by sin. The Shepherds act within the law. The Princes are beyond its bounds and can produce miracles. The Alter Rebbe concludes that:

> *There are two types of souls. There are souls who are God-fearing and as perfect as an* 'olah temimah *(unblemished burnt offering), yet are incapable of teaching God's Torah to their fellows. And there are souls who are masters of Torah, but are not as utterly perfect and without fault as the aforementioned souls. This is because the souls of the God-fearing and perfect derive from the "hidden world" (*'alma d'itakasia*). Thus they are not the leaders of their generation because they are from the hidden world, whose qualities are hiddenness and concealment, and [which] is safeguarded from all contact with [anything negative or mundane]. Nevertheless, they are not that much masters of the Torah, since they [derive] only from the external element of the supernal. The masters of the Torah, [on the other hand], derive from the inner element—it is only that they are from the inner element of a lower level, the "revealed world" (*'alma d'itgalia).[72]*

This brings us back to the dialectical nature of the parting[73] of the Red Sea. Now we have the key: because the

---

72. *Torah Ohr, Mikketz* 34c.
73. See sections "A Path in the Sea" and "Moses, the Human Fish."

Torah is revelation and visible, the masters of the Torah, the Shepherds, act within each of us in the visible, or in other words, the comprehensible sphere. By contrast, the righteous ones are part of the absolute transcendence of the hidden world.

A.S.: All these complementary opposites, such as the teacher and the righteous, the seven and the eight, what acts within me and what makes me act, capture the essence of Sukkot, which has either seven days or eight, if we include Simhat Torah. This is why living in the *sukkah* is, as you said, fully associating the two major facets of the relationship to the Divine. The Shepherds enter into me and I internalize the law. I, in turn, enter into God by living in the *sukkah* of peace.

PART III

THE TIMES
OF
MAN

SIXTH GATE

Purim

THE ACE OF SPADES

And all the king's courtiers in the palace knelt and bowed low to Haman, for such was the king's order concerning him; but Mordecai would not kneel or bow low . . . When Haman saw that Mordecai would not kneel or bow low, Haman was filled with rage. But he disdained to lay hands on Mordecai alone; having been told who Mordecai's people were, Haman plotted to do away with all the Jews, Mordecai's people, throughout the kingdom of Ahasuerus . . . Haman then said to Ahasuerus, "There is a certain people scattered and dispersed among the other peoples in all the provinces of your realm, whose laws are different from those of any other people and who do not obey the king's laws and it is not in Your Majesty's interest to tolerate them."

The Book of Esther 3:2–8

Josy Eisenberg: The Torah decrees five holidays: Rosh Hashanah, Yom Kippur, and the three pilgrimage festivals— Pesaḥ, Shavuot, and Sukkot. Two holidays, Purim and Ḥanukkah, were promulgated by the Sages. Purim is included in the Bible, but not Ḥanukkah, which commemorates an event that took place in the second century B.C.E. These two holidays stand out because men, not God, sanctified them. To view this sanctification in another way: The Jewish people were mature enough to recognize that an event was providential and did not "need" God's commandment to make the day holy.

Purim and Ḥanukkah view historical events through their specific prisms and for that reason are considered to be complementary opposites in Jewish exegesis. Both holidays commemorate a miraculous redemption. Purim, however, takes place in exile, whereas Ḥanukkah takes place in the Holy Land. On Ḥanukkah the Jews took up arms against the Greeks. On Purim, victory was achieved through more undercover means. The Ḥanukkah victory of a handful of freedom fighters against the Greek armies was a particularly spectacular miracle. On Purim, the miracle that Mordecai and Esther believed in was extremely subtle and operated through the most natural of means.

This section looks at these two features of Purim. The first theme is man's level of awareness, which is one of the classic themes in Jewish thought; and the second is the ambiguity of the miracle that does not really seem to be a miracle at all.

Briefly, the Purim story, as told in the Book of Esther, is as follows. Ahasuerus, the king of Persia—probably one of the Artaxerxeses—marries a young and beautiful Jewess, Hadassah, known as Esther, without knowing anything about her background. Esther has a cousin, a noble Jew named Mordecai. He refuses to bow down to the king's courtier, Haman, who, to revenge himself, orders all the Jews of Persia and Media to be exterminated. He draws lots—*pur*, in Persian—to set the date for the first "final solution" of the Jewish people in exile.[1]

Mordecai warns Esther, and she asks all her fellow Jews to fast for three days. She then goes to the king and successfully pleads for their lives. Haman is hanged and Mordecai takes his place.

Adin Steinsaltz: This story has several levels of interpretation. First of all, Purim takes place at a crucial point in our history. The Jewish community of Persia, which was the

---

1. In Egypt, too, Pharaoh ordered the Jews to be killed, but the extermination was partial in that only male children were to be thrown into the Nile.

largest Jewish community in the world at that time, is threatened with extermination and only escapes death through the set of circumstances you described. The saving of the Jewish people is the first and foremost reason we celebrate Purim.

J.E.: Philosophers and kabbalists tend to emphasize symbolic and mystical interpretations of this event, but we should never lose sight of the original meaning. How could we forget the other Purim persecutions that have devastated the Jewish people throughout our history? This is so true, and the image of Haman as the archetypal anti-Semite is so fixed in our minds, that Hitler is said to have claimed, *"The Jews will not have a second Purim."*

A.S.: We have indeed had other Esthers and Mordecais over the course of our history. We have also experienced too many Hamans. This makes the reading of the story of Esther a little difficult, because we have waited so often for the miracle to reoccur. This said, Purim needs to be interpreted on another level, in terms of the interplay of the forces that go beyond the framework of the story. The theme of our survival is interwoven throughout the biblical account. The main characters should be seen as the protagonists of any classical drama but also the models of the key forces that have manifested themselves throughout our history—Good and Evil, the enemies, the friends, and those who remain neutral.

J.E.: Esther and Mordecai are the friends, Haman is the enemy, and Ahasuerus is the neutral. They could be assigned other identities. During the Holocaust, the fate of the Jewish people constantly depended on the power play between these three forces, which no one needs to name.

A.S.: Hatred, alliance, and neutrality are the forces that act in this world on all levels, from the family circle to international relations. From this standpoint, Purim is always a contemporary event; and this is what, perhaps, gives a universal meaning to the verse from the Book of Esther that proclaims the holiday: *"These days shall be observed at their proper time . . . by every family, every province, every city."*[2]

Every era has its Ahasuerus and Haman, forming the basis for the psychological and ethical interpretation of Purim. This analysis is complemented by the perspective the mystics prefer, which centers on the cosmic and metaphysical events recounted in the story of Esther. Here, the four characters—Esther, Haman, Mordecai, and Ahasuerus—are seen as dual personalities. This is true in particular for Ahasuerus. Is he merely an earthly king? The kabbalists consider that his reign does not reflect temporal power but rather Divine Kingship in a flesh-and-blood sovereign. In the mystical interpretation, the Divine characters incarnate metaphysical forces that they are undoubtedly unable to perceive or grasp. This is not simply an arbitrary interpretation. Every individual has more than one facet of existence. By existing, we activate and serve as the instrument for cosmic forces. I would say that our bodies and souls are only the actors, or the performers, of this play we call life. Life is a *Purim spiel*, a Purim "play," and we act out things from the World Above via our personal carnival.

Totalitarianism and Idolatry

J.E.: You are alluding to one of the most colorful Purim traditions. There is a very old custom for people to wear

---

2. Esther 9:28. In Hebrew, the Book of Esther is called the *Megillat Esther*, the scroll of Esther, because it is written on a roll of parchment.

costumes on Purim, both at the synagogue and at home. Purim is a carnival holiday, and long ago there were performances of what in Yiddish are called *Purim spiel*, Purim plays, similar to medieval theater. We will comment later on the underlying meaning of this disguise. Like the characters in a Greek tragedy or the *commedia dell'arte*, we all wear masks and merely act out a certain role, a certain script (sometimes more than one) in life. This is true for every one of us, but even more so for biblical heroes. In Jewish exegesis, and in particular in the Kabbalah, the main figures in the Bible are almost totally depersonalized. Abraham is the human incarnation of goodness; Moses represents knowledge; David, royalty; and so on. Similarly, the four main characters in the Book of Esther are cast as the main figures of a universal drama, where they represent either ethical values or, as the mystical interpretation would have it, the philosophical and allegorical interpretation of transcendental values.

Let us begin with the philosophical interpretation, by defining what Ahasuerus, Haman, Esther, and Mordecai stand for. The biblical text constantly emphasizes the conflict among them.

And all the king's courtiers in the palace knelt and bowed low to Haman, for such was the king's order concerning him; but Mordecai would not kneel or bow low.[3]

Both protagonists live out this conflict, each in his own way, yet the two personalities are alike in many respects. Both Haman, the unbeliever, and Mordecai, the believer, are extremists. What characterizes both of them is that neither

---

3. Esther 3:2.

can do something halfway. Take Mordecai, for example: His refusal is radical. Perhaps he could be made to agree to a compromise later on, but not with Haman. The drama starts because Mordecai does something that appears to be deliberate provocation. He refuses to do as everyone else does and bow down to the king's courtier.

J.E.: It may be interpreted as provocation, but Mordecai did not mean it to be one. Rather, it is dictated by Haman's arrogance.

A.S.: Naturally, Mordecai did not want to challenge Haman, but the conflict is inevitable. It stems from the fact that if Mordecai bows, he ceases to be Mordecai. Mordecai represents Good. The problem of Goodness is that it is absolute. I cannot do good just when I feel like it.

J.E.: On the contrary, Good disturbs others.

A.S.: This is the difference between the righteous man and the opportunist. The righteous one cannot stop being himself; and, as a result, his existence is a provocation. By remaining true to himself, the righteous person knows that he can cause crises, yet he has no choice. He needs to stick to his chosen path without straying. This is the meaning of his existence. Had Mordecai bowed down, he would have permanently ceased to be Mordecai.

J.E.: I would like to point out that Mordecai is the first figure in the Bible to be called "the Jew." Prior to this, the Bible uses the term *Israel*. As a deported Judean, Mordecai is the incarnation and the archetype of the Jew in exile. We could easily and at length extrapolate on his existence. If the Jews had accepted to bow down, they would have ceased being

Jews. This is so obvious that there is no reason to elaborate. Mordecai is challenged, as is always the case, by that other strong personality, Haman.

A.S.: Haman is an astonishing figure. Mordecai irritates him:

When Haman saw that Mordecai would not kneel or bow low, Haman was filled with rage.[4]

But clearly, Mordecai is only a pretext. He symbolizes the refusal of what Haman represents: totalitarianism. Totalitarianism is much worse than dictatorship. In a totalitarian system, if one single person refuses to submit, power crumbles. If there is a single particle of freedom in a totalitarian country, it upsets the whole system. This is what Haman cannot accept. Here the two men are not fighting a duel; rather, they represent two differing conceptions of power and freedom. On the one hand, there is Mordecai, who says: "I am who I am," and on the other, Haman, who states: "I am the absolute master of all reality, and you must submit to my will." There is a midrash that says that Haman was wearing an idol around his neck.

J.E.: Which justifies Mordecai's refusal even more.

A.S.: Yes, but it is a symbol. Haman himself had become an idol. In this sense he is the symbol of cosmic forces, because from a metaphysical point of view, the definition of Evil itself is unlimited power.

---

4. Esther 3:5.

J.E.: This is what the kabbalists call the world of *tohu*, the world without laws or limits.[5] In fact, we need to situate Evil on its true level, which is not only political. I say "political" because the duty to resist totalitarianism—be it religious, political, or both—is also one of the classic interpretations of the story of Esther. Freedom fighters of all countries identify with Mordecai, just as the *refuseniks*[6] did. People commonly compare the situation of the Jews in the former Soviet Union to that of the Jews in Persia. The similarities are troubling. In both cases, only the Jews are described as being marginal or rebels. This interpretation is both legitimate and impor-tant, but, nevertheless, the conflict between Haman and Mordecai goes beyond the problem of centralized power and minorities.

A.S.: This is because a much more important aspect of freedom than democracy is at stake; namely, the right to be oneself, which every individual should be granted. This is what Purim stands for. This type of problem arises for all individuals. How can I remain true to myself, how can I resist an external force that wants to change my being, how can I resist a temporal power that acknowledges no limits?

A Woman of Action

J.E.: In Jewish thought, unlimited power incarnates Evil not only because it necessarily violates human rights, but also

---

5. See the sections "Passing through Exile" and "The Great Croco-dile."

6. Soviet Jews who, in the years of oppression, applied for a visa to Israel and were not only refused, but also consequently suffered economically, socially, and otherwise.

because it takes the place of God as the source of values. This was the case for Pharaoh, who is described as having made himself into a god,[7] and this was also clearly the case for Haman, who is nothing more than the resurgence of the Pharaohs. Jewish mysticism draws a parallel between these two tyrants and captures their political philosophy in a particularly striking phrase: "*Me, and me alone!*"[8]

The conflict between Mordecai and Haman could also be summed up as "*I want to be myself,*" as compared to "*There is no one else but me.*" The contrast is extreme. The contrast is less marked between the two other key figures in the story, Esther and King Ahasuerus.

A.S.: In the interpretation we give to the Book of Esther, which embodies a drama where the radical and unreconcilable forces of Good and Evil confront each other, Ahasuerus represents a power that takes no part in this confrontation.

J.E.: He is the one you called the "neutral."

A.S.: Ahasuerus stays neutral. He is ready to adopt any solution. In fact, he only reacts to suggestions made to him. When Haman has his favor, he agrees, without batting an eyelid, to sign the decree of extermination of the Jews:

And the King said, "The money and the people are yours to do with as you see fit."[9]

---

7. See the section "The Great Crocodile."
8. Isaiah 47:8.
9. Esther 3:11.

When, on the contrary, he is touched by Esther's appeal, he makes an abrupt about-face and condemns Haman immediately: "*'Impale him on it!' The king ordered.*"[10]

In other words, Ahasuerus is buffeted by the forces of good and evil, which toss him in either direction. In fact, he is fundamentally neutral. He reacts rather than acts. This neutrality, which sometimes results in passivity, is in my opinion the real nature of power.

J.E.: That is a little paradoxical.

A.S.: Only superficially. The major forces in the world are not always oriented toward Evil. Sometimes they only do Evil because they have been made to do so. It is enough to put pressure on them for them to reverse their actions and put their power to work for the forces of Good. To do so, someone has to push them. Basically, power, whether it is political or physical, is amorphous.

J.E.: It is true that the word *power* implies potentiality. King Ahasuerus emerges as a particularly weak and irresolute person. Of the four main characters in the Book of Esther, he is the one who knows the least what he wants. It is not surprising that he is influenced by the two strong personalities who attempt to sway him—Haman being the first, followed by Esther, the revolutionary defender.

Esther acts, whereas Ahasuerus, who is neutral, only reacts. She is the main character of the story and the deus ex machina who changes the course of history, making it fitting that the book be named for her. Purim is the feast of Esther. Esther is a woman. Of course, it is not the first or only time in Jewish history that a woman plays the redemptive role.

---

10. Esther 7:9.

Moses was saved because of Miriam, the prophetess Deborah leads the tribes of Israel into battle, and Judith, which means "Jewess"—although her story does not appear in the Bible—also saved her people. Nevertheless, it is striking that in this story, a woman is the key to our redemption.

A.S.: Esther is a complex figure, but basically she incarnates the Jewish people. The Jewish people is always described in the Bible as having the characteristics of a woman. Sometimes the allusion is purely mystical—for example, in the Song of Songs. But aside from mysticism, the recurrent image in the language of the Prophets is that of the bride, companion, wife of God. Marital symbolism, as found in Hosea, Isaiah, Jeremiah, and Ezekiel, is one of the most striking features of biblical prophecy. It has its roots in what the mystics would later call *Knesset Israel*, the community of Israel, the mystical unification of the source of Jewish souls, which collectively forms the interlocutor and the "wife" of the Divinity. The entire history of the world can be seen as a marital relationship, a more or less successful marriage of love (depending on the era) between God and Israel.

Esther is the main figure of this story, but not because she is a heroine. Rather, she represents the Jewish people as a whole. The Jewish people are represented as a woman, because she has two functions. The first is the function of love: This is what the world should give to God. The second is to preserve the home. Home can be a specific land or the whole world, but in any case women are always defined as "the pillar of the home."[11] She watches over the home both in daily life and on the cosmic level. In a certain way, the whole universe is feminine. It is instructed to fructify, and it must undergo suffering in order to create. This is the definition of

11. Psalms 113:9.

301

the world itself. The world is the womb of reality, the place where things are born. This dual feature of passivity and creativity characterizes Esther's attitude. At first she under-goes events and refuses to act. Then, when she does act, she changes the course of history.

The Esther Syndrome

J.E.: Esther's ambiguity prompts me to make another inter-pretation of this story. We saw that Mordecai and Haman represent the forces of Good and Evil, freedom and totalitari-anism, monotheism and atheism. Ahasuerus is neutral. This neutrality is not necessarily neutral. For many scholars, Ahasuerus also represents God, Who gives people their free will but Who is also the judge. The forces of Good and Evil, under the scrutiny of the judge, can cancel each other out, except when a fourth figure intervenes. Esther's function, the function of the Jewish people, is to tip the scales in favor of Good. The mission of Israel is to assume this responsibility.

A.S.: A time will come when the Jewish people will be called upon to determine the end of history. This is one of the lessons of the Book of Esther. Just when Esther is tempted to stay neutral, when she explains to Mordecai that she cannot go see the king without being invited, Mordecai says to her: "*If you keep silent in this crisis, relief and deliverance will come to the Jews from another place, while you and your father's house will perish.*"[12]

Every individual and every nation is familiar with the temptations of neutrality. Mordecai's message, however, is clear. If we do not act, our lives will be worth nothing. Esther

---

12. Esther 4:14.

must act, or else she is condemned to oblivion. Inevitably, we are faced with the duty to act and to decide which dangers we are ready to face.

J.E.: The issue of the responsibility of the Jewish people has become even more crucial for Jewish conscience since the founding of the State of Israel. Theologians define the responsibility of the Jewish people in terms of its specific mission for the human race. This opinion has often been defeated in modern Israel, where many hope to normalize Jewish destiny and make Israel "a people like any other."[13] Israel may be suffering from what could be called an "Esther syndrome," comparable to Esther when she tries to stay neutral and safe in the royal palace. Is Israel this Esther, or the one who, when chided by Mordecai, resolves to take all the risks and shoulder her difference?

A.S.: This is indeed the question that each Israeli must face individually and that the State must deal with collectively. You are right in stressing the fact that Esther herself was not very happy to singularize herself. She was comfortable in the royal palace, and she wanted to live a quiet, happy life as queen in the strictest neutrality. When the situation forces her to act, she does not do so willingly: Mordecai has to force her to do so. He reminds her that her own safety is illusory and that the reason she came to the throne was to save her people: "*And who knows, perhaps you have attained this royal position for just such a crisis.*"[14] This same comment is made frequently to the Jewish people today. In the past Jews could be followers. Today, "the royal role" of statehood calls for another position. The sole justification of history is to

---

13. 1 Samuel 8:5.
14. Esther 4:14.

attain the status of decision maker, and this role justifies both the past and the present. If you cannot assume this role, people will say—as Mordecai said to Esther—"*You and your family will perish,*" and history will cease to have a meaning.

J.E.: In other words, the first Esther, the one who hesitates, who is passive and hides, is the Jewish people in exile. The second Esther is modern Israel, which can freely decide upon its destiny.

A.S.: Esther did not make this decision lightly, and things are not always easy for the State of Israel. Do not forget that Esther is a young Jewish woman whom the king married and who hid her background as though she wanted to make a break with her past and her family: "*Esther did not reveal her people or her kindred.*"[15]

J.E.: You could almost say a "closet Jew." She went even further and changed her name.

A.S.: That is true. She dropped a purely Jewish name, Hadassah, for an apparently Persian name, Esther, which means "star,"[16]—a very common name in all civilizations, like Stella. The only thing she has left is a vague connection with her cousin Mordecai, but aside from that she is as anonymous as the other wives of Ahasuerus, or the 169 members of the United Nations. She tries to blend in with the others, to assimilate. Suddenly, she has to cope with a frightening decision that challenges her past, present, and future: "*You and your family will perish.*" What finally makes her decide is not only that Mordecai is Jewish but that she,

---

15. Esther 2:10.
16. *Asteros* (star) in Greek.

the queen, is, too. This decision is replete with danger because she must identify with Mordecai, and with her people, but also realize that she is directly targeted by the extermination that threatens all Jews. This is what it is to be Jewish and has been the lot of Jews throughout history, with periods of more heightened resolution, such as Esther's.

THE PSEUDONYM OF GOD

"Yet I will keep My countenance hidden on that day, because of all the evil they have done in turning to other gods . . ."[17]

This we should know: In exile, we cry, "Abraham does not know us, and Israel does not recognize us";[18] *but regarding Isaac this is not said. Indeed, the Talmud says that Isaac will redeem us.*

It is known that, in earlier generations, everything was manifest. Whatever they asked for was given to them, both in material matters and spiritual matters. They also had prophets. All this was because the attributes of "Abraham" and "Israel" were manifest in a manner that "fills the worlds." This is why they were able to see miracles and wonders like the Splitting of the Red Sea and the Exodus from Egypt. Whereas in this exile, "we see not our signs"[19]*—we cannot see the signs [of manifest Godliness]. Not because there are no signs, God forbid, but only that we cannot see the signs. Indeed, "These are [the very indications] of His awesomeness; these are His might."*[20] *"There is no longer a prophet, and none amongst us who knows until when."*[21]

This is all because "Abraham does not know us" . . . [For] when "You, God are our redeemer,"[22] *it is not possible to perceive the miracles in a revealed way.*

---

17. Deuteronomy 31:18.
18. Isaiah 63:16.
19. Psalms 74:9.
20. Babylonian Talmud, Tractate *Yoma* 69b.
21. Psalms, ibid.
22. Isaiah, ibid.

Though in truth even today, when obtaining a livelihood is most difficult, this is [a miracle] precisely like the Splitting of the Red Sea. It is only that it comes clothed within natural processes. It is for this reason that Yoḥanan the High Priest ended the practice of the "awakeners" [in the Holy Temple] who would proclaim: "Awake, why do You sleep O God?"[23] *He canceled this, since there is no need to wake Him,* "For, behold, He does not slumber or sleep";[24] *it is only that we cannot see, as per above. . . .*

This is why the miracle clothes itself in the ways of nature. So it was on Purim—the entire story of the Megillah *occurred by natural means.*

Torah Ohr 93a

Josy Eisenberg: The Book of Esther can be read on several levels. The most obvious interpretation of this story could be subtitled, "The difficulty of being Jewish and the need to want to stay so." We stressed that this interpretation has direct implications today. In Jewish thought, this particular feature is so obvious that it requires no further comment. The Sages tend to highlight the original features of this story and emphasize three points.

The first, and certainly most remarkable thing about the Book of Esther, is that the name of God never appears. This is, as one might expect, something unique in the Bible. This striking absence makes the Book of Esther the basic text for one of the fundamental themes in Jewish mysticism, the concealment of God.

Second, the Sages attribute extreme importance to the

---

23. Psalms 44:24.
24. Ibid., 121:4.

fact that Mordecai, Esther, and their contemporaries decreed a new holiday. The terms in which the Bible describes this decision—"*The Jews undertook and irrevocably obligated themselves and their descendants*"[25]—is akin to the words used to describe Israel's acceptance of the Torah: *kabbalat haTorah*, receiving and acceptance.

The Sages thus view this event as a new revelation, or at least a new covenant between Israel and God—one that was made spontaneously and with God's silence. In contrast, at Sinai this presence was overwhelming: "*They confirmed [on Purim] what they had accepted long before [at Sinai].*"[26]

We will discuss this feature as well. Purim, the holiday of liberation, bears some similarities to Pesaḥ and to Shavuot as a time of revelation. However—and this is the third idea developed by the Sages—Purim bears the most resemblance to Yom Kippur. In the Bible, this holiday is called *yom haKippurim*, literally the "day of pardons." The Sages read this as *yom ke-purim*, a day *like Purim*. The most solemn holiday and the happiest one are thus placed on the same level in a way that never ceases to astonish. I suggest we start our discussion with this mysterious connection.

Adin Steinsaltz: Kippur and Purim are like two poles in the revelation on a human scale. On the one hand, we have Kippur, a solemn day, portentous, and serious. On the other hand, we have Purim, a carnival day where we disguise ourselves, play, and sometimes drink too much. A holiday where we are forbidden to eat or drink and a holiday where it is a mitzvah to feast seem to have nothing in common.

To understand how such extremes could intersect, we first need to define how Purim fits into the other Jewish

---

25. Esther 9:27.
26. Babylonian Talmud, Tractate *Shabbat* 88a.

holidays. This holiday was created by the Jews themselves, long after the giving of the Torah, at the start of the diaspora. It symbolizes the situation of the Jews in exile.

Exile has a dual connotation in Jewish thought. First of all, it connotes men's absence from a location, since Israel had to leave its homeland. But this purely geographic feature of exile is not the most critical, for above all, exile means the absence of God. The real polarity is not possessing and being dispossessed of the Holy Land, but rather the contrast between a time and a place where God is present among His people, and a time and a place (the diaspora) where God is apparently absent. When Israel was exiled, the talmudic Sages say, the *Shekhinah*, or Divine Presence, was also exiled. "*When they were exiled in Egypt, the* Shekhinah *was with them. When they were exiled to Babylonia the* Shekhinah *was with them.*"[27] Purim heralds a new time: a dual exile. It is naturally symbolized by Esther, whose name means both "star" and "concealed."

God in Hiding

J.E.: One of the cornerstones of Jewish theology is that the Holy Land is the "land that God inhabits." Although He is everywhere in the world, the Holy Land is sacred to His Presence and the perception of His Presence. In Jerusalem, God is "visible," according to the biblical connotation of "seeing" as certainty of knowledge. When Israel received the Ten Commandments, the Israelites "saw the voices." In exile, this presence is less felt and less obvious. Jews have always felt somewhat lonely, vulnerable, or even abandoned in exile. Although God continues to perform miracles, the least we can

---

27. Babylonian Talmud, Tractate *Megillah* 29a.

say is that they are less obvious and spectacular than those of the exodus from Egypt. This is why exile is considered to be the time of God's concealment. This is not an arbitrary interpretation. Before he died, Moses warned Israel about exile, and speaking in God's name he said: "*Yet I will keep My countenance hidden on that day.*"[28] In the language of the Bible, showing one's face is synonymous with presence and grace: "*Three times a year all your males shall appear before the Sovereign the Lord.*"[29]

Hiding one's face and disappearing is a sign of disgrace, absence, and silence. When Moses says, "*My countenance will be hidden,*" he uses the term *haster astir*, which is written exactly like the name Esther. This is what enables the Sages to say that Esther was predicted in the Torah. It is written, "*And I,* haster astir, *I will hide My face.*"[30]

In other words, the name she chooses is no accident. It was chosen because she is living at the start of exile, of the time when God hides His face. Both the Hebrew etymology of the name, which means "hide," and the Greek root for the word *mystery*, clearly define a time of concealment. This explains why the name of God does not appear in the book of Esther.

A.S.: This is indeed a mystery. What does it mean that God conceals Himself? Who has disappeared? Who is hiding? No one. An anecdote helps us to understand the meaning. The grandson of a famous hasidic master was playing with a friend. Suddenly, he came crying to his grandfather. "What is wrong?" "Grandfather, I hid, but my friend didn't even look for me!" The rabbi started to laugh and said to the child: "You

---

28. Deuteronomy 31:18.
29. Exodus 23:17.
30. Babylonian Talmud, Tractate *Hullin* 139b.

see, it is exactly what God says: 'I hide, but no one comes to look for Me.'"

In other words, there are two ways of hiding. You can hide so as not to be seen or so that no one can find you, in which case you are silent. On the other hand, if you tell everyone that you are going to hide, then you are hiding for the others to find you. This is exactly what God is doing. When He says in the Torah, "Watch out, I'm going to hide," it is to tell us, "I exist even if you do not see Me, and I hide only so that you will look for Me."

This concept of a "God Who hides" differs radically from the idea of the "death of God," which has attracted so much attention in the Western world since Nietzsche. Just because I cannot "see" God, it does not mean that He does not exist. This is why the fact that God is concealed is not perceived in Judaism as basically tragic. Indeed, what do we do on Purim? We do not celebrate a revelation of God but, paradoxically, the fact that God is hiding, that He exists even though He is hiding, and perhaps because He hides. In the *Ḥabad* movement, the words to the verse "*You are indeed a God Who conceals Himself*"[31] have been put to music. This song is not melancholy at all, because it means "I am concealed, but I exist." This is the prime lesson of Purim: In the darkness, in the shadows, in concealment, even in persecution, even there I exist, I am there.

This is why the various festivities that make up the Purim celebrations are so bright and lively. In an ordinary situation where I see and hear, where I know where everything is clear, I can live calmly. But when I do not see anything, where I am in a tunnel, where I search endlessly and suddenly I discover, and I see—then, naturally, I am full of joy.

This is what happens throughout the Book of Esther. All

---

31. Isaiah 45:15.

in all, life and history are sometimes like a novel. For it to be interesting, there has to be excitement and adventures. With Esther begins the adventure of exile, a new process, a new and long era of seeking. From time to time we find what we are looking for, and then we are filled with joy. This is what Purim is about.

Miracles Are Normal

J.E.: It is true that the story of Esther unfolds like a novel full of vicissitudes. I deliberately use the word *unfold* because the scroll of Esther is read according to a specific ritual. Before reading the scroll, the reader unrolls the entire parchment, revealing the whole story. In Hebrew, the verb unroll (*GLL*) is akin to the verb reveal (*GLH*). The unfolding (or unrolling) of this story is an unveiling, which clearly indicates that there was concealment. Not only God's name is concealed in the scroll of Esther, but also His intervention.

The chapters in this story are like those in a well-designed adventure movie, suggesting that the Jews were saved because of an amazing set of special circumstances. First of all, out of all the beautiful women in the kingdom who were brought to the harem, the king chooses Esther. Then Mordecai hears about a plot to assassinate the king, he tells Esther who tells the king, and it is written into the chronicles of the kingdom that Mordecai the Jew saved the king's life. Thus, even before Haman attacks the Jews, the time bomb of deliverance is placed in a book in the heart of the king's palace. The king has to suffer from insomnia before he reads this book. What providential luck!

Then there is another piece of "luck." Haman asks the king for Mordecai's head just when the king has sent for someone to reward Mordecai for saving his life. Haman has to reward Mordecai for his devotion by walking him trium-phantly around the streets of Shushan. In short, this whole story could be interpreted as a series of lucky breaks. Esther and Mordecai, however, can read between the lines. They understand that God is pulling the strings, and that from now on miracles will be disguised in what passes for reality. God is always present but is hidden in what appears to be the natural course of events.

For the Alter Rebbe, this represents a fundamental change in Jewish history:

In exile, we cry, "Abraham does not know us, and Israel does not recognize us"; but regarding Isaac this is not said. Indeed, the Talmud says that Isaac will redeem us.

It is known that, in earlier generations, everything was manifest. Whatever they asked for was given to them, both in material matters and spiritual matters. They also had prophets. All this was because the attributes of "Abraham" and "Israel" were manifest in a manner that "fills the worlds." This is why they were able to see miracles and wonders like the Splitting of the Red Sea and the exodus from Egypt. Whereas in this exile, "we see not our signs" — we cannot see the signs [of manifest Godliness]. Not because there are no signs, God forbid, but only that we cannot see the signs. Indeed, "These are [the very indications] of His awesomeness; these are His might." "There is no longer a prophet, and none amongst us who knows until when."

This is all because "Abraham does not know us" . . . [For] when "You, God are our redeemer," it is not possible to perceive the miracles in a revealed way. Though in truth even today, when obtaining a livelihood is most difficult, this is [a miracle] precisely like the Splitting of the Red Sea. It is only that it comes clothed within natural processes. It is for this reason that Yoḥanan the High Priest ended the practice of the "awakeners" [in the Holy Temple] who would proclaim: "Awake, why do You sleep O God?" *He canceled this, since there is no need to wake Him,* "For, behold, He does not slumber or sleep"; *it is only that we cannot see, as per above.* . . .

This is why the miracle clothes itself in the ways of nature. So it was on Purim—the entire story of the Megillah *occurred by natural means.*[32]

There was a time when the Patriarchs and the Prophets vehicled the Divine Presence or the perception of the Divine in the world. This was the time of meditation and immanence. In exile there is no meditation or immanence. God has withdrawn to transcendence. But, unlike Achilles who retreats into his tent, God does not sleep. He now continues to govern the affairs of the world directly, but from higher and farther away, and thus His presence is no longer visible to the naked eye. A fundamental principle of the Kabbalah is that the stronger the Divine light, the more filters men need in order to perceive it. Divine providence is now clothed in shades of nature.

A.S.: A philosopher, who incidentally was not Jewish, said one day: *When God wants to use a pen name, he signs* "*nature.*"[33] What the Alter Rebbe is saying goes far beyond the classic view of God that is revealed in Nature.

---

32. *Torah Ohr* 93a.
33. Voltaire.

J.E.: God as the Creator: the "heavens tell the glory of God,"[34] and so on.

A.S.: Here, the Alter Rebbe goes beyond another classic idea that he himself developed. Holiness and transcendence can be incarnated in the world of matter and nature. Here he is dealing with the much vaster issue: the contrast between miracle and law. For the Alter Rebbe, a miracle destroys a law but is part of a very simple structure similar to a deus ex machina. Reality is destroyed, but then rebuilt, and once again everything falls into place.

J.E.: Making a miracle is something like dealing the cards another way. It is toying with the law, in order to make a new law immediately afterward.

A.S.: On the other hand, revelation through nature is a much more complex operation, which integrates all the components of reality without altering them. It is as though I were given the words to a paragraph and were asked to write a new text using the same words. This is why working a miracle through nature is the greatest of miracles.

Generally speaking, the Alter Rebbe always stressed what he calls "the permanent miracle of life." He constantly marvels over all these small miracles that make up reality rather than the miracles that change the law. God truly reveals Himself in these daily miracles. The greatest of all miracles, and the greatest source of wonder, is when men realize that daily life is a miracle. Creating the cherubs or the angels was easy for God, but creating a world that does not know it was created was prodigious. The real miracle is that the world lives only because God gives life to it, but God is the only One

---

34. Psalms 19:2.

that the world does not see. This is a law of nature, as it is the law of history.

What do men know and what do they remember? We remember great events in history and famous people who played a role in shaping them. We have completely forgotten the most important things in life and whom we have to thank for them. We do not remember the name of the person who invented the wheel. It is amazing. We do not know who invented the things that completely changed the history of humanity. This is why the most important, and the most amazing, thing created by God is nature. Just like all great inventions, we do not see it.

J.E.: The kabbalists have often pointed out that nature is simply the visible manifestation of the hidden presence of God. The numerical value of the letters of the name of God the Creator, *Elohim*, is 86, exactly the same as for the word *haTeva*, "nature." Does that mean that the distinction between the natural and the supernal is at times completely artificial? Both are "miracles." What differentiates them is that the natural "miracle" is permanent, whereas the supernatural "miracle" is not. In Jewish thought, the permanent is always more admirable than the accidental.

A.S.: The most ordinary and the most extraordinary: these extremes meet. This brings us back to the question you raised earlier. What do Purim and Yom Kippur have in common? What they have in common is being the extremes. On the one hand, we have Yom Kippur, the time of absolute transcendence, the most dense presence that rips through all reality, the only day of the year when the High Priest utters the sacred name of God in the Holy of Holies. On the other hand, we have Purim, a festival of natural events, with not even the slightest mention of holiness, without even the name of God being mentioned. The high and the low meet. There are only two extreme situations: one where we must take everything into account and the other, the time of forgiveness, which is above all accounts. This is why the relationship the Sages describe is not arbitrary, since absolute transcendence meets absolute immanence.

The Healing of the Snake

J.E.: On Purim we disguise ourselves. What appears to be folklore now takes on another coloration. Nature is the mask of God. It is His clothing, His cloak, His garment. Jewish mysticism uses all these terms to suggest that God puts on all sorts of disguises and masks in this world. To live is to seek out what is behind the mask.

A.S.: Even though wearing costumes on Purim is a later Jewish tradition that does not appear in the Bible, it is true that the whole story of Esther is one long disguise. This is the real key to the story. Esther does not say who she is, and neither the king nor Haman suspect that she is Jewish. The most dramatic moment in the story, its Gordian knot, is when Esther reveals herself.

The king again asked Esther at the wine feast, " What is your wish Queen Esther, it shall be granted you. And what is your request? Even to half the kingdom it shall be fulfilled." Queen Esther replied: "If your majesty will do me the favor, and if it pleases Your Majesty, let my life be granted me as my wish, and my people as my request."[35]

---

35. Esther 7:3.

Here, Esther incarnates the Jewish people even more. She is the Divine Presence, hidden in the world, whose nature we do not know.

J.E.: Until she reveals herself.

A.S.: Purim demonstrates that God is in the world not as a separate presence but as a force that acts within the world. The world moves like the fingers, each doing its job. It is a little as though the world were a puppet. Each finger plays its role. The Hand Above guides each puppet. I only see the puppet; I do not see the hand.

J.E.: In my opinion, we constantly experience the ambiguity of this absence, which is really an invisible Presence. It is easy to understand why Purim occurred when the Jews began their long march into exile. The era of prophecy had ended, and God had apparently retreated from history. Mordecai and Esther were fully able to decode the events of the day and send the Jews a message of hope: "You do not see Him any more, but God is present. Be patient; one day you will see what the Prophets promised":

For every eye[36] shall behold the Lord's return to Zion.[37]

Exile represents ambiguity, a tug-of-war between Good and Evil. Exile is a world in which man's vision is, in a sense, cross-eyed. The messianic era, the time of return, is the time when men's vision will be restored, and where the visible and the invisible God will be One.

---

36. Literally, "look into each other's eyes."
37. Isaiah 52:8.

This undoubtedly accounts for one of the strangest obligations in the Talmud: *One must drink at Purim until one cannot tell between "cursed be Haman" and "Blessed be Mordecai."*[38] This commandment is astonishing, given that the Sages could not stand drunkenness (except to say that *"wine makes man's heart light"*).[39] It is clear that we are not dealing with drinking. The inability to differentiate Good from Evil can represent amorality but also signifies the coming of the messianic era.

A.S.: This is the great revelation promised for the time of the Messiah; the time when Evil will vanish, the time when *He will destroy death forever*[40] and *The wolf shall lie with the lamb, the leopard lie down with the kid.*[41] That day, Good and Evil, the hangman and the victim, will attain such a level of harmony that we will not be able to differentiate them. The Midrash tells us that at the end of time, the snake will be cured and will become man's helpmeet. We will have come full circle. The snake is Haman.

J.E.: In Jewish thought, the snake, the source of temptation in the Garden of Eden, is the symbol of Evil. It is identified with the Evil intent as well as with death. Haman thus belongs to the world of the snake. The Sages find a subtle allusion to Haman in the story of the snake. When Adam eats the forbidden fruit, God says to him, *"Was it from the tree from which I had forbidden you to eat, that you ate?"*[42]

---

38. Babylonian Talmud, Tractate *Megillah* 7b.
39. Psalms 104:15.
40. Isaiah 15:8.
41. Isaiah 11:6.
42. Genesis 3:11.

The phrase "was it from" in Hebrew is *haMin*, which can also be read as *Haman*. Haman is connected to the source of conflict between Good and Evil. Adam will be redeemed when the snake is cured of its wickedness, ceases to be the enemy of man, and becomes his helper.

A.S.: The essence of the story is to "repair" the Evil that the snake brought into the world. This repair, *tikkun*, is even more important for the snake than for man. Naturally, man is incomplete and fragmented, and he also needs to repair himself. However, man is not basically evil. He simply needs to change a little, as Esther did. The transformation of the snake and of Evil is much more radical. The ideal is for Evil to become Good. Purim is not over until Haman stops being Haman. Haman can be eliminated, he can be hanged; but the transformation of Evil is on a higher level than its elimination. We need to reach that stage when Haman exists but is no longer Haman.

J.E.: The world of metaphysics mirrors life in society. The ideal is not the death of the sinner but rather his return to society. This mutation is the goal of creation itself. The kabbalists call it the "*transformation of darkness into light.*"[43] History is divided into two phases. In one, we need to combat Evil by destroying it. It is a violent period corresponding to the exodus from Egypt. The other is the messianic age where Evil will become Good. This is one of the Alter Rebbe's favorite topics.

. . . This is because darkness has been transformed into light, and not only that the Other Side has been sup-

---

43. *Hakdamat Sefer haZohar* 4a.

pressed so that [the forces of Evil] are nullified and conquered, as is the case in the other exiles, regarding which it is written, "Who smote the firstborn of Egypt."[44] *Rather,* "For then I will turn to the people a pure language,"[45] *and* "And many people shall go and say, Come, and let us go up to the mountain of the Lord."[46]

Now, a semblance of this was [realized] in the miracle of Purim, when Ahasuerus's heart was transformed to good. The very same mouth that said [to Haman], ". . . and the people also [is in your hands], to do with as it seems good to you,"[47] *said [to Mordecai and Esther],* "Write also for the Jews, as it seems good for you."[48] *This is the concept of "the transformation of darkness into light," and that the glory of God is revealed, specifically in the place of darkness.*[49]

The Alter Rebbe rightly points out that on Purim, when the Jews enter the night of exile, the process of transmission has already begun and has already succeeded with Ahasuerus. Things went less well with Haman. He refused to submit and had to be eliminated. At the end of days, though, his time will come. It is only at that time, an inebriating moment, that we can drink and permanently cease to differentiate Haman from Mordecai, the benediction from the malediction. Haman will have ceased to exist just as the snake, the bearer of

---

44. Psalms 135:8.
45. Zephariah 3:9.
46. Isaiah 2:3.
47. Esther 3:11.
48. Ibid., 8:8.
49. *Torah Ohr* 94b.

malediction, will no longer exist. Drinking each year at Purim is a way of saying "cheers" to this future success.

A.S.: There is a strange text in the Talmud that says, *"The descendants of Haman studied Torah at Bnei Brak."*[50]

J.E.: It is like announcing that Hitler's grandchildren had become rabbis.

A.S.: "Bettering" Evil, or making the bitter into sweet,[51] as the kabbalists say, is more powerful than destruction. This is the meaning of the feast that Esther prepares for the king and Haman. She invites Haman to "change, or cease to exist."

Victory over Destiny

J.E.: To return to our original question, the transmutation of Evil is the second great similarity between Purim and Yom Kippur. The Day of Pardon is not only the day when sins are absolved but also the day when, through *teshuvah*,[52] our sins can become merits. On both holidays, chance—this travestied Presence—plays the same role. Haman drew lots to determine the date of extermination of the Jews, and it was precisely on that day that the Jews triumphed over their enemies and instigated Purim. Similarly, at the Temple in Jerusalem, people drew lots to see which goat would become the scapegoat, designated to expiate for all the sins of Israel and to eradicate Evil. In both cases, "chance" led to the transformation of Evil.

---

50. A small town in the Land of Israel, located in a different place than the contemporary town of the same name near Tel Aviv.

51. *Hakdamat Sefer haZohar* 4a.

52. Return. See "The Head of the Year" and "The Royal Trumpets."

A.S.: On Yom Kippur, the difference between a good deed and a sin is obliterated through forgiveness. Evil vanishes, as it disappears during the feast of Purim.

J.E.: Once again, extremes meet. From a moral perspective, fasting and drinking produce the same effects.

A.S.: Purim complements Kippur as much as it resembles it. The process at Kippur is metaphysical: Forgiveness comes from Above. The process at Purim is human, and redemption comes from Below. Purim corresponds to the awakening Below. This is why it is also the time when men decide to accept the Torah. According to the Sages, Purim completes Shavuot. When the Book of Esther says, *"The Jews accordingly assumed the obligation,"*[53] the Sages interpret this as *"They accepted in Persia what they had received at Sinai."*[54] This is the dual articulation of the revelation. In the time of God, at Sinai, the movement is from Above to Below, from God to man. On Purim, in exile, men's free will aspires toward God. By promulgating Purim, the Jews of Persia reinforce the acceptance of the Law.

J.E.: It is worth pointing out that although the Israelites spontaneously accepted the Law by saying *na'ase venishma'*,[55] they could scarcely reject it. The Talmud expresses this idea by saying that God upturned the mountain like a tureen over Israel and said: *"If you accept, that is good; if not, this is going to be your grave."*[56] The Talmud then asks whether this means that because the covenant was extorted,

---

53. Esther 9:23.
54. Babylonian Talmud, Tractate *Shabbat* 88b.
55. See Shavuot, section "Seeing Voices."
56. Babylonian Talmud, Tractate *Shabbat* 88a.

it has no validity. The answer is that Purim constitutes voluntary and deliberate acceptance.

Kippur represents the highest level of the Holidays Above, as Purim is the highest of the Holidays Below. Exile and redemption are the left side, and the right side is rigor and love. They face each other. In exile these values are permutated. The holidays Above, decreed by God, are complemented by the holidays Below, decreed by men, who restore the light of the revelation to God. This is why Purim is such an important holiday, as the Sages point out in an odd statement: "*Even if all the holidays are abolished, Purim will remain.*"[57]

This parallels what is said in the Prophets: "*A time is coming when it shall no more be said 'As the Lord lives who brought the Israelites out of the land of Egypt,' but rather, 'as the Lord lives who brought the Israelites from the land of the north, and from all the lands He had driven them'; and I will bring them back to their land which I gave to their fathers.*"[58]

In other words, what will be revealed at the end of exile will be greater than the revelation in Egypt. This final redemption is announced at Purim. This event implies and proclaims that the transmutation of Evil represents such a high spiritual level that it will change the meaning of all things. To say that Purim will never be abolished is to say that at the end of days, the holidays decreed by God will only be minor events compared to the ones decreed by men: They will also have succeeded in changing reality and will have solved the enigma of the world.

---

57. Jerusalem Talmud, Tractate *Taanit* 2:5.
58. Jeremiah 16:14–15.

SEVENTH GATE

Ḥanukkah

MAN-OF-LIGHT

For a mitzvah is a lamp, and the Torah, light.

Proverbs 6:23

The soul of man is the lamp of God, Revealing all his inmost parts.

Proverbs 20:27

In reference to the verse "for a mitzvah is a lamp and the Torah, light; an instructive rebuke, a way of life" . . . *The meaning of the comparison of the mitzvah to a lamp and Torah to light is as follows: "lamp" (ner) is a reference to the oil, as in the words of our Sages "a ner of oil" "a ner of wax." Oil, on its own, possesses no light; on the contrary, it extinguishes a light that falls into it. Nevertheless, from it and via it is drawn the flame of fire that also holds the wick, in the bit of oil that is drawn through the wick; for when the oil runs out, the light is extinguished. The very same is true of the mitzvah; although it is the will of the king, without any reason and rationale, and there is no comprehension of it, nevertheless, from it and via it is drawn and revealed the light of [Divine] wisdom [Hokhmah]* . . .

The mitzvah is like a king who rules his people: he is above them and they do his will without any [comprehension of its] reason and rationale, [but] because it is the command of the king, and "one cannot investigate the heart of kings"[1] [for] an understanding of [their] commandments . . .

Nevertheless, [the fulfillment of the king's command] is analogous to grasping the king by one of his limbs and

---

1. Proverbs 25:3.

> *drawing him to oneself, in which case also the vitality within [the king's limbs] is drawn after it. Thus it is written, "and his right arm embraced me."[2] For the 248 positive commandments[3] are the 248 limbs of the king, and through the drawing down of mitzvot, the Divine Unity itself is automatically drawn down after them. . . .*
>
> *Torah Ohr, Mikketz 32b–d*

Josy Eisenberg: The cycle of the seven holidays in the Jewish calendar ends with Ḥanukkah, the Festival of Lights. Ḥanukkah was the last holiday to be proclaimed. Like Purim, it was decreed by men, not by God. Unlike Purim, which is mentioned in the Bible, Ḥanukkah is postbiblical, and its institutionalization by the Sages sets it apart from other holidays. This in no way detracts from its importance or its impact. The main holiday observance is particularly lovely,[4] and it is easy to see why Ḥanukkah is a joyous and popular festival for both children and adults.

Like Purim, Ḥanukkah commemorates a miraculous deliverance. In the year 165 B.C.E., the Jews revolted against the Syrian occupants of the Holy Land, who had tried to impose forced Hellenization upon the Jews. Spurred on by Judah Maccabee, a great leader, they overcame several Syrian armies, freed Jerusalem, and founded an independent Jew-

---

2. Song of Songs 2:6.

3. In Jewish tradition, the Torah includes 613 commandments; 365 are negative and 248 are positive. Each positive commandment is called a "limb of the King" in Jewish mysticism, since by accomplishing them the individual can "grasp" the Divine.

4. One flame is kindled on the first night; two on the second night and so on, until on the eighth night all eight flames of the *hanukkiah*, the eight-branched candelabrum, are lit. Customarily, children also light their own candelabra.

ish state. In Jerusalem they rid the Temple of Greek idols that had desecrated it and held a solemn re-dedication. According to tradition, they wished to rekindle the seven-branched lamp in the Temple at that time, but only ritually pure oil could be used. One tiny cruse of such pure oil was found, with just enough oil for one day—yet this oil burned for eight days. Hanukkah commemorates both this miracle and the miraculous military victory of a small band of insurgents, recounted in the Hanukkah liturgy:

> *You in Your great mercy stood by them in the time of their distress. . . . You delivered the strong into the hands of the weak, the many into the hands of the few, the wicked into the hands of the righteous. . . .*

Compared to other holidays, Hanukkah is unique in that it has inspired Jews regardless of degree of observance. It was the first war fought for religious freedom in our history, and for a considerable length of time this fact was stressed. Secular Jews have shown greater responsiveness to the political aspect of the military victory. Hanukkah has been used to glorify both martyrdom and resistance. As such, it was the natural reference during the pogroms and the Holocaust to those who were bowed into submission and those who struggled to resist. A great deal could be said about references to Hanukkah in the Warsaw ghetto and the concentration camps, and recent history has tragically re-actualized the debates of yesteryear on submission and revolt. It is noteworthy that in the Israeli army, men and women are sworn in either in front of the Western Wall or at Modi'in, where Judah Maccabee was born.

Despite all this, rabbinic tradition tends to emphasize the purification of the Temple and the miracle of the cruse of oil rather than the Hasmonean victories, capturing the notion of a tiny flame, which should have burned out and which survived far beyond its physical capacities. What a fitting description of the fate of Israel! Thus, the Sages primarily viewed Hanukkah as a wellspring of symbols, since in Judaism, as in other religions, light plays a major role in symbolism and mysticism.

The Alter Rebbe contributes to this vast literature on light as the symbol of spirituality, by focusing on two of its most classic features: light as the image of the soul, and light as the image of the Torah. This chapter examines his original views on these two topics.

The Alter Rebbe deals primarily with two verses from the Book of Proverbs. The first sets down relationships between the law and the commandments: "*For the mitzvah is a lamp, and the Torah, light.*"[5] The other verse compares the soul to a lamp: "*The soul of man is the lamp of God.*"[6] The word *ner* (lamp) designates both soul and mitzvah. This parallel needs to be clarified. First of all, however, we need to explain why light is so full of symbolic meanings in Jewish thought.

Adin Steinsaltz: Remember that light is one of the first phenomena a human being is aware of. The newborn first discovers light.

J.E.: Birth is often said to be "seeing the light of day."

A.S.: As the infant develops, his ability to discriminate light increases. In fact, the infant almost immediately needs to cope with one of the major problems in physics—namely, the existence of an element that plays a fundamental role in our

---

5. Proverbs 6:23; a mitzvah is a commandment.
6. Proverbs 20:27.

lives but that, apparently, is not concrete. In general, though, we seek out symbols that are easy to understand. Everything about light is simple, because it is real and symbolic at the same time. It is both immateriality and materiality. Because of its extreme simplicity, it is a symbol par excellence. Light is characterized by its duality. It lies midway between the material and the spiritual, and forms the most basic and natural tie that binds them.

The strength of this symbol comes not only from the fact that man feels a natural attraction to light, but also because light straddles two universes. Incidentally, in modern science, light plays this same fundamental role. It is the most stable indicator of the existence of the world. In a universe governed by relativity, the speed of light is the sole constant. There is even a theory that claims that light is not an accidental phenomenon but rather the universal yardstick. This helps to show why in Judaism light symbolizes so many things—most of which, however, are desirable, such as the Revelation, Creation, the soul, the Torah, the messianic era, and the World to Come, which is called the "day when all will be light."[7]

Light, Lights

J.E.: Light is an object and the means of vision. Light can be seen. I identify light and differentiate it from darkness. The newborn, opening his or her eyes, mentally reenacts the first gesture of Creation: "*God saw that the light was good; and God separated the light from the darkness.*"[8] The second function of light, as an enabler of vision, allows us to discover

7. Midrash on Proverbs 1.
8. Genesis 1:6.

the world around us, to differentiate shapes, colors, objects; in short, it represents the intellectual and communicative function of vision. The Book of Job contains a remarkable description of light. When there is light, "*it changes like clay under the seal till [its hues] are fixed like those of a garment.*"[9] Without light, the world is a lump of clay, and things are meaningless. Light alone enables us to understand them. The world around us is, in a sense, born of light and emerges in the light of day.

A.S.: Everything is born of light, and it would be more accurate to say that everything we see is only a category of light. In other words, we do not see things; we see their light. This is also true for the foremost symbol of light in Jewish mysticism: the Infinite Light, *Or En Sof.* We cannot know the *En Sof,* the Infinite, but only what emanates from it, its light, *Or En Sof,* which is both the principle and the essence of all reality. Just as we can perceive only the light of the physical world, we cannot know the Infinite God, only His emanation.

J.E.: In fact, the light of the Infinite, which is also infinite light, is the matter and the means through which God reveals Himself. Traditionally, the two types of revelation emanate from God: nature and Torah. I can know God by contemplating His works, and I can know Him by studying His words. It is striking that the world was created by ten utterances, and the Torah was revealed by ten commandments.[10] The world is external light, or external reality, and the Torah is internal reality, the meaning and the structure of things. This explains the statement "*The mitzvah is a lamp and the Torah, light.*"

---

9. Job 38:14.

10. See Armand Abecassis and Josy Eisenberg, *A Bible Ouverte*, (Albin Michel, 1980), pp. 55–61.

Nevertheless, the verse makes a clear distinction between Torah and mitzvah, between the Divine word in the general sense, and the commandments. This distinction has become a classic one in Jewish thought. People often speak of doing *Torah u-mitzvot,* study and its applications. Here the Bible appears to refer to two types of light: light in general (the Torah) and light in particular (the mitzvah). The word *ner,* which we translated as "lamp," also means light in the sense of flame. We could translate it as "*The mitzvah is flame and the Torah, light.*"

A.S.: Although they are very similar, there are nevertheless several appreciable differences between the Torah—"light"— and the mitzvah, the "lamp" or the "flame." The Torah is permanent. You can turn off a lamp or a flame, but you cannot turn off light. The existence of a mitzvah is man's doing. Someone can choose to "light" or not "light" a mitzvah. In contrast, the existence of the Torah does not depend on anyone. One of the main themes in Jewish mysticism is that there was a primordial light, the light of *En Sof,* through which one could see from one end of the universe to the other. This is the light. This light was too strong for men, and the Sages tell us that "*God hid the light and concealed it for the righteous in the end of days.*"[11] This is why we receive partial light, the light of the sun and the moon, and not total light. "Where did God hide this light?" asked the founder of Hasidism, the Ba'al Shem Tov, and answered: "In the Torah!"

J.E.: The similarity in pronunciation between the word *torah* and the word *orah,* one of the Hebrew words for "light," has been amply commented upon.

---

11. Babylonian Talmud, Tractate *Ḥagigah* 12a.

A.S.: This is why anyone who perceives the essence of the Torah perceives the total light of the Infinite. This is the basic difference between the Torah and the mitzvah. The Torah reflects the infinite light, whereas the mitzvah sheds light on a specific individual in a specific situation. In this sense, the mitzvah has an advantage over the Torah, in that the Torah is like the Aurora Borealis. It is beautiful but a little distant. A mitzvah, on the other hand, is close to men. It is a lamp that I can hold and move. The latter part of the verse compares the soul to a lamp and shows that the lamp helps us to see the details better: *"The soul of man is the lamp of God, revealing all his inmost parts."*[12] I can see all the nooks and crannies with a lamp.

The "flame" (the other meaning of *ner*) differs in yet another way from light. There is more than light to a flame. A flame is also fire—or, in other words, heat and energy. This is why fire is used for referring to God, Who is called the "consuming fire,"[13] as well as to the angels and the altar. The fire of the mitzvah is that small flame connected to the consuming fire of God. Like fire, the mitzvah acts upon things. The light enables us to see; fire transforms things. This is the function of the mitzvah, to change the world by illuminating it.

J.E.: Divine light is revealed in the world below in the Torah and in the mitzvot. These two forms of light correspond to the two functions you defined earlier, namely, shedding light (which is more the function of the Torah) and transforming (which is more the function of the mitzvot). These two functions also correspond to the respective functions of light and fire. Knowledge and action are the two extremes of existence. Interestingly enough, the Alter Rebbe called his first com-

---

12. Proverbs 20:27.
13. Deuteronomy 9:3.

mentary on the Torah *Torah Ohr*, "Torah Light," drawing the title specifically from the verse that is the basis for his commentary on light: "*For the mitzvah is a lamp/flame and [Torah Ohr] the Torah is a light.*"[14]

Nevertheless the many commentaries he wrote on this verse place greater emphasis on "flame" than on "light." What most captured his attention was the fact that *ner* ("flame" and "lamp") designates both the mitzvah and the soul. He attempted to clarify the symbolism of the lamp and its components, and gives several interpretations of this symbolism by focusing alternatively on the oil or on the wick.

We will start with two key texts by the Alter Rebbe:

The meaning of the comparison of the mitzvah to a lamp and Torah to light is as follows: "Lamp" (ner) is a reference to the oil, as in the words of our Sages "a ner of oil, "a ner of wax." Oil, on its own, possesses no light; on the contrary, it extinguishes a light that falls into it. Nevertheless, from it and via it is drawn the flame of fire that takes hold of the wick, in the bit of oil that is drawn through the wick; for when the oil runs out, the light is extinguished. The very same is true of the mitzvah: although it is the will of the King, without any reason and rationale, and there is no comprehension of it, nevertheless, from it and via it is drawn and revealed the light of [Divine] wisdom (Ḥokhmah).[15]

The lamp includes oil, the wick, and two hues of flame: the dark flame that is [directly] above the wick, and the bright flame. The flame, which is the main component of the lamp, adheres specifically to the wick; the oil, on the other hand, cannot hold the flame on its own, only by

---

14. Proverbs 6:23.
15. *Torah Ohr, Mikketz* 33b.

*means of the wick. Nevertheless, it is the oil that the
flame consumes, while a single wick can facilitate the
consumption of much oil.*

*Likewise, the deeds of the mitzvot in this world are the
"oil," as the Zohar states [in the name of] "the child" in
[parshat] Balak—the "holy anointing oil" whose source is
in the Supernal Wisdom (Hokhmah illa'ah) and the Supernal Will (ratzon ha'elyon).*[16] *But because it has evolved
and descended to the physicality of this world, there is no
way for the infinite light of the Blessed One to take hold
in it save via the medium of the "wick," which is the
Godly soul that observes mitzvot, and thereby draws into
them a revelation of the infinite light of the Blessed
One. . . . This is by the means of the soul's* bittul
*(self-abnegation) to God. Thus the [soul] is analogous to
the wick that holds the flame, this being through the said*
bittul, *which is not in the oil. For the soul is spiritual, and
therefore possessive of this* bittul, *which is not the case
with the deeds of the mitzvot, which are physical, and
are thus analogous to the oil that is consumed by the
flame [only via the wick]. By the means of a single wick,
much oil is consumed, for a single soul fulfills and does an
immeasurably great number of mitzvot in the course of
its lifetime. The bright light [in the flame] stems from the
oil . . . and the dark light from the wick . . . since the
wick is the Godly soul as it is clothed in the animal soul.*[17]

A.S.: The basic idea is very clear. A lamp is made up of
several parts. The utensil that holds these various parts
together, which unites them and enables them to work, is the
lamp, which stands for the body.

---

16. The *sefirah* of Hokhmah (Wisdom) is the second of the ten
emanations through which the Infinite gave birth to the finite world.
17. *Torah Ohr, Mikketz* 33b–c.

J.E.: A lamp, like the body, is physical and opaque. In olden times, lamps were made of clay, a fitting reference to the body. There is a beautiful line where men are called *"Those who inhabit houses of clay."*[18]

A.S.: Then there is the oil, the wick, and finally the flame. The wick is crucial because it transforms the oil into flame. If we assume that the wick stands for the soul and that the oil is our material existence, it is easy to grasp the true function of the soul. The soul is the chain drive connecting the oil and the flame. Here, the soul is not considered to be a pure and transcendent essence but rather the soul within man, incarnated in the individual, a wick without which nothing can take place.

J.E.: A wick floating in oil.

A.S.: Yes, but which oil?

J.E.: We could give a very mundane interpretation and say that the wick is life, and the oil is the energy, calories, or gas that life needs to burn in order to survive. But we are not dealing with bodily existence here.

A.S.: We are dealing with the life of the soul, which, like the body, needs "fuel." This fuel is the oil from Above, the mitzvah. I said earlier that light and fire are both material and immaterial. Burning oil to obtain a flame is initiating the process that transforms the material into the immaterial, immanence into transcendence. Oil is a storehouse of energy that must be released to produce fire. To do so, however, we need the intermediary of the wick.

---

18. Job 4:19.

The Mark of the Commandments

J.E.: In other words, the Alter Rebbe is suggesting a very complete definition of life. This definition is founded on a postulate and on an observation that is one of the leitmotifs of his work. The postulate is that man was created to carry out God's commandments. I say "carry out" rather than observe. Through the commandments, Divine Will is accomplished. Our actions take on their true meaning in this way, not through the observance of certain rules. This theory is crucial to demystify a misconception about Judaism and religion in general, which assumes that religion is simply a matter of discipline and ethics. The postulate is that we need to learn how to transform the oil into flame, and this is why God gave us the wick (the soul), which is capable of choosing a course of action.

The Alter Rebbe's observation is that this action—more specifically, the 613 commandments in the Bible, and in particular the 248 positive commandments[19]—must be carried out in the physical world in a material way. This is true for rituals, such as the phylacteries made of cowhide, or the "four kinds" taken on Sukkot, which are plants and fruits, and for deeds that are connected to interpersonal ethics. Charity, for example, requires making a gesture, which in turn requires a certain attitude regarding the use of material wealth.

---

19. According to tradition, the Bible contains 613 commandments: 365 negative ones and 248 positive ones. The negative commandments, what one should not do, form a specific category of spirituality: They are there to *preserve*. In contrast, the positive commandments are meant to be carried out and are courses of action and human *doings*. These two categories of commandments were handed down to Adam, because it is said that God put him in the Garden of Eden to "*cultivate it and to guard it*" (Genesis 2:15).

Thus, oil represents matter; not in the sense of pure matter as contrasted with pure spirit, but on the contrary: matter containing or capturing the spirit. This view, so akin to the weltanschauung of Judaism that everything is material and spiritual at the same time, is captured by the symbolism of the oil and the commandments. In fact, the Alter Rebbe goes so far as to state that the commandments in themselves are as opaque as inert oil. They are the expression of the will of God, which is formulated in the Torah without being explained or justified: without light. If the human soul, the wick, knows how to burn the oil, it can draw out the pith of the Divine light.

This explains the verse, "Sing and rejoice O daughter of Zion."[20] In galut *(exile) the Community of Israel[21] is called the "daughter of Zion." The concept of Zion will be understood by first explaining the verse, "The Lord shall reign forever, Your God O Zion for all generations; praise the Lord."[22] The meaning of this is that in order that the sovereignty of God should extend "to the world"—the aspect of space—and "for all generations"—the aspect of time—this is achieved by the aspect of "Zion."*

It is written: ["Let Us make man in] Our image and Our likeness,"[23] *this being the 248 commandments, the 248 limbs of the King. Namely, the spirituality of the mitzvot and the spirituality of the Torah as they are above, within*

---

20. Zachariah 2:14. This is the beginning of the text in which the Prophet sees a "lamp stand of gold"; this text is one of the main sources used by the Alter Rebbe in his study of light.

21. The heavenly, ideal Israel made up of all Jewish souls.

22. Psalms 146:10. The etymological root of the word *Zion* means "mark," or "sign."

23. Genesis 1:26.

the infinite light of the Blessed One, where these are verily "in Our image." But as for the physicality of the mitzvot, as they have been enclothed in physical ele-ments—tzitzit[24] of wool, tefillin[25] [inscribed] on parch-ment—they are only a ziyyun, a mark,[26] as in the phrase Zion hametzuyenet[27] ("distinguished Zion"), meaning that the physical mitzvot signify the spiritual element, since in them and via them is drawn down the spiritual infinite light of the Blessed One. For example, the woolen tallit *and tzitzit [represent the Divine attribute referred to in the verse] "He dons light as a garment."[28] And so with all the mitzvot. The same is true regarding the Torah: through the physical study of the Torah, as it has been enclothed in physical subjects, one draws down the supernal, spiritual light of Torah, which speaks of spiritual matters. Thus the physical Torah and mitzvot are signs and markers of the spiritual element.[29]*

A.S.: In a famous work of kabbalistic commentary, the *Sefer Ḥasidim,*[30] each organ and limb is associated with the 613 commandments of the Torah. Each commandment thus corresponds to a specific part of the body. Man is an array of lights, and each mitzvah gives off its own small light. Our

---

24. Fringes of the prayer shawl or *tallit.*
25. Phylacteries.
26. *Ziyyun* (spelled in Hebrew exactly like the word *Zion*) some-times means "a milestone"; and this definition, which is found in the Bible, is the one the Alter Rebbe refers to here. We could translate it as a *milestone that marks.*
27. Prayer for Hosha'na Rabba, based on Psalms 87:2, and the Babylonian Talmud, Tractate *Berakhot* 8a.
28. Psalms 104:2.
29. *Torah Ohr, Mikketz* 37b–c.
30. "The Book of the Devout."

lives consist of lighting one light here, one light there, and all these lights together make up a human being, the ideal image of the person, as though man were merely a brace, or a stand, for the 613 lights.

J.E.: The soul, whose function is to make the light that is implicit within the oil emerge, is the "wick" of the Divine.

A.S.: That is man's role. Jewish tradition has two etymologies for the word *adam*, "man." The first defines his physical existence, and in this case the three letters of the word, aleph, dalet, and mem,[31] stand for *efer* ("ashes"), *dam* ("blood"), and *marah* ("bile").

J.E.: Man is often described in the Talmud as a being of "flesh and blood."

A.S.: The second definition derives the word *adam* from the phrase *"edame la'elyon,"*[32] "I resemble the Supernal One." Man is in God's image, as was written at the time of Creation: *"And God created man in His image; in the image of God He created him."*[33]

The word *image* should be taken seriously. According to the laws of optics, when a broad ray of light goes through a small aperture, it nevertheless preserves the shape of its luminous source. Similarly, Divine light travels through the universe, is reflected through this tiny slit, and remains, on a

---

31. Because biblical Hebrew writing only uses consonants, the word *adam* has three letters in Hebrew, although it has four in English.
32. Isaiah 14:14.
33. Genesis 1:27.

human scale, Divine light. The function of a mitzvah is thus to "reflect" God in the physical reality of this world; by lighting the lights of the mitzvah, man reveals on earth the infinite light in all things and restitutes the image Above.

J.E.: In other words, physical life is metaphysical in essence. The Alter Rebbe develops a very complex view of anthropology, which involves other topics we will deal with later. At this stage, what you have to say about the metaphysical nature of light explains the role, importance, and context of the festival of Ḥanukkah. The Sages have always contended that the struggle of the Hasmoneans, the defenders of pure monotheism against the Syrian invaders and Greek culture, epitomized more than the classic struggle for freedom and independence. It is said in the Talmud that the Greeks had "defiled all the oils." Further, King Antiochus Epiphanes ordered that a statue of Zeus be put in the Temple in Jerusalem. Thus, the real battle was ideological and could have remained on the level of philosophical debate, had there not been a war. One ideology championed a purely rationalistic and materialistic view of the universe. Our world, says Plato, is a dark cave, all matter is dark, and oil is nothing more than oil. The other believes that oil captures the secret of the luminosity of the world, its ultimate transparency.

A.S.: Ḥanukkah is above all a religious war; there have been others since then, but this one was the first. Everything revolves around light and darkness. The little cruse of holy oil that was used to rekindle the lamp stand of the Temple was hidden and hard to find. The challenge our ancestors faced was to reveal the light. We relive this need and this lesson every year on Ḥanukkah, by lighting an additional light each evening for the eight days of the holiday.

J.E.: On his deathbed, Goethe said: "*Mehr licht*" "(more light"). Did he mean he should have lived with more light, or that he was finally about to receive more light as he entered the next world? I tend to favor the second interpretation. This relationship between light and the world beyond is the focus of the next chapter.

THE GARMENTS OF LIGHT

The mitzvot are garments through which the soul is able to comprehend and enjoy the [Divine] pleasure and effulgence in the Garden of Eden. The mitzvah is like a garment, in that just as the garment does not enter into the person to become his inner vitality, like food which becomes literally one with the person and vitalizes him, . . . [but rather encompasses the person and shields and protects him,] in the same way, the mitzvot are rooted in the level of makifim,[34] [the Divine light that "encompasses all the worlds," which is why their revelation below in this world] does not come in a manner of inner unity, only in physical deed. . . . But through the doing of mitzvot is created a makif ("encircler") and "screen," so that via the mitzvot [the soul] can enjoy the pleasure in the light of the Infinite. This is the purpose of the soul's descent [to earth], "a descent for the purpose of ascent" . . .

Because the mitzvot are rooted in the gulgalta ("skull"), when the soul clothes itself in garments of mitzvah it enjoys the pleasure of the light of the Infinite.
Maamarei Admor HaZaken, Hanaḥot HaRaP, p. 124

Josy Eisenberg: The fundamental feature of the flame as a symbol is its dual capacity to shed light and to transform. This symbolism is captured in the three elements we discussed earlier—namely, the oil, the wick, and the flame—which for the Alter Rebbe also correspond to commandment, soul, and Torah. The first approach to this symbolism is

---

34. The general structures of being. This term was discussed in the section entitled "The State of Grace."

straightforward. The commandments are connected to this world. They apply to finite times, places, and things. This is their "definition." Where, when, and how should the law be applied? The main concern of the talmudic Sages was to find responses to these questions.

The Torah, on the other hand, comes from the Infinite, from the infinite light of the *En Sof*, or Divine infinite. The soul does not perceive it; it only perceives its rays. The entire universe is nothing other than the light that comes from the *En Sof* and that the *En Sof* caused to extend so that men would know it. It is the garment of the Infinite. I cannot know the essence of the king; but I can recognize his functions through his crown or his purple vestments. Similarly, it is written that God is "*wrapped in a robe of light.*"[35]

Light is the first emanation of God, and so is the Torah. We can say that Torah and light are entirely synonymous. This is the meaning of the verse "*The mitzvah is a lamp and the Torah, light,*"[36] which is the pivot of the Alter Rebbe's thesis. What Torah and what light are we talking about? The kabbalists provide a dual interpretation. They distinguish the Torah Above, which is infinite and invisible light, from the Torah Below, which is finite and visible light. In other words, what men define as "Torah" is only the tip of the Divine iceberg. The biblical text is the projection, into our world, of the infinite Torah, just as the light we perceive is only a finite part of the spectrum of the infinite light that forms the true matter of the universe. Einstein was not far off the mark.

The Torah Below, with its 613 commandments, is hence the earthly reflection of the Torah Above. By lighting the 613 mitzvot one after the other, man creates the physical conditions for Divine light to be present in the physical world. This

---

35. Psalms 104:2.
36. Proverbs 6:23.

is the meaning of man's existence. He alone can perform this operation, because it stems from both the infinite and the finite. This is why the soul, the wick, acts as the mediator between the oil and the light.

> *Likewise, the deeds of the mitzvot in this world are the "oil," as the* Zohar *states [in the name of] "the child" in [parshat]* Balak — *the "holy anointing oil" whose source is in the Supernal Wisdom (ḥokhmah illa'ah) and the Supernal Will (ratzon ha'elyon). But because it has evolved and descended to the physicality of this world, there is no way for the infinite light of the Blessed One to take hold in it, save via the medium of the "wick," which is the Godly soul that observes mitzvot and thereby draws into them a revelation of the infinite light of the Blessed One.*[37]

Adin Steinsaltz: Man's duty is to make light. This is why the individual is a combination of the elements that make up a lamp. Just as the body needs calories, the soul needs energy to subsist. This is provided by the "oil" of the commandments. The Sages often talk about the three liquids that are necessary to life. These are water, the basic element without which we cannot survive; wine, which brings joy; and oil, which gives off light and heat.

J.E.: I have always been struck by another triplet that is similar to the one you just mentioned—wheat, wine, and oil. These are the three gifts that Moses and the Prophets refer to so often. Three times daily in the portion of the *Shema'* we repeat this promise:

---

37. *Torah Ohr,* Genesis 33c.

And if you will diligently obey my commands which I give you today, to love the Lord your God and to serve Him with all your heart and with all your soul, I will give rain for your land at the right season . . . that you may gather in your grain, your wine, and your oil.[38]

To reinforce what you said, these three gifts are dependent on rain. When Hosea chastises Israel for having forgotten God, he refers to these three gifts: "And she did not consider this: it was I who bestowed on her the new grain and wine and oil."[39]

In his many commentaries on Ḥanukkah, the Alter Rebbe develops the following argument. In the Jewish calendar there are three festivals that commemorate a deliverance. Pesaḥ, which commemorates the exodus from Egypt; Purim, which celebrates the preservation of the Jews of Persia; and Ḥanukkah. The three observances we are instructed to perform during these holidays are to eat matzah on Pesaḥ, drink wine on Purim, and light the oil of the lampstand on Ḥanukkah. The first two deal with the body and the third with the spirit. Grain, wine, and oil are all represented. Furthermore, they are in an order that reflects the basic needs of life, and they end with the feast of lights, which is seen as the ultimate stage of revelation.

Bittersweet

A.S.: The Alter Rebbe devotes a great deal of commentary to the fact that oil as a vehicle of fire has enormous advantages

---

38. Deuteronomy 11:13–14.
39. Hosea 2:10.

over grain and wine, in that it can transmit without losing its substance. The more I share my grain and wine, the less I have. In contrast, a flame can be used to light a thousand other flames, and a soul can kindle a thousand others.

J.E.: The Torah and the commandments are sometimes called "food for the soul." They serve a dual function of consumption and communication, and it is natural that their nobler feature is communication—or, in other words, revelation.

A.S.: Like oil, the mitzvah nourishes our existence, and it is often called "food for the soul."

In this case, however, we are dealing with much more than "spiritual nourishment." The mitzvah is Divine. It reveals God's will, and in addition we can say that God reveals Himself in the mitzvah. Mitzvot are sometimes called the "emmissaries of God." An "emmissary" (*shaliah*) is, in a certain sense, the very equivalent of the person he represents. In this sense, the mitzvah represents Divine Presence in the world. This presence is concealed in the oil. It is up to man to penetrate this physical envelope and release the light.

J.E.: Recall that a mitzvah is compared to a lamp and to the soul. In other words, there is a profound similarity between them. It is as though God needed the oil in order to hide and to be clothed but also needed the lamp in order to be revealed.

We have yet to deal with one other contrasting pair related to concealment-revelation; namely, to burn oil is also to destroy it. This is why the Alter Rebbe suggests a second symbolism for oil and the flame whereby oil, which is on the level of matter, no longer represents the mitzvah, but rather materialism, sensuality, and the various pleasures of life. The dimension of revelation of the spirituality imprisoned in matter is now linked to asceticism and elevation. Carrying out the commandments becomes a form of catharsis. The mitzvah is a crucible in which we separate the slag from the pure metal of Divine love. The slag falls and disappears and, like fire, the love freed of the fetters and seduction of materiality can rise up to God.

Now when a person contemplates and understands all this, his soul will dissolve and yearn to nullify itself to God, to the extent that it will desire to divest itself from the pleasures of this world, to completely transform its heart and cleave to Him. In the Zohar[40] it is said: "He who does not taste bitterness as sweetness and transform darkness into light, has no portion here."

"Bitterness" is the lusts of this world and the pleasures that derive from the halls of kelipah.[41] For there is nothing [on earth] below that does not have a corresponding "chamber" above,[42] from which the thing and its effects derive. All the material pleasures, even the most trivial thing, even curling one's hair—the vitality of the thing derives from the chambers of impurity. This is why Joseph was punished, and sat twelve years in prison, because he curled his hair. One must transform his heart to taste [this bitterness] as true sweetness— "taste and see that God is good;"[43] "Then you shall delight yourself in the Lord."[44]

---

40. *Zohar* 1:4, 1.
41. *Kelipah,* "shell" or "husk."
42. *Kelipah* is the symbol of Evil; in the World Above, there are sources, or chambers, for Evil that are the counterparts of those where the idea of Good is nourished. Without these supernal "chambers," Evil would not have reality or consistency.
43. Psalms 34:9.
44. Isaiah 58:14.

This was the concept of the korbanot—*that the fat of the animal soul is transformed and ascends to be included within the supernal flame. This should be the function of prayer, which comes in place of the* korbanot: *to inflame one's soul in the supernal fire and experience delight in God.*

The concept of "transforming darkness into light" is that the material darkness of this world—the terrestrial and celestial creation which presents itself as a being and a physical thing—should be transformed into light, so that should be revealed in it the infinite light of the Blessed One, so that its "beingness" should be nullified to the Blessed One, "and the glory of God should be manifest"[45] below as it is above.

This is to say that through "tasting bitterness as sweetness," which is [man's effort] from the below upward to transform his heart and lusts of this world into a craving and thirst to cleave to God, one causes the light of God to shine from above downward into the place of darkness, so that the world should not conceal[46] the light and holiness of God.

This is also the concept of "mitzvah is a lamp and Torah is light." The lamp of the mitzvah is the elevation from below upwards, and Torah as light is the drawing down, from above downward. Through "mitzvah is a lamp," "Torah is light" is attained.[47]

J.E.: This text on the symbolism of the oil and the flame highlights one of the Alter Rebbe's key ideas: the transmuta-

---

45. Isaiah 40:5.
46. The word *'olam*—"world"—also means "concealment."
47. *Torah Ohr, Mikketz* 42a.

tion of living matter. From this standpoint, Ḥanukkah transmits the same message as Purim. Changing Evil into Good is expressed in a series of metaphors that the Alter Rebbe liked to refer to, such as the transformation of bitterness into sweetness or the transition from darkness to light. Oil is bitter to the taste and thus represents, first of all, the shallowness of earthly pleasures. By refining the oil, we obtain the source of all pleasures. This is the true purpose of a mitzvah, which goes far beyond its various functions and motivations—including morals—that are generally assigned to it. The mitzvah establishes a specific connection between the physical and the metaphysical, and elevates the world toward God.

Clothe the Naked

A.S.: In the Tabernacle in the desert, and later in the Temple in Jerusalem, the golden lamp stand was destined, according to the biblical phrase, to "burn from evening to morning before the Lord."[48] Fire and light have always symbolized the desire for elevation and a return to the supreme source that in Jewish thought is inscribed, and sometimes buried, in the world and in the individual.

J.E.: The Sages often refer to the "fire of love" that King Solomon called "*darts of fire, a blazing flame.*"[49]

A.S.: Fire consumes things, but with the purpose of transforming them. By transforming them, it elevates them. In fact, this transformation of the physical world through the

---

48. Exodus 27:20.
49. Song of Songs 8:6.

love of God, through His instrument the mitzvah, is on the order of reconstitution or restitution rather than change. To elevate things is to bring them back to their true nature, and to reinstate their true identity. What we said about exile[50] is also true for the oil that bears light. To fulfill a mitzvah, to transform oil into light, is to accomplish for the world something similar to the work of a psychoanalyst. You take a man or a thing and tell them: "You have forgotten who you are and where you come from." Our true vocation as men is to free the world of its complex by creating change and to upset the laws of a static world by transforming things through the fire of the mitzvah.

J.E.: Everything we have said so far about the symbols of light and flame, which shed light, change it, bring it back to its true source, purify it, and so forth, have focused on the world. To the extent that they account for what we need to accomplish in this world, they are basic concepts in Jewish anthropology. Paradoxically, though, this anthropology is not really anthropocentric. In other words, the various types of symbols for the oil lamp, which we have talked about, do not imply that man is the crucial entity. In the oil-wick-flame triplet, man-wick plays the role of a mediator or instrument. He is merely a drive belt, an amplifier that is needed but whose action—making the oil luminous—is only designed to redeem matter, draw the sweet from the bitter, and transform the opaqueness of the world into an infinite luminosity. This is an enormous undertaking, and aside from the satisfaction of having a deed well done and being God's Brave Soldier Schweik on earth, what rewards does the soul get from this?

The Alter Rebbe's basic postulate is that the soul de-

---

50. See the section "The Passage through Exile."

scends to earth so as to ascend higher than before its incarnation. This is captured in the phrase *Yeridah tzorekh 'aliyah,* "a descent for the sake of ascent," so often cited in his works. This leads to a second interpretation of a mitzvah. Beyond elevating and transforming the world, the mitzvah elevates and transforms the soul. The real originality of the Alter Rebbe's thought lies in this interpretation.

A.S.: It is true that we have only dealt with man as the agent of the mitzvah. The soul is incarnated in an individual who has been assigned a mission here below. Yet this incarnation has an additional function of maturation. The soul must go through a form of initiation rite. The function of life is to assist the soul in becoming adult. There is a kind of reciprocity. From above to below, the soul enables Divine light to illuminate the world by kindling the flame of the mitzvot, and in this way it serves the world. In return, life on earth enables the soul to develop, and here it uses the world. The mitzvot that we carry out, the various duties we accomplish, and the obstacles we encounter are the phases of the maturation of the soul.

J.E.: What is the "maturation of the soul"?

A.S.: The soul needs to solve the problem of distance. There is a chasm between the created and the Creator. Souls are called the "children of God," and it is God's wish that his children establish a means of communication with Him. Communication can only take place by using the ladder that God built for this purpose. A very old commentary shows that the numerical value of the word *Sinai* is the same as the word *sulam,* "ladder." This ladder is used in both directions to descend from the World Above and to ascend from the World Below.

J.E.: This is the meaning of Jacob's dream and the famous ladder he sees in his dream, where the "*angels of God were going up and down on it.*"[51] Traditionally, this ladder is said to represent prayer, which rises to God from the world of men and whose effects, the responses, descend. Saying that Sinai, the source of the Torah, is also a ladder demonstrates that there is a whole series of means of communication between God and man, which are all revealed and which proceed from the World Above. These forms of communication are prayer (note that the word *prayer* in Hebrew—*tefillah*—is the anagram of the word *petillah*, or "wick"), the Torah, and finally, the commandments.

A.S.: These ladders are like bridges made by God over the chasm of the Infinite. Another image we can use is that of a man gripping a mountainside. To reach the top, someone has to give him a hand. This is the function of the mitzvah. There is a well-known hasidic interpretation that derives the word *mitzvah* from *tsavta*, which means "being together." A mitzvah is the special place where the Divine and the human cohabit; it is the instrument that enables me to reach God.

This reverses the perspective. Man is no longer the recipient or the wick; rather, he becomes the contents. When King Solomon says that "the soul of man is the lamp of God,"[52] he means that the soul is a flame, and this is why it needs to be clothed in the commandments and the oil of the Torah.

The soul is referred to as the "wick" particularly when it is enclothed in the body; then it is a "wick" in relation to the mitzvot, which are the "oil," to imply that the light can take hold only in the wick. For as they descend to earth,

---

51. Genesis 28:12.
52. Proverbs 20:7.

354

the soul is spiritual and the mitzvah is physical. This, however, is not the case in their upward ascent to Gan Eden *(the Garden of Eden). There, the reverse is the case: the infinite light [of God] is revealed to the soul via the garments created from the observance of the mitzvot. Consequently, there the mitzvot are the "wick" and the soul is the "oil" that is consumed in the infinite light of the Blessed One by means of the "wick."*

This being the case—that the soul is a "wick" only because of its investment in the animal soul[53]—it is the soul that produces the dark flame . . . [while] the deed of the mitzvah produces the bright flame, which is the joy of mitzvah.

So the soul is referred to as ner, *and the mitzvah is also called* ner; *[the latter] in reference to [when] the soul is the "wick" element (i.e., when it is enclothed within the animal soul) and the mitzvot are the "oil," producing two aspects of light, as it is written, "Ve'ahavta" ("and you shall love")[54] which is twice the numerical value of* ohr *("light").*

When a lamp is lit, there first rises the [portion of the] flame that encircles the wick, which is the dark flame, following which the bright flame is drawn forth and revealed. Similarly, there must first be an upward striving on the level of "with all your might,"[55] following which "a spirit brings a spirit and draws down a spirit"[56]—the

---

53. In Hasidism, two "souls" cohabit in all men: the Divine soul, seeking out spirituality and attracted upward; and the animal soul, or all the functions and pleasures, both physical and mental, that attract men to the world below.
54. Deuteronomy 6:5.
55. Ibid.
56. *Zohar* 2:162, 2.

> *revelation of the infinite light of the Blessed One through the doing of the mitzvot.*[57]

J.E.: In this text, the Alter Rebbe indicates another function of the mitzvot: to clothe the soul, to prepare it for eternal life. Here light becomes a garment, the raw material of the World to Come. This idea is pivotal to Jewish mysticism. If we "go down in order to go up," it is because the time the soul spends on earth will give it the additional "something" that the Sages call the "garment."

The idea is the following: The soul itself is naked. Like a baby, it cannot communicate lucidly with its Father. In fact, the ladder we mentioned earlier stands for the language that the soul needs to learn in order to communicate with God. This language, this maturation of the soul, is called a "garment." The naked soul is immature, and the clothed soul is what I would call the "socialized Divine." This garment is the mitzvah. Without it, without this interstitial cloth that the soul weaves around itself throughout its life on earth, the soul would return naked to the Garden of Eden.

This symbolism of nakedness and clothing connected to the fulfillment of the commandments is extremely old. When the Bible says that in the Garden of Eden[58] Adam and Eve realized that they were naked after the sin, the Sages comment that "*They saw that they were naked, naked of the commandments, for God had only given them a single commandment and they had not observed it.*"[59]

Thus, life is lighting the oil of the commandments and the

---

57. *Torah Ohr, Mikketz* 33c.
58. The Garden of Eden below, located in our world and where the ascent to the Garden of Eden Above is prepared for.
59. Genesis 19.

Torah in this world, and weaving the garment of light needed for eternity. Incidentally, the Alter Rebbe draws attention to the fact that a certain number of metaphors concern the World to Come and bear a certain resemblance to life here below. Like the body, the soul has the basic requirements of food and clothing, lodging and nourishment. The Torah, the light, is its food, and the mitzvah, the oil, makes its garment. Food stands for what we assimilate and internalize. Clothing stands for what covers us and surrounds us. This helps clarify the Alter Rebbe's comments on *penimiut* (what is internal) and *makif* (what is encompassing), which are the two complementary opposites of the Kabbalah. We can internalize a light when we understand what is said to us, and as we can live within an atmosphere (which we described for Sukkot)[60] that surrounds or clothes us.

Living the Torah and the mitzvot here, in the World Below, is hence preparing the double provisions that the soul needs in the Garden of Eden to impregnate itself with the two gifts it was promised—namely, to know the intimacy of the Divine light and to be bathed in it.

The mitzvot are garments through which the soul is able to comprehend and enjoy the [Divine] pleasure and effulgence in the Garden of Eden. The mitzvah is like a garment in that just as the garment does not enter into the person to become his inner vitality, as food which becomes literally one with the person and vitalizes him, [but rather] encompasses the person and shields and protects him, in the same way, the mitzvot are rooted in the level of makifim [the Divine light that "encompasses" all the worlds], which is why their revelation below [in this world] does not come in a manner of inner unity, only in

---

60. See the section entitled "The State of Grace."

> *physical deed . . . But through the doing of mitzvot is created a makif ("encircler") and "screen," so that via the mitzvot [the soul] can enjoy the pleasure in the light of the Infinite. This is the purpose of the soul's descent [to earth], "a descent for the purpose of ascent."*
>
> *Because the mitzvot are rooted in the gulgalta ("skull"), when the soul clothes itself in garments of mitzvah it enjoys the pleasure of the light of the Infinite.*

A.S.: What is called the Garden of Eden is not a place but rather a situation that we can compare to a change of phase. The soul experiences joy from contact with the Divine. This contact calls for an instrument of transformation.

J.E.: It is as though the voltage of the Divine light was too strong for the soul; it needs a transformer, which the Alter Rebbe calls a screen, but it could also be called a filter, a decoder, a kind of asbestos garment.

A.S.: This garment, woven by our deeds, is called in the Midrash the "Sages' garment," *ḥaluka de-rabbanan;* and woe, says the *Zohar*, to the person whose garment has holes.

J.E.: He might be burned by Divine light. This garment is often called a coat of mail, referring to the verse "*He donned victory like a coat of mail.*"[61] The Alter Rebbe makes a series of comments on these complementary opposites: the food that fortifies me from the inside, and the clothing that protects me from the outside. We do not need to eat continually; normally, people eat three meals a day. On the other hand, we cannot go around without clothes.

---

61. Isaiah 59:17.

This helps explain another comment. The Jews as a whole do not use up all the light of the Torah, but rather all fulfill one commandment or another. Thus, all have their place in the World to Come. Yet naturally, those with the skimpiest garments will have to stand a little farther away from the Divine light.[62]

In the final analysis, it comes down to what could be called a question of compatibility of light. The naked soul is unable to perceive Divine light and benefit from it, although it was expressly created for this purpose, if we refer to the well-known talmudic saying: "*In the World to Come there is no eating and drinking but the righteous sit with their crowns on their heads feasting on the brightness of the Divine Presence.*"[63]

Life on earth thus becomes a rite of passage. God encloses His light in the Torah and the mitzvot, which serve as the outer shell protecting the essence that men must extract. Man will make light come from the darkness of oil and, little by little, clothe himself in light. Thus, when the soul returns to its primary source, it is already formed of a cloth compatible with the light of *En Sof.* In kabbalistic terms, this additional elevation of the soul takes place in the following way. At the start, the soul emanates from Divine wisdom, *Ḥokhmah,* the second *sefirah.* Through the mitzvot it can attain the inner core of *Keter,* the first *sefirah,* Supernal Will. It goes up a notch: This is "descending in order to ascend." The numerical value of *Keter* is 620. This is also the number of mitzvot,[64] and the Kabbalah speaks of 620 columns of light that connect the World Above to the World Below.

---

62. For these two comments, see *Hanaḥot HaRaP,* p. 80, and *Maamrei Admor haZaken* 5565 (1805), p. 348.

63. Babylonian Talmud, Tractate *Berakhot* 17a.

64. The 613 biblical commandments and the seven rabbinical prescriptions.

A.S.: The Alter Rebbe's commentary is based on two verses in which the Torah is called light and the mitzvah and the soul is called a lamp. We can now see why mitzvah and soul are equated. Just as the oil of the mitzvah is transformed into light, so man's soul becomes the light of God: "The soul of man is the lamp of God."[65]

---

65. Proverbs 20:27. See Tanya 1:5; *Hanahot HaRaP*, p. 79; *Likkutei Torah* 38d, 44.

Index

Aaron, 270–271
Aaron of Karlin, Rabbi, 26
Abraham, 47, 48, 49, 235–
    236, 270–271, 272, 274,
    277, 295
Adama (Earth), 84
Adam (man), 83–84, 341
Ahasuerus, 292, 294, 295,
    299–300, 302, 304
Akedah, 47, 48, 49
Akiva, Rabbi, 29–30, 59–60
Al Ḥet prayer, 28
Alter Rebbe, 245
    De profundis, 34
    Ḥanukkah, 330, 334–336,
        338, 339, 342, 344,
        345, 347–348, 348,
        352–353, 356, 357,
        358, 360
    Moses, 208, 209, 211
    Passover (exile), 107, 108,
        109, 110, 111, 112,
        113–114, 116, 117,
        118, 119, 121, 123

Passover (exile in Egypt),
    128, 130, 132, 133,
    135
Passover (food), 144, 148–
    151, 152, 153–154,
    155–157, 158, 162,
    164, 169
Passover (Red Sea), 173,
    174, 179, 180–181,
    184, 185, 187, 193,
    195–196, 203, 204,
    205, 206–207, 209
Purim, 313–314, 315,
    320–321
on renewal, 33
Rosh Hashanah, 10, 13,
    14, 18, 39, 40, 41
Shavuot and giving of the
    Torah, 222, 224, 226
Sukkot, 256, 258, 261,
    262, 264, 269
Sukkot (Eight Princes of
    Man), 279, 280, 281,
    282, 283–284

Alter Rebbe (*continued*)
Sukkot (Seven Shepherds),
270, 271, 273, 277
on wrongdoing, 41–42
Yom Kippur, 56–57, 58,
63, 64, 74, 89, 91, 93,
95, 96
Yom Kippur and purifica-
tion and holiness, 66,
67–69
Yom Kippur and the soul,
80, 81, 84, 86, 87, 92
Yom Kippur and thoughts,
77, 78–79
Amos, 281
Angels, 218–220
Antiochus Epiphanes, 342
Anti-Semitism, 135
Aphar, 130
Ari, 46
Assif, 277
Atik yomin (Ancient of Days),
70
Atzilut, 178, 183, 184, 188,
190–191, 192, 194, 198,
207
Awe, concept of, 19–22,
233–238

Ba'al Shem Tov, 147
Ba'al teshuvah, 64
Binah (understanding), 149,
155, 209, 223, 224, 227
Book of Life, 21

Causality, 40, 159–160, 183,
184
Cave, myth of the, 122–123
Children
child and the sage and
Passover holiday,
163–167
food and verbal and non-
verbal relationships,
151–154, 155–157,
158
Chosen people, concept of
the, 18–19, 136
Circumcision, 130
Commandments, 338–343,
345, 348–351, 356–357
Creation
birth and creation of man,
46–50, 155, 190
of the world, 8, 14–19,
132–133, 148, 177–
181, 182, 183–184,
331
Crocodiles, battle between
two, 127–129
Crying, 63

David, 61, 242, 270–271,
272, 277, 281, 295
Deborah, 301
De profundis, 34
Diaspora, 105, 116, 117,
119, 210
Dietary observances, Pass-
over *seder*, 140–169

Din, 257
Dispersion, 116, 119–120
Divine emanations, ten, 16,
  34
Divine energies, 129, 147
Divine Essence, 57
Divine forgiveness, 55–56
Divine light, 334, 339–340,
  341–342
Divine mercy, 74
Divine names, 57–58, 69
Divine power, 129
Divine Presence, 21, 121
Divine sovereignty, 18,
  22–27
Divine sparks, 119–120,
  122, 123, 145
Divine thought, 223–224,
  229
Divine transcendence, 20,
  66, 71
Divine Will, 130, 183, 184,
  205, 230, 233, 242, 338

Ecclesiastes, Book of, 75–76
Eight Princes of Man,
  279–285
Eisenberg, Josy
  Hanukkah, 328–330, 331–
    332, 333, 334–336,
    337, 338–340, 341,
    342, 343, 344–346,
    347, 348–351, 352–
    353, 354, 356–358

Moses, 195–196, 197–198,
  199, 200–201, 202,
  203–207, 208, 209,
  210–211
Passover (exile), 103, 104–
  105, 106, 107, 108,
  109, 110–112, 113,
  114–115, 116–117,
  118, 119–120, 121,
  122, 123, 124
Passover (exile in Egypt),
  125, 126, 127–129,
  130–132, 133, 134,
  135, 136–137, 138,
  139
Passover (food), 142–143,
  144–145, 146, 147,
  148–151, 152–154,
  155–157, 158, 164,
  165–166, 167, 169
Passover (Red Sea), 172–
  174, 175–177, 178,
  179–181, 182, 183,
  184–185, 187, 188–
  190, 191, 192, 193–
  194
Purim, 291–292, 293,
  294–296, 297, 298–
  299, 300–301, 302,
  303, 304, 307–308,
  309–310, 312–314,
  315, 316, 317, 318–
  319, 320–322, 323–
  324

Eisenberg, Josy (*continued*)
Rosh Hashanah, 6–7, 8–9,
10, 13, 14, 29–30,
32–33, 34, 37, 38, 39,
40–42, 43–44, 45
Rosh Hashanah and the
chosen people, 18–19
Rosh Hashanah and con-
cept of awe, 20, 21
Rosh Hashanah and
creation, 14–15, 16,
47, 48, 49, 50
Rosh Hashanah and
Divine sovereignty,
22–24, 25, 26
Rosh Hashanah and
Hokhmah-Binah, 35,
36–37
Rosh Hashanah and
remembrance and
forgetting, 27, 28
Shavuot and giving of the
Torah, 216–218, 219,
220, 221, 222–224,
225, 226–227, 228–
229, 230–231, 233–
234, 235, 236, 237,
238, 239, 240, 241,
242, 243, 244–245
Sukkot, 250–252, 253,
254, 255–256, 257–
258, 260, 261, 262,
263–265, 266, 269–
271, 272, 273–275,
276, 277, 278–281,
282, 283–285
Yom Kippur, 54–55, 61, 62,
63, 65, 73–74, 75–76,
88, 89, 90–91, 91,
92–93, 95–96, 97
Yom Kippur and purifica-
tion and holiness, 66–
67, 68–69, 70
Yom Kippur and spiritual
life, 84, 85, 86, 87
Yom Kippur and thoughts,
76–77, 78, 80–82
Yom Kippur and YHVH, 56,
57–59
Elijah, 263, 281, 282
En Sof, 80–81, 178, 269, 274,
332, 333, 345, 359
Esther, Book of, 291, 292,
293, 294, 295–305, 307–
308, 309, 310, 311–312,
313, 317–318, 322, 323
Ethics, 40
Evil, 127, 132, 135–139
good and, 297–298, 299,
300, 302, 318, 319–
320, 322–323, 351
Exile, Jewish, 104–124,
309–310, 318
Exodus, Book of, 170,
215–216
Ezekiel, Book of, 112, 120,
125, 186, 301

Fear, 233–238
Felix culpa, 135
Fire, 351–352
Fish, 128–129, 191–194,
    209–211
Forgetting and remem-
    brance, 27–28

Galut (exile), 107, 109, 117,
    122
Garden of Eden, 356, 358
Genesis, Book of, 61, 174–
    175, 184
Genitalia, revealing, 130, 131
Geulah (redemption), 107,
    109, 122
Goethe, 343

Habad movement, 21–22, 29,
    261, 311
Haggadah ritual, 163, 165,
    166, 169
Halevi, Yehudah, 139
Halevy, Judah, 216
Haman, 292, 293, 294, 295–
    296, 297, 298, 299,
    300, 302, 312–313, 317,
    319–320, 321–322
Hanina Ben Dosa, 283
Hanukkah, 291–292
  bittersweet, 347–351
  clothe the naked, 351–360
  the garments of light,
    344–360

light, lights, 331–337
man-of-light, 327–343
mark of the command-
    ments, 338–343
Hashov, 78
Hashuv, 78
Hasidism, 27, 83, 85, 164,
    225–226
Hasidut, 144
Hesed, 256, 257, 258, 260
Hiding, concept of a God who
    hides, 309–312
Hokhmah-Binah, 34–37
Hokhmah (Thought), 41, 45,
    92, 149, 155, 209, 223,
    224, 226, 227, 228,
    229, 230, 359
Holiness, 66–71
Holocaust, 135, 293
Hosea, 95, 262, 301

Idolatry, 294–298
Imma, 156
Isaac, 47–48, 49, 235, 262,
    264, 270–271, 274, 277
Isaiah, 38, 194, 301

Jacob, 210, 264, 270–271,
    272, 274, 354
Jeremiah, Book of, 59–60,
    301
Jesse, 281
Job, Book of, 97, 200–201,
    332

Joseph, 111, 270–271, 272
Judah Maccabee, 328, 329
Judith, 301

Kabbalah
    atik yomin (Ancient of
        Days), 70
    concept of time, 10, 12
    creation, 15, 16, 133, 155
    Divine Name and Divine
        Essence, 57
    food, 144, 145, 149
    Ḥokhmah, 92
    Ḥokhmah-Binah, 34
    Keter, 242
    Kingdom, 21, 228
    Purim, 293, 295, 314
    Red Sea, 85, 174, 178, 183,
        185, 198
    "secret of the cutting," 46
    the soul, 359
    sounds and musical notes,
        45
    Sovev kol 'almin, 71
    sparks, 119
    "sparks of holiness," 114
    Sukkot, 253, 264, 275,
        282, 283
    thought and action, 224,
        225, 226, 227
    tohu and *tikkun*, 118
    Yiḥud, 69
Kadosh, 66
Kant, Immanuel, 224
Katan, 156

Keter (Crown and Will), 15,
    24, 34, 41, 92, 180, 223,
    228, 242, 359
Keter Elyon, 24
Kiddush, 143
Kingship, 14–19, 20, 21–22,
    46
Knesset Israel, 301
Kol pashut, 44

Ladder symbolism, 353–354
Leviticus, Book of, 249
Light, 114–115, 123,
    331–360
Likkutei Torah
    Balak, 72–73
    Deuteronomy, 5–6, 32,
        53–54
    Numbers, 53
    Song of Songs, 140–142

*Maamrie Admor haZaken
    Taksav*, 170–172, 344
Maggid of Dubno, 87
Maharal of Prague, 108, 119,
    137, 139
Makif, 254, 255, 256, 259,
    260, 264, 265, 282, 357
Makifim, 253, 254, 282, 283,
    284
Malkhut (Kingdom), 15, 21,
    46, 154, 155, 181, 188,
    226, 228, 229
    Divine sovereignty, 18,
        22–27

Manicheism, 129, 136
Marriage, 187–188
Melekh, 15
Meod, 95–96
Mercy, grace and, 255–261
Messiah, 266, 281, 282–283
Micah, Book of, 267, 270, 281
Midot, 152, 155, 156, 274
Miracles, 312–317
Miriam, 301
Mitzrayim, 126
Mohin, 152, 155
Mordecai, 292, 293, 294, 295–297, 298, 299, 302, 303, 304–305, 308, 312–313, 318, 321
Moses
  exile, 127, 128, 130, 138, 310
  Purim and depiction of, 295
  redemption, 301
  Red Sea, 185
  rescue of, 63
  revelation of the Torah, 50, 216, 219, 233–234, 239, 240
  and Seven Shepherds, 270–271, 272, 274, 275, 277
Moses in Egypt, 195–198
  it's him, I recognize him, 198–203
  land of men, 207–209

like a fish on land, 210–211
Moses: you will always cherish the sea, 203–207
Mount Sinai, giving of the Torah on, 49–50, 199, 201, 209, 217, 222, 225, 229, 230–231, 232, 244–245
Mysticism, Jewish
  Hanukkah, 332, 333, 356
  Passover, 115, 127, 128, 136, 192, 193, 207
  Purim, 299, 307

Na'ase, 225, 226, 227
Naso, 70
Neck symbolism, 130, 131
Nefesh, 80, 81, 90
Neshamah, 80, 81, 90
Nessirah, 46
Nishma, 225, 227
Nora, 237

Oref, 130

Pa'am, 11
Paganism, 127
Par'oh, 130
Passover, 6–7, 103
  B-A-Ba: Abba, 151–154
  the bread of healing, 167–169

Passover (*continued*)
the bread of knowledge,
140–169
the bread with no taste,
161–163
the child and the sage,
163–167
a chromosome called
Israel, 113–115
clash of the worlds,
132–134
continuity in change,
112–113
dormant Israel, 109–112
exile, an organized dis-
order, 117–121
the forces of evil, 135–139
the great crocodile,
125–139
king is causality, 159–160
leap into the unknown,
154–159
memories from beyond life,
121–124
Moses, the human fish,
195–211
passage through exile,
104–124
a path in the sea, 170–194
Red Sea, 170–194
the rejectionist front,
127–132
seder, 140–169
sow or spread, 115–117

tell me what you eat,
146–151
to eat is to know, 144–146
whoever sows Israel, reaps
humanity, 106–108
Paul, 235
Penimiut, 357
Peri Etz Ḥayyim (Vital), 254
Pesaḥ. *See* Passover
Plato, 122, 222
Polarization, 119
Prayer, 354
Princes of Man, Eight,
279–285
Proselytism, Jewish,
234–235
Proverbs, Book of, 327, 330
Psalms, Book of, 30, 33, 35–
36, 78, 87–88, 260, 276
Purification and holiness,
66–71
Purim
the ace of spades, 291–305
the Esther syndrome,
302–305
God in hiding, 309–312
the healing of the snake,
317–322
miracles are normal,
312–317
the pseudonym of God,
306–324
totalitarianism and
idolatry, 294–298

victory over destiny,
322–324
a woman of action,
298–302
Purim spiel, 294, 295

Rahamim (compassion),
256–257, 260, 263
Rain, 261–266
Ratso-vaShov, 10
Rava, 280
Redemption, 300–301
Red Sea, 88–89, 103, 170–
174, 216, 284
in the beginning was the
sea, 174–181
free as water, 181–187
Israel: a pilot fish,
191–194
Moses and, 195–207, 209,
211
our mother the sea,
187–191
Remembrance and forget-
ting, 27–28
Reverential fear, 237
Roman exile, 104–105
Rosh Hashanah
God outside the law, 34–37
head of the year, 5–31
mostly positive?, 29–31
and in the name of the
Father, 22–27
in the name of the King,
19–22

a new world symphony,
37–45
point of origin, 9–10
a programmed moment,
13–14
remember to forget, 27–28
the royal trumpets, 32–50
this newborn world, 46–50
who made you king?,
14–19
the year is dead: long live
the year, 10–13
Ruah, 80, 81, 90

Samuel, 281
Sartre, Jean Paul, 135
Saul, 281
Seder, 119
Seed, the, 115–117
Sefer Hasidim, 340
Sefer Taksav, 249–250
Sefirot, ten, 359
Passover, 149, 152, 154,
155, 180–181, 209
Rosh Hashanah, 16, 21,
34, 41, 45
Shavuot, 223, 224, 226,
228, 230
Sukkot, 256, 257, 274
Seven Shepherds, 270–275,
277, 278–281, 281, 283,
284, 285
Shanah, 13, 43
Shavuot, 7, 103, 196
awe yes, fear no, 233–235

Shavuot (*continued*)
  the end of amnesia,
    220–224
  a God who desires me,
    242–245
  Hear O Israel, 230–232
  hear what I see, 224–225
  I, *Anokhi*, 238–242
  know-how, 225–228
  my kingdom for a mitzvah,
    228–230
  the secret of the angels,
    218–220
  seeing voices, 215–232
  suddenly, so close,
    235–238
Shema' Israel, 231
Shema prayer, 95, 346–347
Sheni, 43
Shofar, 37, 38, 42–43, 44–
    45, 46, 47, 49–50, 216
Simḥat Torah, 251, 285
Sins, repairing, 91
Solomon, 75, 168, 354
Song of Songs, 158, 254,
    255–256, 266, 269, 275,
    278, 301
Soul, the, 79–82, 90, 92,
    221–222
  clothe, 356–360
  fish representation of
    souls, 128–129
  light and the, 344, 345,
    354–356, 359

maturation of, 353–354
  spirit l life, 84–88
Sovev l ͻt 'almin, 71
Sowing, 115–117
Sparks, Divine, 119–120,
    122, 123, 145
Sparks of holiness, theory of
    the, 114–115, 147
Spiritual life, 84–88
Steinsaltz, Adin
  Ḥanukkah, 330–331, 332,
    333, 334, 336–337,
    340–341, 342, 346,
    347–348, 351–352,
    353, 358, 360
  Moses, 196–197, 198–
    199, 200, 201–202,
    203, 207, 208–209,
    210
  Passover (exile), 105, 106,
    107, 108, 109, 110,
    112–113, 114, 115,
    117–118, 119, 120–
    121, 122, 123–124
  Passover (exile in Egypt),
    125–126, 127, 129–
    130, 132–133, 134,
    135–136, 137, 138–
    139
  Passover (food), 143, 144,
    145, 146, 147, 151,
    152, 154, 155, 158,
    163–164, 165, 166–
    167, 168–169

Passover (Red Sea), 174,
177, 178, 179, 181,
182–183, 184, 185–
187, 188, 190–191,
192–193
Purim, 292–293, 294,
296, 297, 298, 299–
300, 301–302, 303–
304, 305, 308–309,
310–312, 314, 315–
316, 317–318, 319,
320, 322, 323
Rosh Hashanah, 7–8,
9–10, 11, 14, 29, 30–
31, 33, 37, 38–39, 40,
42, 43, 44
Rosh Hashanah and the
chosen people, 18
Rosh Hashanah and
concept of awe, 19–
20, 21–22
Rosh Hashanah and
concept of time,
11–13
Rosh Hashanah and
creation, 15, 16, 46–
47, 48, 49–50
Rosh Hashanah and
Divine sovereignty,
24–25, 26–27
Rosh Hashanah and
Ḥokhmah-Binah,
34–35

Rosh Hashanah and
remembrance and
forgetting, 27–28
Shavuot and giving of
the Torah, 218–219,
220, 221–222, 224–
225, 226, 227–228,
229, 230, 231–232,
234, 235–236, 237–
238, 239, 240–241,
242–243, 244, 245
Sukkot, 252–253, 254–
255, 256–257, 258–
260, 261, 262–263,
265–266, 271, 272,
275–276, 277–278,
281, 282–283, 285
Yom Kippur, 55–56, 60–
61, 62, 63, 64–65, 66,
74–75, 76, 89, 90, 91,
92, 93–95, 95, 96–97
Yom Kippur and purifica-
tion and holiness, 66,
67, 70, 71
Yom Kippur and spiritual
life, 85, 86, 87–88
Yom Kippur and thoughts,
77, 78–80, 82–84
Yom Kippur and YHVH,
56–57, 59
Sukkot, 25, 103
between grace and mercy,
255–261
the dew and the rain,
261–266

Sukkot (*continued*)
  God's embrace, 253–255
  God's friends, 275–277
  princes of the future,
    281–285
  reconstructed man,
    277–281
  seven figures in search of
    a *sukkah*, 267–285
  the state of grace, 249–266
  substance and subsis-
    tence, 272–275
Supreme Will, 34, 36, 41, 47,
  56–57

Tallits, 67
Targum, 76
Te'amim, 45
Ten Commandments, 110,
  216, 230, 233, 238–239,
  241, 242, 243, 309, 332
Ten Days of Repentance
  (*Teshuvah*), 7, 39, 45,
  54–55
Teru'ah, 43
Teshuvah
  Rosh Hashanah, 39, 45
  Yom Kippur, 55–56, 58–
    59, 60–61, 62, 64–65,
    69, 70, 71, 74–75, 76,
    77, 82–83, 84, 87, 90,
    93, 94, 96
Tetragrammaton, 12, 56–57,
  58, 69, 74, 205

Thoughts, 76–84
Tikkun, 118, 119, 120, 121,
  137, 320
Time, concept of, 10–13
Tohu, 118, 119, 120, 121,
  133, 135, 137
Torah Ohr, 306–307, 335
  Beshallah, 104, 195
  Mikketz, 267–269,
    327–328
Totalitarianism, 294–298
Transcendence, 66, 71,
  254–255
Tsohoraim, 67

Vespasian, 26
Vital, Hayyim, 254

Water, 62–63
  rain, 261–266
Wrongdoing, concept of,
  41–42

Yabbashah, 174–175
Yam Suf, 175
Yihud, 69
Yohanan Ben Zakkai, 283
Yom Hadin, 7, 27
Yom Kippur, 7, 28
  before YHVH there is God,
    56–60
  the haven of God, 72–97
  the pure and the holy,
    66–71

Purim and, 308, 316–317,
  322–324
reasons of the heart, 95–97
spirit, are you there?,
  84–88
thoughts make the man,
  76–84
up to God, 88–95
the weeping waters, 53–71
where are you?, 60–66

Zechariah, Book of, 120, 249,
  252–253
Zedekiah, 281
Zephaniah, 281
Zera', concept of, 113–114
Zerubabel, 116–117
Zohar, 62, 110, 111, 149,
  169, 179, 192, 206–207,
  207, 358

About the Author

Rabbi Adin Steinsaltz, scholar, teacher, mystic, scientist, and social critic, is internationally regarded as one of the leading rabbis of this century. The author of many books, he is best known for his monumental translation of and commentary on the Talmud. In 1988, Rabbi Steinsaltz was awarded the Israel Prize, his country's highest honor. He and his family live in Jerusalem.

Rabbi Josy Eisenberg is a television producer, director, and writer who was born and educated in France. He received his rabbinical ordination from the Paris Jewish Rabbinical Seminary while also completing a degree in history. He served as the Rabbi of Montmartre, Paris, between 1957 and 1967. In 1962, he started a weekly program on Jewish subjects on French television, called *La Source de Vie* ("Spring of Life"), which continues to this day.